Computer-Supported Collaborative Learning:
Best Practices and Principles for Instructors

Kara L. Orvis
Aptima Inc., USA

Andrea L.R. Lassiter
Minnesota State University, Mankato, USA

 Information Science Publishing

Hershey • New York

Acquisition Editor:	Kristin Klinger
Senior Managing Editor:	Jennifer Neidig
Managing Editor:	Sara Reed
Development Editor:	Kristin Roth
Copy Editor:	April Schmidt and Laura Kochanowski
Typesetter:	Jamie Snavely
Cover Design:	Lisa Tosheff
Printed at:	Yurchak Printing Inc.

Published in the United States of America by
    Information Science Publishing (an imprint of IGI Global)
    701 E. Chocolate Avenue
    Hershey PA 17033
    Tel: 717-533-8845
    Fax: 717-533-8661
    E-mail: cust@igi-global.com
    Web site: http://www.igi-global.com

and in the United Kingdom by
    Information Science Publishing (an imprint of IGI Global)
    3 Henrietta Street
    Covent Garden
    London WC2E 8LU
    Tel: 44 20 7240 0856
    Fax: 44 20 7379 3313
    Web site: http://www.eurospan.co.uk

Library of Congress Cataloging-in-Publication Data

Computer-supported collaborative learning : best practices and principles for instructors / Kara L. Orvis and Andrea L.R. Lassiter, editors.
    p. cm.
  Summary: "This book answers the demand for a thorough resource on techniques to facilitate effective collaborative learning in virtual environments. This book provides must-have information on the role of the instructor in computer-supported collaborative learning, real-world perspectives on virtual learning group collaboration, and supporting learning group motivation"--Provided by publisher.
  Includes bibliographical references and index.
  ISBN 978-1-59904-753-9 (hardcover) -- ISBN 978-1-59904-755-3 (e-book)
  1. Group work in education. 2. Computer-assisted instruction. I. Orvis, Kara L. II. Lassiter, Andrea L. R.
  LB1032.C5748 2008
  371.39'50785--dc22
                      2007040230

British Cataloguing in Publication Data
A Cataloguing in Publication record for this book is available from the British Library.

Computer-Supported Collaborative Learning:
Best Practices and Principles for Instructors

Table of Contents

Section I:
Setting the Stage

Section II:
Student Development Case Studies

Section III:
Professional Development Case Studies

Section IV:
Diversity in CSCL Environments

Section V:
Looking Forward

Preface

Abstract

In collaborative learning, interaction among learners is essential for effective knowledge acquisition and increased understanding. Computer-supported collaborative learning (CSCL) environments often inhibit or cause problems with learner-learner interactions. This book takes an applied perspective of what the instructor can do to identify and manage learner-learner relationships in a CSCL environment. This information will provide insight to both corporate trainers and K-12 and university educators on how instructors can promote appropriate and positive learner-learner interaction in CSCL environments.

Computer-Supported Collaborative Learning

Computer-supported collaborative learning (CSCL) allows group learning to take place in computer-mediated environments. To receive the full benefit of social learning, collaborative learners must interact with each other, share information, and coordinate actions. Unfortunately, research has indicated computer mediation creates potential barriers to learner-learner interaction. Specifically, members of computer-mediated teams tend to experience slower development of trust, cohesion, efficacy, and shared cognition, all of which impact whether learners interact effectively. A concern for instructional developers and designers is how to foster effective learner-learner interactions in CSCL environments.

In 2006, Orvis and Lassiter proposed that instructors have the ability to influence and promote effective learner-learner interactions by identifying problems and stepping in to facilitate their processes. However, an assertion was made that CSCL course developers and instructors have not focused on the instructor's role of promoting learner-learner interaction. Rather, attention has been paid to the choice of technologies used to support this interaction, even though research on virtual teams has found that a leader is able to influence the processes (e.g., coordination, information sharing) and relationships (e.g., cohesion, efficacy, trust) between team members (Zaccaro, Ardison, & Orvis, 2004; Orvis, 2004). That research incorporated virtual team and CSCL research to focus on the role of the CSCL instructor as a promoter, facilitator, and manager of positive learner-learner relationships and interactions. This was, in part, due to the minimal amount of published research on the topic of the instructor and how they are able to facilitate learner-learner interactions in a CSCL environment.

The Contribution of This Book

The purpose of this book was to pull together chapters which focus on the role of instructors in promoting learner-learner interactions in a CSCL environment. Our vision for the book was twofold: First, to provide a document which would help corporate trainers and K-12 and university educators learn how to promote appropriate and positive learner-learner interaction in CSCL environments; second, to promote additional research in the area of instructor-group interactions. To accomplish this goal, we bring together academics and practitioners from a variety of disciplines, including business, communication, education, psychology, and information technology. In addition, this is a multinational effort with contributions from the USA, Greece, Poland, Turkey, and the United Kingdom.

The Organization of This Book

This book has XIV chapters, divided into four sections. Here we briefly describe each section and its accompanying chapters.

Section I: Setting the Stage

The first section of the book includes two chapters which offer interesting findings and ideas to consider throughout the rest of the book.

In Chapter I, Traci Sitzman of the Advanced Distributed Learning Co-Lab in Alexandria, Virginia, Katherine Ely of George Mason University, and Robert Wisher of the Department of Defense present results from a meta-analysis that compares the effectiveness of Web-based instruction (WBI) to classroom instruction (CI). They identify which instructional methods incorporated in WBI are the critical factors in determining trainees' knowledge acquisition. Among those instructional methods were providing the appropriate kind of learner-learner interactions. Based on their meta-analytic findings, the authors of this chapter make several recommendations for Web-based course design.

In Chapter 11, Orlando Olivares, a professor at Bridgewater State College, examines CSCL in the context of cooperative and collaborative learning, highlighting similarities and differences between the two. Dr. Olivares also makes suggestions for how the instructor should approach the digital classroom, based on the conceptual differences between collaborative and cooperative learning.

Section II: Student Development Case Studies

Section II is made up of five chapters which describe and draw conclusions from case studies involving CSCL environments. Although each chapter proposes guidelines for what instructors could do to promote learner-leaner interactions, each case is supported by different technologies and/or focuses on different instructional methods. This section highlights the variety of approaches to studying this area of research.

In Chapter III, Stephanie Cawthon and Alycia Harris from Walden University report student and instructor reactions concerning how social factors influence learning outcomes during an online research lab. They use Community of Practice theory as a lens for this exploration. The chapter includes strategies used by the instructor, perspectives from students, and recommendations for ways to overcome obstacles to a successful online research community.

In Chapter IV, Stephanie Brooke of the University of Phoenix presents the case method as one pedagogical approach for teaching online courses and promoting collaboration among learners. Pedagogical approaches to working with novice and seasoned online students are addressed.

In Chapter V, Evelyn Johnson of Boise State University and Jane Pitcock of Walden University present a brief overview of the importance of social learning theories and existing research that supports learner-learner interaction as an important aspect of learning. They then report and discuss findings from a qualitative study examining the use of an ecological assessment tool to evaluate an online course's ability to support learner-learner interaction. Throughout the chapter, they focus on the instructor's role in supporting learner-learner interactions.

In Chapter VI, Erman Yukselturk and Kursat Cagiltay of the Middle East Technical University monitor the input, processes, and outcomes of a selection of online learning groups through semi-structure interviews. They focus on describing how such groups work collaboratively, how to facilitate them and what makes work in such groups satisfactory and successful. They find that group homogeneity and the opportunity for face-to-face communication play a major role in successful group work.

In the final chapter of this section, Donna Ashcraft of Clarion University of Pennsylvania and Thomas Treadwell of West Chester University examine problems instructors and students experience in collaborative learning by drawing on social psychological literature and their personal experiences in implementing online collaborative learning. They make propositions for how instructors should manage learner-learner interactions though a social psychology lens. The authors draw on their experiences with CORAL (Collaborative Online Research and Learning) in order to demonstrate these phenomenon and recommendations.

Section III: Professional Development Case Studies

CSCL environments are not exclusive to the K-12 or college courses. CSCL is increasingly being used to develop professionals in the workplace. The selection of chapters in Section III presents approaches and lessons learned within the context of CSCL professional development efforts.

In Chapter VIII, Ellen Nuffer of Keene State College examines principles of adult learning and cognition as well as theories and perspectives on collaboration that inform best practices in supporting faculty as they find creative ways to work together. These best practices are examined in their applications to faculty collaboration using course management system software. Four projects are described and analyzed. Recommendations are then discussed.

In Chapter IX, Eileen B. Entin of Aptima, Inc., Jason Sidman of Aptima, Inc., and Lisa Neal of eLearn Magazine discuss considerations and tradeoffs in developing an online teamwork skills training program for geographically distributed instructors and students. The chapter focuses on supporting active engagement of learners and meaningful and thoughtful learner-learner interactions for a professional training program. The authors propose lessons learned in leveraging the advantages of both self-paced and group learning, providing opportunities to practice the teamwork concepts being trained, creating social presence, and promoting interaction and reflection among the course members.

Section IV: Diversity in CSCL Environments

Diversity is a topic which is becoming increasingly important as technology enables collaboration to take place over barriers of time and space. Multinational collaborations offer an additional challenge to learner-learner interactions and instructors in CSCL environments. The fourth section of this book offers three chapters which investigate the influence of diversity on real world student collaborations.

In Chapter X, Anna Michailidou and Anastosios Economides of the University of Macedonia discuss the impact of demographic diversity in learner-learner interaction in CSCL teams. They pull from the virtual teams literature and assert that instructors must invent new ways to implement successful collaboration, particularly in cross-cultural learning collaborations.

In Chapter XI, Janice Whatley of the University of Salford, Elena Zaitseva of Liverpool John Moores University, and Danuta Zakrzewska of the Technical University of Lodz introduce peer reviewing as a form of collaborative online learning which encourages students to engage in reflective critical evaluation of each other's work. They describe two cases in which this method was applied and discuss challenges particular to a multinational collaborative setting.

In Chapter XII, Derrick L. Cogburn of Syracuse University and Nanette S. Levinson of American University report on a nine-year case study of collaborative learning in cross-national and cross-university virtual teams. They define a triple track approach to the opportunities and challenges of cross-cultural collaborative learning. The authors analyze alternative delivery modes, identify best practices, and highlight critical success factors including trust-building, cross-cultural communication, and collaborative learning champions.

Section V: Looking Forward

The chapters in this section offer some interesting research areas moving forward, specifically that of shared cognition in CSCL environments and the role of instructor assessment in managing learner-learner interactions.

In Chapter XIII, Marissa L. Shuffler of the University of North Carolina and Gerald F. Goodwin of the Army Research Institute explore the concept of shared mental models within the context of CSCL environments. They present the challenges that a dispersed environment brings to establishing a shared understanding and explore what instructors can do to facilitate the development of shared knowledge among learners.

In Chapter XIV, John LeBaron of Western Carolina University and Carol Bennett of the WRESA Elementary & Middle Grades Curriculum Coordinator, discuss the issue of self-assessment in CSCL environments. The chapter outlines recommendations on how instructors can assess whether they are actually managing leaner-leaner engagement in the ways they intended. They advocate the use of multiple data sources collected over time. This chapter offers an interesting area for further research.

Conclusion

Research surrounding the instructors role in CSCL is still in its infancy. Though this book highlights research being conducted within that topic, much of the research is anecdotal in nature. Although we learn valuable lessons from these studies and gather additional insight into the challenges facing CSCL instructors and suggested solutions, we propose that there is also a role for more rigorous empirical research. Therefore, we encourage future research to examine some of the topics and findings highlighted in this book within the context of more structured research methodology.

Acknowledgment

This book would not have been possible without the support of several people. We would first like to thank the chapter authors. Without their scholarly achievements, applied experience, and informative contributions, this book would not exist. Each and every one was a pleasure to work with, across boundaries of time and space. We are equally grateful to our reviewers (many of which were chapter authors) who helped with the blind review process. This was instrumental in producing such an outstanding publication.

In addition, we would like to thank S. Pixy Ferris and Susan Godar, the editors for "Teaching and Learning with Virtual Teams." A chapter we published in their book spawned the idea for this collection. In addition, we would like to thank Dr. Steve Zaccaro, whose work on team leadership formed the foundation of our approach to understanding the role of the instructor in promoting learner-learner interactions.

We would also like to thank our editors, Kristin Roth and Jessica Thompson. We appreciate all their competence, time, and expertise as they supported us in this process. They knew exactly when to be flexible and when to push.

Finally, we would like to thank our husbands, Scott Lassiter and Brendan Crowley, both of whom helped on the home front while their wives spent many after-work hours on the computer to get this publication finished.

Section I

Setting the Stage

Chapter I

Designing Web-Based Training Courses to Maximize Learning

Traci Sitzmann, Advanced Distributed Learning Co-Laboratory, USA

Katherine Ely, George Mason University, USA

Robert Wisher, U.S. Department of Defense, USA

Abstract

This chapter presents results from a meta-analysis that compares the effectiveness of Web-based instruction (WBI) to classroom instruction (CI). The results suggest that when the same instructional methods are used, WBI and CI are equally effective for teaching declarative knowledge. However, the instructional methods and course design features incorporated in WBI are critical factors in determining trainees' knowledge acquisition. Specifically, the chapter examines the influence of lecture, human interaction, and learner control on the effectiveness of WBI. Based on the findings, the authors provide the following recommendations for increasing learning in WBI: (1) require trainees to be active, (2) incorporate a variety of instructional methods, (3) offer computer and Internet skills courses, (4) provide trainees with access to lecture notes, (5) incorporate synchronous human interaction, and (6) provide trainees with learner control.

Introduction

Web-based instruction (WBI) is becoming an increasingly popular delivery medium for training and education. Recent surveys report that 37% of companies used technology-delivered instruction in 2005 (Rivera & Paradise, 2006) and 63% of traditional undergraduate institutions offered undergraduate courses online in 2004 (Allen & Seaman, 2005). The *Washington Post* reported that in 2007, 1.78 million college and university students were enrolled in online courses (Mendenhall, 2007). When properly employed, WBI can reduce training costs while simultaneously increasing training accessibility and strengthening human capital for organizations (Welsh, Wanberg, Brown, & Simmering, 2003). Due to the potential benefits and increasing prevalence of WBI, it is important to understand how instructors and course developers can design Web-based training programs that optimize learning outcomes.

The overarching goal of the current chapter is to examine the influence of instructional methods on the relative effectiveness of WBI and classroom instruction (CI). Specifically, this chapter will address three important issues relevant to the effectiveness of WBI. First, we will examine if any observed differences between WBI and CI are driven by the delivery media (i.e., WBI vs. CI) or the instructional methods (e.g., lecture, tutorials). Second, we will investigate whether the incorporation of lecture, human interaction, and learner control during WBI influence the extent to which trainees learn during training. Third, we will synthesize our findings and present practical implications for designing Web-based training courses that research suggests will maximize learning. Specific examples of training courses that follow the recommendations from the study results will be provided to help instructors visualize how training courses can incorporate the current guidelines.

A few key terms are necessary to understand the study results and their implications. WBI refers to courses where all of the training materials are delivered via the Internet, whereas CI refers to courses where the training materials are delivered face-to-face via an instructor. We define instructional methods as techniques used to convey course content such as lecture, group discussion, reading, and assignments. Delivery media is defined as technological devices such as computers, video-teleconferencing, and the Internet used for the purpose of instruction. We conducted a meta-analysis to compare the effectiveness of the two delivery media for teaching declarative knowledge, and to examine the effect of instructional methods on learning. Meta-analysis is a statistical technique for combining the results of studies that address a set of similar research questions. Finally, declarative knowledge is trainees' memory of the facts and principles taught in training (e.g., trainees' ability to define key terms and to describe a theory covered in training).

Instructional Methods vs. Delivery Media

Our review of the education and training literature identified 76 studies that compared declarative knowledge outcomes from WBI and CI, and were included in the meta-analysis. Each study evaluated Web-based and classroom-based versions of a course on the same topic. All of the courses were adult work-related training, and included both organizational and university courses. For example, Weems (2002) provided data comparing test scores from Web-based and classroom versions of a university algebra course. Combined, these studies report data collected from 11,943 trainees across 155 courses.

We calculated an effect size for differences in declarative knowledge between the Web-based and classroom versions of courses.[1] The results indicate that across 155 courses, WBI was 5% more effective than CI for teaching declarative knowledge. This suggests that if the average test score in classroom training is 75%, then the average test score in the comparison Web-based training course will be 80%. Additionally, the relative effectiveness of WBI compared to CI for teaching declarative knowledge was similar for both college students and organizational employees, suggesting these results are valid for both groups of trainees.

Educational theory can be used to shed light on the meaning of the current results. Clark (1983) proposed delivery media are "mere vehicles that deliver instruction but do not influence student achievement any more than the truck that delivers our groceries causes change in our nutrition" (p. 445). In making this assertion, Clark (1983, 1994) noted the need to distinguish between the effects of instructional methods and delivery media on learning outcomes. Clark argued that while delivery media influence the cost and accessibility of material, the medium used is inconsequential in affecting learning—trainees' learning outcomes are driven by the instructional methods. Clark's theory suggests our finding that WBI is 5% more effective than CI for teaching declarative knowledge is driven by the instructional methods incorporated in WBI, rather than a true difference in the effectiveness of WBI and CI. Thus, if identical instructional methods are used in both Web-based and classroom versions of a course, the two delivery media should be equally effective for teaching declarative knowledge.

To test Clark's theory, we isolated studies that compared declarative knowledge from WBI and CI when similar instructional methods were used. Studies were coded as having similar instructional methods when all of the instructional methods included in the Web-based version of the course had a comparable instructional method in the classroom version of the course (e.g., when lecture is provided in CI, a comparable instructional method in WBI is an online video of the lecture). Studies were coded as having different instructional methods when an instructional method was present in WBI or CI, and there was not a comparable instructional method in the other delivery medium.

The results of the current meta-analysis support Clark's theory, and indicate WBI and CI were equally effective for teaching declarative knowledge when similar instructional methods were used. This result is consistent with a growing body of evidence that reports no significant difference between classroom instruction and distance learning (Russell, 1999). This suggests instructional methods rather than delivery media are the causal factor in determining trainees' achievement levels. Therefore, course designers should choose instructional methods that will maximize learning outcomes.

Our analyses also indicate that when different instructional methods were used to deliver the two courses, WBI was 11% more effective than CI for teaching declarative knowledge. These findings highlight that the most effective Web-based courses were not merely Internet versions of CI, but rather they leveraged the instructional advantages afforded by WBI. These courses tended to incorporate a wide variety of instructional methods and chose activities, such as learner collaboration and tutorials, which require learners to be active during training. This suggests instructors should look for ways to use technology to support and enhance learning in order to design Web-based training courses that will maximize the acquisition of declarative knowledge.

The Impact of Self-Selection

Clark (1983, 1994) also argued that many of the empirical studies comparing the effectiveness of WBI to CI failed to institute experimental controls sufficient to rule out alternative explanations for group differences. It is possible that trainees who self-select into Web-based courses may exhibit different characteristics than trainees who choose CI. For example, trainees who are more knowledgeable about the course topic, or trainees who are higher in cognitive ability or motivation might choose Web-based courses over CI, resulting in the appearance that WBI is more effective than CI for teaching declarative knowledge.

To examine the effect of self-selection on the effectiveness of WBI, we isolated studies where trainees were allowed to choose their delivery medium. In these studies, WBI was 6% more effective than CI for teaching declarative knowledge. However, in studies where trainees were randomly assigned to delivery media, CI was 6% more effective than WBI. These findings highlight a need for additional research on individual differences that might influence trainees' success rates in WBI and CI. Specifically, which trainees are most likely to be successful in WBI or CI? Are there instructional methods that can be incorporated in the delivery media to guarantee all trainees will be successful? These results also suggest that requiring trainees to participate in WBI may lead to lower learning outcomes if trainees lack the computer and Internet skills required for success in WBI.

Overall, the results support Clark's (1983, 1994) theory and suggest that instructional methods and experimental design influence the relative effectiveness of WBI and CI for teaching declarative knowledge, rather than true differences in the effectiveness of the delivery media. In the following pages, we will examine the effect of instructional methods and course design characteristics on learning declarative knowledge during WBI.

Is Lecture Beneficial in WBI?

Lecture is the most common instructional method in CI, and is used in almost all classroom courses (Van Buren & Erskine, 2002). When designing WBI, many instructors also attempt to incorporate lecture by uploading PowerPoint slides to the Web, creating audio-visual materials (e.g., streaming video of lectures, audio recordings of lectures along with PowerPoint slides or other visual aids), or providing trainees with access to online lecture notes.

Seventy-three percent of Web-based training courses included in the current review utilized lecture as one of their instructional methods, and all of the comparison classroom courses utilized face-to-face lecture as one of their instructional methods. About 50% of the Web-based courses that included lecture utilized audio-visual materials, 41% utilized lecture notes, and 9% utilized PowerPoint slides without accompanying audio. With the majority of courses utilizing lecture, instructional designers need to be aware of whether or not lecture is an effective instructional method for teaching declarative knowledge in WBI.

Our analysis indicated that various forms of online lecture differed in their effects on learning declarative knowledge. When lecture notes were provided online, WBI was 16% more effective than CI for teaching declarative knowledge. In addition, lecture notes were the only form of online lecture that resulted in WBI outperforming CI to a greater extent than when WBI did not include any form of lecture. WBI was 10% more effective than CI for teaching declarative knowledge when WBI did not include lecture, and 3% more effective than CI when WBI included audio-visual lectures. Finally, WBI and CI were equally effective for teaching declarative knowledge when WBI utilized PowerPoint lectures without accompanying audio. This suggests trainees are more likely to benefit from lecture notes than audio-visual or PowerPoint lectures in WBI, and including audio-visual or PowerPoint lectures did not improve the effectiveness of WBI, relative to CI, over Web-based courses that did not utilize lecture.[2]

Is Human Interaction Beneficial in WBI?

Human interaction refers to the extent to which trainees communicate and interact with both the instructor and other trainees during training. While human interaction is prevalent in CI, through advances in technology, human interaction can also be built into WBI through features such as e-mails, chat rooms, group projects, and discussion boards. In a narrative review of the distance education literature, Zirkin and Sumler (1995) concluded that the more interactive the instruction, the more trainees learn.

Brown and Ford (2002) proposed there are two potential benefits of human interaction in training. The first is informational—trainees receive more relevant information when collaborating, discussing, and sharing information. Listening to classmates express their ideas can provide trainees with additional perspectives and information that can increase the accuracy and complexity of their mental models. The second benefit is motivational. Human interaction provides the opportunity for collaborative learning, which is hypothesized to influence trainees' adoption of learning goals (Brown & Ford, 2002), and create a sense of community by fostering a sense of mutual interdependence, trust, shared values, and goals (McMillan & Chavis, 1986; Rovai, 2002). In turn, this sense of a collaborative community reduces participants' feelings of isolation (Haythornthwaite, Kazmer, Robins, & Shoemaker, 2000; Morgan & Tam, 1999), improves attitudes towards the course (Ludwig-Hardman & Dunlap, 2003), and correlates positively with learning outcomes (Rovai & Jordan, 2004). Based on previous research, we hypothesize trainees will learn more declarative knowledge in Web-based courses with a high—rather than a low—level of human interaction.

In the current review, we classified Web-based courses as having a low level of human interaction if less than half of the trainees' time was spent interacting with the instructor or other trainees. An example of a Web-based course with a low level of human interaction would be a semester-long course in which trainees participated in an online discussion once a week or less. Courses in which the majority of the trainees' time involved interacting with the instructor or other trainees were classified as having a high level of human interaction. An example of a Web-based course with a high level of human interaction would be a course in which trainees frequently collaborated on group projects and regularly participated in online discussions.

In the human interaction analysis, all of the classroom courses were high in human interaction. This allowed us to examine the effect of varying the level of human interaction in the Web-based training courses. The results indicated that the effectiveness of WBI, relative to CI, did not differ when WBI had a high or a low level of human interaction. This suggests, when averaging across all communication channels, human interaction is not beneficial in WBI.

When discussing human interaction in WBI, one important factor to consider is the form of the human interaction (e.g., chat sessions, discussion boards, e-mail). Thus, we examined the effect of the synchronicity of the communication medium. Synchronous communication occurs in real time, and includes communication media such as chat sessions where trainees receive immediate feedback to their questions and comments. Asynchronous communication involves a time delay in communicating with the instructor or other trainees, such as with e-mail or discussion boards. As many Web-based courses utilize multiple forms of human interaction, each article was coded for the percentage of interaction that was synchronous.

The results suggest trainees tended to learn more in courses that utilized synchronous rather than asynchronous communication during WBI. Thus, we recommend utilizing chat rooms and virtual classrooms rather than e-mail and discussion boards to communicate with trainees during WBI.

Is Learner Control Beneficial in WBI?

Learner control refers to the extent to which trainees have control over their learning experience by affecting the content, sequence, or pace of material (Friend & Cole, 1990). In WBI, the absence of learner control is character- ized by program control, in which the instructional software controls most or all of the decisions.

WBI typically provides trainees with more control over their learning ex- perience than CI (Sitzmann, Kraiger, Stewart, & Wisher, 2006). During classroom instruction, the instructor typically guides trainees' instructional experience—providing little control to trainees. Classroom instruction as- sumes all trainees begin a course with the same knowledge level and requires trainees to learn the same content in the same timeframe. However, WBI often allows trainees to tailor the course to meet their needs by providing trainees with control over their learning experience.

Previous research consistently finds that adults react favorably to receiving control during instruction (e.g., Kraiger & Jerden, 2007). Adults tend to be- lieve they know what material they need to review and how much time they must spend reviewing the material (Knowles, 1990). However, research also shows that the impact of learner control on actual learning is either negligible or non-existent. A meta-analysis by Niemiec, Sikorski, and Walberg (1996) concluded that while the learner control construct is theoretically appealing, the effects of learner control on learning are "neither powerful nor consis- tent." Kraiger and Jerden (2007) also conducted a meta-analysis to assess the effect of learner control on learning outcomes. They found learner control had a small, positive effect on learning declarative knowledge. This research suggests that while trainees *like* to control the means by which they engage instructional material, they do not necessarily benefit from it. Since prior research has not consistently demonstrated an effect for learner control on trainee achievement, we cannot develop a directional hypothesis regarding the effect of learner control on the effectiveness of WBI. However, given the great potential for individual customization in online courses, we were interested in the effect of learner control during WBI.

In the current review, courses in which trainees had little control over the content, sequence, or pace of material were coded as having a low level of learner control. Examples of Web-based courses with low learner control would be non-interactive, lecture-based classes and computer-controlled sequences of activities completed in a set amount of time. Studies were coded as having a high level of learner control when trainees had at least some control over two of the three dimensions: pace, content, or sequence. Examples of courses with high levels of learner control would be managerial courses where trainees selected material they found relevant to their jobs, or online tutorials that trainees accessed when they needed to practice job-related skills.

In the learner control analysis, all of the classroom courses were low in learner control. This allowed us to examine the effect of varying the level of learner control in the Web-based training courses. Our results indicated trainees learned more declarative knowledge when they received a high—rather than a low—level of learner control during WBI. When trainees received a high level of learner control, they learned 9% more declarative knowledge from WBI than CI. These results may be inconsistent with previous research because Niemiec et al. (1996) incorporated both adults and children in their meta-analysis, and Kraiger and Jerden (2007) found learner control was more likely to be beneficial in recent— rather than in older—studies. Together, the current and previous meta-analytic results suggest learner control is beneficial for the modern, adult learner.

Guidelines for Designing More Effective Web-Based Training Courses

Overall, the results indicate course design characteristics determine the extent to which trainees learn declarative knowledge from WBI. It is possible to design Web-based courses where learning will be much greater or much less than CI. The current study identified three instructional methods and course design characteristics which increased learning from WBI. Specifically, the extent to which trainees in WBI learned more declarative knowledge than trainees in CI was greatest when WBI contained lecture notes, included synchronous communication, and provided trainees with control over their learning experience. In contrast, it is also possible to design Web-based courses in which learning levels will be inferior to CI. Specifically, CI was more effective than WBI when the latter failed to incorporate synchronous human interaction, and provided little control over the learning experience. Thus, careful attention to course design features is critical for maximizing learning declarative knowledge during WBI. The following paragraphs outline six guidelines for designing Web-based courses to maximize learning.

First, require trainees to be active during WBI. Trainees are highly active when they are asking questions, collaborating with other trainees, discussing training content, completing learning exercises, or practicing new skills, and are inactive when they are listening to lectures and reading a textbook. Webster and Hackley (1997) developed guidelines for teaching in distance learning, and stated that "learning is best accomplished through the active involvement of the students" (p. 1284). They proposed instructors must actively engage trainees for trainees to learn the course material. Spending time practicing the key task components of training should help trainees develop an understanding of the deeper, structural features of the task (Newell, Rosenbloom, & Laird, 1989). Online courses that require trainees to be active tended to also incorporate self-assessments such as quizzes, tests, and puzzles (Moore, 2005).

One approach to promoting active learning is through online instructional tools such as Psychology Computer Assisted Learning (PsyCAL; Buchanan, 1998, 2000). After completing lessons, PsyCAL provides trainees with a series of questions, and then provides immediate feedback on which questions were answered correctly. For each incorrect answer, the program provides trainees with a reference on where to find the correct answer, thus requiring trainees to actively engage with the material they did not understand. After reviewing the material, trainees are then advised to repeat the test-learn-retest cycle until all the material is mastered.

Second, incorporate a wide variety of instructional methods in WBI. One of the main benefits of WBI is the ability to customize instruction to the needs of different trainees. Incorporating a variety of instructional methods allows trainees to tailor the courses to be consistent with their learning styles (Salomon, 1988). Through the incorporation of a variety of instructional methods, WBI permits trainees who are having difficulty understanding the course material to continue to review the material in different ways. Additionally, including instructional methods that increase learner collaboration (e.g., discussion boards, group projects) may facilitate the learning of declarative knowledge by providing trainees with opportunities to learn the material from multiple perspectives. For example, a trainee who is not grasping the materials presented in an audio lecture may be able to learn and understand the content after reading other trainees' discussion board comments.

An example of a course with a wide variety of instructional methods was the Principles of Accounting I course at Montana State University (Campbell, Floyd, & Sheridan, 2002). Trainees had access to online learning objectives for each chapter of the course textbook, PowerPoint lectures, and relevant resource material. Frequent communication was also encouraged. Trainees participated in seven one-hour chat room sessions in which they could discuss course material with their instructor and other trainees, and the instructor posed questions for discussion. Trainees could also participate in small group chat room sessions, and e-mail the instructor or other trainees. In addition, homework and practice quizzes were available online to allow trainees to assess their progress towards mastering the training material.

Third, offer a computer and Internet skills course for trainees participating in Web-based courses. Organizations should be cautious about completely replacing CI with WBI, because some trainees may not have the computer and Internet skills that are required to navigate Web-based training courses. Providing trainees with access to a computer and Internet skills course may enable all trainees to be successful in WBI. For example, Long Beach City College developed an orientation for all online trainees that included basic Internet skills, such as using computers and Web browsers to access the Internet (Moore, 2005).

Fourth, provide trainees with access to online lecture notes. One of the main benefits of WBI is that it enables the instructor to provide trainees with control over the pace of instruction. When an instructor is lecturing during CI, all trainees are forced to learn at the pace set by the instructor. In contrast, online lecture notes enable trainees to review the course content at their own pace. Trainees can skip sections they are already familiar with, and read the notes as many times as desired.

Online lecture notes can also serve as advanced organizers (i.e., devices that provide the trainee with the structure of the information that will be presented in the course) and study tools for preparing for the exam. Advanced organizers are theorized to facilitate effective training by focusing the trainees' attention

(Mayer, 1989), and assisting trainees in organizing the information presented in training (Kraiger, Salas, & Cannon-Bowers, 1995). When trainees are responsible for taking their own notes, research has shown notes tend to contain only 35% of the presented material, and are sometimes incorrect (Kiewra, 1985). Knight and McKelvie (1986) found that trainees who only reviewed complete lecture notes outperformed trainees who attended a face-to-face lecture, took their own notes, and then reviewed their own notes. In addition, research examining learner utilization of online lecture notes has shown that accessing lecture notes was correlated positively with course achievement (Grabe, 2002). Online lecture notes guarantee all trainees have complete and accurate information, and can improve learning from WBI.

Fifth, incorporate synchronous human interaction in WBI. Synchronous communication lays the foundation for discussion and collaboration among learners. Synchronous communication also reduces frustration that can be associated with lengthy time delays between asking a question and receiving a response. When engaged in asynchronous discussions, a lack of immediate feedback can lead trainees to procrastinate on commenting, or even withdraw from the discussion (Mikulecky, 1998).

Research suggests that learners may be hesitant to engage in online discussions with individuals they do not know (Vonderwalle, 2003). In order to establish a community of learners, instructors should provide trainees with the opportunities to get to know each other (e.g., posting short biographies), communicate clear expectations for participation in discussions, and model and reinforce effective communication (Tallent-Runnels, Cooper, Lan, Thomas, & Busby, 2005). Additionally, to encourage learner interaction, instructors may consider scheduling specific chat times when trainees may gather to discuss course topics, and creating a conversational space to allow trainees to reflect on ideas and learning experiences. Requiring learner-led discussions, and encouraging trainees to post responses that are relevant and thought provoking, provides trainees with opportunities to think deeper about the course material, and build more complex understandings of the domain (Moore, 2005). Within this conversational space, instructors should foster a norm of open discussion, and should provide feedback on trainees' ideas.

Instructors and instructional designers are encouraged to utilize chat rooms, instant messaging, and virtual classrooms to maximize opportunities for synchronous human interaction. When incorporating synchronous interaction in WBI, the role of the instructor is to facilitate learner interaction, to oversee the accuracy of the information exchanged between learners, and to monitor discussions and debates to limit conflict (Arbaugh, 2000; Coppola, Hiltz, & Rotter, 2002). Instructors can serve as powerful facilitators of online instruction, and provide individualized guidance to assist trainees in mastering course content. In addition to discussion providing a sense of camaraderie and building a learning community, it is an active learning approach that can enhance understanding of the course material (Tallent-Runnels et al., 2005).

Sixth, design WBI to provide trainees with control over the content, sequence, and pace of instruction. Learner-controlled environments allow trainees to spend as much time as they want or need learning the material. Learner control provides each trainee with time to reflect on the material, prepare ideas, and compile responses thoughtfully. This allows trainees to tailor the experience to meet their specific needs and interests, helps trainees take responsibility for their learning and behavior, and accommodates initial differences in aptitude (Gay, 1986). Providing trainees with control should reduce frustration and boredom, since trainees can skip sections of the material they are already familiar with (Large, 1995). In addition, Web-based training courses have the capability of linking to the Internet, making it possible to provide additional content (and more choices regarding content) for learners, than either CI or single workstation training programs.

If trainees are going to be successful in a learner-controlled environment, the course material must include a variety of content and informational resources, a clear statement of the learning objectives, and tools to assess their knowledge or skill acquisition (Wydra, 1980). Learners must understand their goals, have a means to reach them, and a way to know when their goals have been accomplished. Thus, research suggests that it is beneficial to provide trainees with guidance on their progress towards their goals, enabling them to make informed decisions in learner-controlled training courses (Brown & Ford, 2002).

An example of a course with a high level of learner control is WinEcon, an online program for teaching introductory economics, developed by the Teaching and Learning Technology Program Economics Consortium (Lim, 2001). When trainees login to WinEcon, they are presented with a breadth of available modules, providing trainees with control over the content and sequence of instruction. Trainees are active while learning the material, and can learn information in several ways as they deviate from the main body of learning materials. Material is also presented in a non-linear fashion, allowing trainees to choose a wide range of navigation routes. Trainees can set the pace of learning, and can quickly move through sections of the material they are familiar with, and repeat sections when necessary.

Conclusion

The current results suggest attention to course design is critical for maximizing learning from WBI. Across 155 courses and 11,943 trainees, WBI was slightly more effective than CI for teaching declarative knowledge. This suggests that, on average, WBI will be at least as effective as CI for teaching declarative knowledge, and delivery media do not have a large effect on learning outcomes, supporting Clark's (1983, 1994) theory.

The instructional methods incorporated in WBI are the critical factors for determining how much declarative knowledge trainees will acquire from work-related training courses. Specifically, the effectiveness of WBI hinges upon the incorporation of instructional methods that facilitate learning, and it is possible to design Web-based training courses where learning will be far superior or inferior to the comparison classroom courses. Requiring trainees to be active during WBI, incorporating a wide variety of instructional methods, including synchronous human interaction, and providing trainees with control, lecture notes, and access to a computer and Internet skills course will maximize learning declarative knowledge from WBI. However, failing to follow these recommendations may result in classroom trainees having a strong advantage over Web-based trainees when attempting to master the training material. In the current meta-analysis, CI was more effective than WBI when the latter failed to incorporate synchronous human interaction and provided little control over the learning experience. These guidelines are based on empirical research, and provide instructors with suggestions on how to design more effective Web-based training courses. It is our hope that instructional designers will follow these guidelines, and design Web-based training courses that will optimize the instructional advantages of the Internet.

References

Allen, I. E., & Seaman, J. (2005). *Growing by degrees: Online education in the United States.* Retrieved October 15, 2007, from http://www.sloan-c.org/resources/survey.asp

Arbaugh, J. B. (2000). How classroom environment and student engagement affect learning in Internet-based MBA courses. *Business Communication Quarterly, 63,* 9-26.

Brown, K. G., & Ford, J. K. (2002). Using computer technology in training: Building an infrastructure for active learning. In K. Kraiger (Ed.), *Creating, implementing, and maintaining effective training and development: State-of-the-art lessons for practice* (pp. 192-233). San Francisco: Jossey-Bass.

Buchanan, T. (1998). Using the World Wide Web for formative assessment. *Journal of Educational Technology Systems, 27,* 71-79.

Buchanan, T. (2000). The efficacy of a World-Wide Web mediated formative assessment. *Journal of Computer Assisted Learning, 16,* 193-200.

Campbell, M., Floyd, J., & Sheridan, J. B. (2002). Assessment of student performance and attitudes for courses taught online versus onsite. *The Journal of Applied Business Research, 18,* 45-51.

Clark, R. E. (1983). Reconsidering research on learning from media. *Review of Educational Research, 53,* 445-460.

Clark, R. E. (1994). Media will never influence learning. *Educational Technology Research and Development, 42,* 21-29.

Coppola, N. W., Hiltz, S. R., & Rotter, N. G. (2002). Becoming a virtual professor: Pedagogical roles and asynchronous learning networks. *Journal of Management Information Systems, 18,* 169-189.

Friend, C. L., & Cole, C. L. (1990). Learner control in computer-based instruction: A current literature review. *Educational Technology, 20,* 47-49.

Gay, G. (1986). Interaction of learner control and prior understanding in computer assisted video instruction. *Journal of Educational Psychology, 78,* 225-227.

Grabe, M. (2002). *Voluntary use of online lecture notes: Individual variability and frequency of misuse.* Paper presented at the annual meeting of the American Educational Research Association, New Orleans, LA.

Haythornthwaite, C., Kazmer, M., Robins, J., & Shoemaker, S. (2000). *Making connections: Community among computer-supported distance learners*. Paper presented at the Association for Library and Information Science Education Conference, San Antonio, TX.

Kiewra, K. A. (1985). Providing the instructor's notes: An effective addition to student notetaking. *Educational Psychologist, 20,* 33-39.

Knight, L. J., & McKelvie, S. J. (1986). Effects of attendance, note-taking, and review on memory for a lecture: Encoding versus external storage functions of notes. *Canadian Journal of Behavioral Science, 18,* 52-61.

Knowles, M. S. (1990). *The adult learner: A neglected species* (4th ed.). Houston: Gulf Publishing.

Kraiger, K., & Jerden, E. (2007). A new look at learner control: Meta-analytic results and directions for future research. In S. M. Fiore & E. Salas (Eds.), *Where is the learning in distance learning? Towards a science of distributed learning and training*. Washington, DC: American Psychological Association.

Kraiger, K., Salas, E., & Cannon-Bowers, J. A. (1995). Measuring knowledge organization as a method of assessing learning during training. *Human Factors, 37,* 804-816.

Large, A. (1995). Hypertext instructional programs and learner control: A research review. *Education for Information, 14,* 95-107.

Lim, C. P. (2001). Learner control and task-orientation in a hypermedia learning environment: A case study of two economics departments. *International Journal of Instructional Media*. Retrieved October 15, 2007, from http://www.accessmylibrary.com/comsite5/bin/ pdinventory. pl?pdlanding=1&referid=2930&purchase_type=ITM&item_id=0286-6753054

Ludwig-Hardman, S., & Dunlap, J. C. (2003). Learner support services for online students: Scaffolding for success. *The International Review of Research in Open and Distance Learning, 4*(1). Retrieved October 15, 2007, from http://www.irrodl.org/index.php/irrodl/article/view/131/602

Mayer, R. E. (1989). Models for understanding. *Review of Educational Research, 59,* 43-64.

McMillan, D. W., & Chavis, D. M. (1986). Sense of community: A definition and theory. *Journal of Community Psychology, 14,* 6-23.

Mendenhall, R. (2007). Challenging the myths about distance learning. *Distance Learning Today, 1,* 1, 4-5, 11.

Mikulecky, L. (1998). Diversity, discussion, and participation: Comparing web-based and campus-based adolescent literature classes. *Journal of Adolescent and Adult Literacy, 42,* 84-97.

Moore, J. C. (2005). *A synthesis of Sloan-C effective practices.* Retrieved October 15, 2007, from http://www.sloan-c.org/publications/books/ v9n3_moore.pdf

Morgan, C. K., & Tam, M. (1999). Unraveling the complexities of distance education student attrition. *Distance Education, 20,* 96-108.

Newell, A., Rosenbloom, P. S., & Laird, J. E. (1989). Symbolic architectures for cognition. In M. Posner (Ed.), *Foundations of cognitive science* (pp. 93-131). Cambridge, MA: MIT Press.

Niemiec, R. P., Sikorski, C., & Walberg, H. J. (1996). Learner-control effects: A review of reviews and a meta-analysis. *Journal of Educational Computing Research, 15,* 157-174.

Rivera, R. J., & Paradise, A. (2006). *State of the industry.* Alexandria, VA: American Society for Training and Development.

Rovai, A. P. (2002). Building sense of community at a distance. *International Review of Research in Open and Distance Learning, 3.* Retrieved October 15, 2007, from http://www.irrodl.org/index.php/irrodl/article/ view/79/153

Rovai, A. P., & Jordan, H. M. (2004). Blended learning and sense of community: A comparative analysis with traditional and fully online graduate courses. *International Review of Research in Open and Distance Learning, 5.* Retrieved October 15, 2007, from http://www.irrodl.org/index. php/irrodl/article/view/192/274

Russell, T. L. (1999). *The no significant difference phenomenon as reported in 355 research reports, summaries and papers.* Raleigh, NC: North Carolina State University.

Salomon, G. (1988). AI in reverse: Computer tools that turn cognitive. *Journal of Educational Computing Research, 4,* 123-134.

Sitzmann, T., Kraiger, K., Stewart, D., & Wisher, R. (2006). The comparative effectiveness of Web-based and classroom instruction: A meta-analysis. *Personnel Psychology, 59,* 623-664.

Tallent-Runnels, M. K., Cooper, S., Lan, W. Y., Thomas, J. A., and Busby, C. (2005). How to teach online: What the research says. *Distance Learning, 2,* 21-27.

Van Buren, M. E., & Erskine, W. (2002). *The 2002 ASTD state of the industry report.* Alexandria, VA: American Society of Training and Development.

Vonderwalle, S. (2003). An examination of asynchronous communication experiences and perspectives of students in an online course: A case study. *Internet and Higher Education, 6,* 77-90.

Webster, J., & Hackley, P. (1997). Teaching effectiveness in technology-mediated distance learning. *Academy of Management Journal, 40,* 1282-1309.

Weems, G. H. (2002). Comparison of beginning algebra taught onsite versus online. *Journal of Developmental Education, 26,* 10-18.

Welsh, L. T., Wanberg, C. R., Brown, K. G., & Simmering, M. J. (2003). E-learning: Emerging uses, best practices, and future directions. *International Journal of Training and Development, 7,* 245-258.

Wydra, F. T. (1980). *Learner controlled instruction.* Englewood Cliffs, NJ: Educational Technology Publications.

Zirkin, B., & Sumler, D. (1995). Interactive or non-interactive? That is the question! An annotated bibliography. *Journal of Distance Education, 10,* 95-112.

Author's Note

An earlier version of the meta-analysis was published in *Personnel Psychology.* See Sitzmann, Kraiger, Stewart, and Wisher (2006) for additional information on the relative effectiveness of Web-based and classroom instruction.

Endnotes

[1] The Hedges and Olkin (1985) approach was used to analyze the data. The effect size calculated for each study was d, the difference between the Web and classroom training groups, divided by the pooled standard deviation. Effect sizes were corrected for small sample bias and for at-

tenuation using the scale reliabilities reported in each study. The subgroup procedure was used to test for the effects of categorical moderators.

2   There was a lot of variability in the effectiveness of online audio-visuals for teaching declarative knowledge. The quality of the audio-visuals may be an important determinant of the effectiveness of this instructional method.

Chapter II

Collaborative vs. Cooperative Learning:
The Instructor's Role in Computer Supported Collaborative Learning

Orlando J. Olivares, Bridgewater State College, USA

Abstract

A central theme of this chapter is the following: to better understand the role of the teacher within a computer-supported collaborative learning (CSCL) environment, it is necessary to better conceptualize the CSCL construct. Toward this goal, this chapter will examine similarities and differences between cooperative and collaborative learning. Next, CSCL will be examined in the context of cooperative and collaborative learning, and a brief history of CSCL will be provided. It is argued that there has been a lack of definitional and conceptual clarity among these learning constructs—this has resulted in the conflation between cooperative learning and CSCL, as well as a continued focus on individual learning, as opposed to "group mind"-like constructs. It is hoped that better conceptual clarity about CSCL will provide a renewed understanding of the role of the teacher within a CSCL environment.

Overview

Zaccaro, Ardison, and Orvis (2004) developed a model for computer-supported collaborative learning (CSCL) where group characteristics mediate the relationship between instructor processes and individual learning. In this model, individual learning is the outcome variable, and it is assumed (or implied) that the primary purpose of the collaborative environment is individual learning; that is, through the social collaborative process—instructor-driven and computer mediated—individuals acquire knowledge and a deeper understanding of material than if they worked alone (Deatz & Campbell, 2001; Orvis & Lassiter, 2006). However, Orvis and Lassiter (2006) acknowledge that providing the opportunity to collaborate will not necessarily result in collaborative actions, particularly if the socio-emotional processes are ignored. Moreover, it is suggested that the acquisition of knowledge in a CSCL environment is dependent on the level and quality of interaction among learners, and it is the instructor who regulates and influences team processes, namely the cognitive, affective, and motivational processes.

I would argue, however, that to better understand the role of the instructor, and how the instructor may affect team processes and the effective use of technology, it is necessary to better conceptualize the construct in question. One persistent thread of confusion in the literature is the distinction between cooperative and collaborative learning (Olivares, 2005). Moreover, it is suggested that the confusion that exists in the CSCL literature (e.g., Kaptelinin & Cole, 2002; Koschmann, 1996) may be a function of the conflation of CSCL and cooperative learning, the failure to adequately conceptualize and distinguish cooperative and collaborative learning, and, at a more basic level, the failure to adequately conceptualize "group-mind"-like constructs (e.g., shared meaning or group learning) (Klimoski & Mohammed, 1994). As it is difficult to design technologies around fuzzy, ill-defined processes and constructs, an initial positive step in better understanding the role of the instructor within a CSCL framework is to more clearly conceptualize cooperative learning, collaborative learning, and CSCL.

Accordingly, the primary purpose of this chapter is to draw distinctions between cooperative learning and collaborative learning. These distinctions will unveil the differences in the goals of these social processes and, in turn, the role of the instructor. Since technology is a tool of the instructor and aids the instructor in accomplishing his/her task, we can draw some broad conclusions about the role of the instructor in a computer-mediated collaborative environment. However, this chapter will not provide a prescription for technology use. Stahl, Koschmann, and Suthers (2006) suggest that "In order to design technology to support collaborative learning and knowledge building, we must understand in more detail how small groups of learners construct shared meaning using various artifacts and media" (p. 417). Today, our level of understanding of the CSCL environment does not meet this standard and, therefore, guidelines for specific technologies will not be proffered. Nonetheless, recommendations for instructors will be provided.

This chapter will begin with an analysis of cooperative and collaborative learning, followed by a brief overview of the origins of CSCL. This overview will provide an understanding of how CSCL has been conflated with cooperative learning, and why it is necessary to draw distinctions between cooperative and collaborative learning in order to better understand CSCL and the role of the teacher. Then, CSCL and cooperative and collaborative learning will be compared and contrasted. Finally, the role of the instructor in a CSCL environment will be examined.

Cooperative and Collaborative Learning: Confusion in the Literature[1]

In the cooperative learning literature, the terms *cooperative* and *collaborative* have been, for the most part, used interchangeably; therefore, distinctions between cooperative and collaborative learning often are not made. Both cooperative and collaborative learning are considered small group processes that are concerned with knowledge acquisition, problem solving, and/or learning. The Office of Instructional Consultation at the University of California, Santa Barbara Web site (2006) states:

Collaborative learning is the umbrella term encompassing many forms of collaborative learning, from small group projects, to the more specific form of group work called cooperative learning. Cooperative learning is a type of Collaborative learning developed by Johnson and Johnson in the 1960s, and is still widely used today.

Although the Web site identifies the essential elements of cooperative learning, the distinctions between cooperative and collaborative learning are not made. Consistent with the interchangeable usage of the terms, Gokhale (1995) defined *collaborative* learning as "an instruction method in which students at various performance levels work together in small groups toward a common goal," but then cited Johnson and Johnson and the virtues of *cooperative* learning, to with:

Proponents of collaborative *learning claim that the active exchange of ideas within small groups not only increases interest among the participants but also promotes critical thinking. According to Johnson and Johnson (1986), there is persuasive evidence that* cooperative *teams achieve at higher levels of thought and retain information longer than students who work quietly as individuals (my emphasis). Carlsmith and Cooper (2002), in the article* A Persuasive Example of Collaborative Learning, *detailed the process of integrating a 12-week collaboration project within a course. Yet, the authors stated the following: "Several decades of empirical research have demonstrated that cooperative learning is an effective teaching device in higher education" (Johnson, Johnson, & Smith, 1991; Meyers, 1997; Slavin, 1985). In other words, Carlsmith and Cooper (2002), like Gokhale (1995), stated that they were conducting research on* collaborative *learning, but cited* cooperative *learning research to frame and support the effectiveness of* collaborative *learning.*

The extant literature suggests that researchers use the terms *cooperative learning* and *collaborative learning* interchangeably; moreover, the cooperative learning research is cited by collaborative learning researchers as support for the effectiveness of collaborative learning; hence, the (implied) inference is that cooperative learning and collaborative learning are essentially the same constructs. There are, however, some authors who have made the distinction between cooperative and collaborative learning (e.g., Brody, 1995; Bruffee, 1995).

Bruffee (1995) asks: "Is there really any difference between the two?" To which he responds: "Cooperative learning and collaborative learning are two versions of the same thing." Bruffee continues: "And, although members of both groups may disagree among themselves about terms and methods, principles and assumptions, their long-range goals are strikingly similar" (p. 12).

In contrast, Brody (1995) states: "We should not take the distinctions between these two orientations lightly, because the different historical roots of such practices give coherence and structure to instructional practices that can help us evaluate the congruency between our program philosophy and goals" (p. 133). Are cooperative and collaborative learning indeed two versions of the same thing, as suggested by Bruffee (1995), or are they substantively different—that is, they have different group structures, goals, and processes?

Cooperative Learning

The *American Heritage Dictionary* defines *cooperative* as, "engaged in joint economic activity." A more nuanced interpretation, however, suggests that the term *cooperative* connotes some sort of payoff—that is, the joint effort will realize gains for all (i.e., economic activity). Indeed, the cooperative learning literature suggests that the way students interact with each other is a key determinant of who learns and what is learned. Johnson and Johnson (1991) suggest that social skill development is a key element of cooperative learning. Specifically, cooperative learning theory suggests that when students work cooperatively, with concern for others' learning as well as their own, they learn more (Johnson, Johnson, & Holubec, 1998). Johnson et al. (1998) defined cooperative learning as an instructional use of small groups, so that students work together to maximize their own and each other's learning. Central to cooperative learning is the development of social skills whereby group members learn to work together, so that each member and all members of the group are successful. Slavin (1991) argues that concern for the success of each and every member of the group is what *distinguishes* cooperative learning from other group processes.

Cooperative learning is a social process grounded by structured group work, and is concerned with promoting both social and academic outcomes; that is, students learn new social skills and how to work together in order to achieve academic goals. These goals are realized through the imposition of structure and control by the teacher. The teacher holds students accountable for learning, collectively. In doing so, the teacher acts like a manager or director using instructional strategies to engender social skills, positive interdependence, cooperation, and accountability (Brody, 1995). In sum, cooperative learning, although outcome-based, can be considered an inward-looking, individual-centered group process, where the primary goal of the group process is for each and every member of the group to learn.

Key Points

- Individual student success (learning) is central and a distinguishing characteristic of cooperative learning.

- No one succeeds unless everyone succeeds; hence groups are structured in a way to induce positive interdependence of group members' activities.

- Group members help one another to learn, preferably in face-to-face interaction.

- Individuals, and the group, must be held accountable for achieving specific goals.

- Students are taught interpersonal and small group skills so they are able to work more cooperatively.

- Groups need to monitor how members work together and how group effectiveness can be enhanced.

Collaborative Learning

Collaborative is defined by the *American Heritage Dictionary* as "to work jointly with others or together especially in an intellectual endeavor." Indeed, the collaborative learning literature suggests that collaborative learning is, first and foremost, a social-intellectual exercise concerned with the creation of new knowledge, whereby a problem or task is posed, and a solution or solutions sought (Brody, 1995; Bruffee, 1995). Collaborative learning is grounded in social constructivism (e.g., Bruner, 1996; Dewey, 1916; Piaget, 1973; Vygotsky, 1978), and is concerned with creating new knowledge; toward this end, the teacher serves as a facilitator (Ornstein & Hunkins, 1998) or guide (Dewey, 1916) to the social process of discovery.

Accordingly, collaborative learning is concerned with cultivating students' independence, an atmosphere of dissent, a lack of group structure, and a free exchange of ideas. In collaborative learning, the group will seek to answer a question, or generate solutions to a problem; however, there is no concurrent goal that each and every member of the group will learn from the experience. Collaborative learning can be considered an outward-looking, unstructured group process where the primary goal of the group is to generate, through creative interaction, a best solution or solutions—that is, knowledge construction (Brody, 1995).

Key Points

- Individual student success (learning) is NOT a central concern and distinguishing characteristic of collaborative learning; rather, the concern is that joint group activities result in knowledge acquisition or problem solving that is superior to individual efforts.

- Collaborative learning is not a structured group process; it is concerned with cultivating independence, and independence of thought through the collaborative process.

- Small group and interpersonal skills are not taught as part of the collaborative process because this may interfere with the free flow of information and ideas.

Cooperative and Collaborative Learning: A Comparative Analysis

While both are small group processes, cooperative and collaborative learning are substantively different processes with different goals. Cooperative learning is a very structured process characterized by a high degree of individual accountability, positive member interdependence, and social skill development. Positive interdependence is central to the development of a cooperative learning environment and, subsequently, to the commitment of success of each and every member of the group: this is the heart of cooperative learning (Johnson et al., 1998).

In contrast, collaborative learning does not share the elements of cooperative learning, nor does it share the common goal of cooperative learning. Collaborative learning is an unstructured, small group process that cultivates independence, free thinking, and dissent. The goal of the collaborative learning process is to have group members think about and solve abstract problems, problems that may have no specific answers, or multiple solutions. In short, the goal of collaborative learning is to create new knowledge through a social context. Although group members are expected to work together, there is no commitment to group members that each will learn and be successful as a result of the process. Collaborative learning is, fundamentally, an intellectual process within a laissez-faire social framework.

Bruffee (1995) identifies two basic differences between cooperative learning and collaborative learning: (1) cooperative learning imposes much more structure on group members than collaborative learning, and (2) cooperative learning is concerned with the use and development of foundational knowledge (i.e., knowledge that is widely accepted); collaborative learning is concerned with the use and development of non-foundational knowledge (e.g., What is the best way to deal with terrorism?). Accordingly, cooperative learning places tremendous authority in the teacher: the teacher structures group exercises, and ensures that students work associatively. Additionally, the role of the teacher includes ensuring that students learn a variety of social skills, and those students contribute equitably to assignments (Bruffee, 1995; Matthews, Cooper, Davidson, & Hawkes, 1995). In contrast, collaborative learning places the governance of the students in the hands of the students—the teacher does not evaluate group processes, nor should the teacher attempt to influence group processes. Hence, student accountability surrenders to student dissent, and the correctness of solutions is fungible (see Table 1).

The definitions and conceptualizations of cooperative and collaborative learning provide a framework for understanding the origins of CSCL and how CSCL has been conflated with cooperative learning. Moreover, it is argued that the failure to distinguish cooperative from collaborative learning may have served to tarnish the conceptual clarity of CSCL. Accordingly, the next section will provide a brief history of the development of CSCL.

Table 1. Key differences between cooperative and collaborative learning (This table is from Olivares, 2005)

Characteristic	Cooperative Learning	Collaborative Learning
Knowledge	Foundational	Nonfoundational; A social artifact
Epistemological Orientation	Structured Instruction	Social Construction
Process	Achievement-Oriented	Course of Action
Group Structure	High/Positive Interdependence	Low/Laissez Faire/Individualistic
Teacher's Role	Micro Manager Hands-on/Director	Moderator/Facilitator/Guide
Student's/Participant's Role	Cooperative/Agreeable	Dissident/Independent
Goals	Develop Social Skills and Learning for All Members	Knowledge Construction through Conversation; Concern for Problem Solving

The Origins of CSCL

CSCL grew out of two very different streams of research, about 30 years apart: (1) cooperative learning, and (2) "the use of technology to improve learning related to literacy" (Stahl et al., 2006, p. 412). Cooperative learning is a type of structured group learning that was developed in the 1960s by Johnson and Johnson, who suggested that there are advantages for individual learning when working in groups (e.g., Johnson & Johnson, 1991). Johnson and Johnson's early research involved students in K-12 (e.g., Johnson & Johnson, 1986); later research was applied to the college level (Johnson et al., 1991); all their research, however, emphasized the primacy of individual learning in structured group settings.

Stahl et al. (2006) indicate that "CSCL arose in the 1990s in reaction to software that forced students to learn as isolated individuals" (p. 410). Three different projects developed technologies that engaged students to write in new ways (ENFI Project), sought to make writing more meaningful (CSILE Project), or sought to improve reading skills (the 5th Dimension). Stahl et al. (2006) note that:

All of these projects—ENFI, CSILE, and 5thD—shared a goal of making instruction more oriented toward meaning-making. All three turned to computer and information technologies as resources for achieving this goal, and all three introduced novel forms of organized social activity within instruction. In this way, they laid the groundwork for the subsequent emergence of CSCL. (p. 412)

Paralleling the development of individual-centered learning technologies was the development of technologies to enhance or facilitate collaboration—for example, e-mail, chat rooms, Blackboard Learning System™, and the blogosphere, to name a few. Hence, in the 1990s and into the 21st century, academic institutions have continued to focus on individual learning, but within a framework of technologies that sought to enhance collaboration. At the same time, there was a paradigm shift within CSCL whereby the individual as cognitive agent was not the focus; rather, the focus was group cognition or shared meaning making (Koschmann, 2002). CSCL, although a type of social activity like cooperative learning, is concerned not so much with the individual student who learns as it is the collaborative group (Stahl, 2005, p.

79). Thus, in CSCL, the focus of analysis moves from the individual to the group, and from individual learning and cognition to group meaning-making in the context of joint activity (Koschmann, 2002).

Both CSCL and cooperative learning have their origins in academic settings and are concerned with joint activity within a social framework, but they have different historical and research roots (Stahl, 2005). These similarities, and the difficulty of conceptualizing and operationalizing group meaning-making, may be reasons for the conflation of cooperative learning with CSCL. At a more basic level, however, the failure to adequately distinguish cooperative learning from collaborative learning may have served to muddle fundamental distinctions between cooperative learning and CSCL—for example, the concern for individual vs. group learning. The failure to make this distinction is common in the CSCL literature. Shell, Husman, Turner, Cliffel, Nath, and Sweany (2005), for instance, conducted an empirical investigation to examine the effects of CSCL on student learning. They stated: "In conclusion, our findings generally support arguments that implementation of CSCL communities and use of CSCL technologies will enhance students' knowledge building, intentional learning, and perceptions of the classroom" (p. 346). The focus here is on individual learning, not the collaborative group. Zaccaro et al. (2004), and Orvis and Lassiter (2006), also identify individual learning as the outcome variable in the CSCL environment. Koschman (2002), however, has suggested that even excellent CSCL research tends to use a theoretical approach that is inconsistent with group meaning-making in the context of joint activity.

Cooperative Learning, Collaborative Learning, and CSCL

Based on the arguments presented, we can conclude that cooperative and collaborative learning are not interchangeable constructs. Cooperative learning is driven by the goal of individual student learning as central to the social process; collaborative learning is not constrained by this goal. Collaborative learning has the goal of knowledge construction and/or problem solving through conversation—individual learning, if it occurs, may be considered a positive byproduct of this process. Individual learning, however, is not a central concern of collaborative learning. In fact, outside of academic institutions, the collaborative process is often used to develop ideas and better products, solve a problem, design strategy, and engage in a host of organizationally-related goals. In these cases, the primary goal of the collaborative process is not individual learning, or even necessarily group learning; rather, the goal is to satisfy an organizational mandate, goal, or objective.

CSCL reframes collaborative learning, in that it focuses not on (individual) knowledge construction or problem solving; rather, it focuses on meaning-making in the context of joint activity (Koschmann, 2002). CSCL redirects knowledge from the individual to the group—that is, it externalizes knowl-edge—and through social interaction, creates shared cognitions (Hinsz, Tindale, & Vollrath, 1997) or shared mental models (Canon-Bowers, Salas, & Converse, 1993). Koschmann (2002) defined CSCL as "a field of study centrally concerned with meaning and the practices of meaning-making in the context of joint activity, and the ways in which these practices are medi-ated through design artifacts" (p. 18). In sum, cooperative, collaborative, and CSCL are all social processes, but with different primary goals: cooperative learning is concerned with individual learning, collaborative learning is concerned with knowledge construction and/or problem solving, and CSCL is concerned with shared meaning-making or collaborative group cognition (Stahl, 2005). Stahl (2005) argues that "The question for CSCL is: can sets of students be transformed into groups that learn collaboratively in ways that encourage the emergence of collaborative group cognition in a significant sense?" (p. 85). We can extend Stahl's question and ask: how can the instructor facilitate the acquisition of group cognition? Technology is an extension of the instructor, and so it is necessary to first understand teacher behaviors that can facilitate group meaning-making, and then find technologies to support teachers' efforts. To this end, however, it is necessary to better conceptualize the constructs' "group cognition" and "shared meaning-making" before we can pursue technologies to support teachers in their efforts to facilitate the acquisition of "group" constructs.

Over 10 years ago, Klimoski and Mohammed (1994) bemoaned the fact that there has been little progress in conceptualizing "group mind"-like constructs. Today, the concerns of Klimoski and Mohammed have not been allayed. The understanding of "group-mind"-like constructs continues to suffer from a lack of definitional and conceptual clarity. This limitation constrains our ability to develop specific (and effective) technologies for the CSCL environment.

The primary goal of this chapter was to better conceptualize cooperative and collaborative learning. As part of this process, distinctions between CSCL and cooperative learning were made, as well as differences between CSCL and collaborative learning. These distinctions allow for teachers to better understand the differences among these group processes and design curricula and technology accordingly. For example, cooperative learning is a highly-structured group process that is primarily concerned with individual learning. The teacher, then, should be a hands-on director of activities with the intent of facilitating social skill development and promotional interaction. Technologies should be selected or designed that will facilitate instructor-related activities. For example: The technology should provide or induce group structure, harmony, and interdependence, continuously monitor student learning and social skill development, and provide feedback accordingly.

Collaborative learning is an unstructured group process that is primarily concerned with knowledge construction and problem solving. Neither student learning nor the acquisition of social skills is a requirement of this social process. Any efforts to impose structure or seek harmony may interfere with the free flow of ideas, knowledge acquisition, and problem solving. Olivares (2005) defined collaborative critical thinking, a type of collaborative learning, as follows: "A relatively unstructured social process that results in judgments being made or problems solved through the process of conversation, and through the use of evidence, inference, interpretation, logic, and reflection" (p. 10).

In contrast with cooperative learning, the role of the teacher in collaborative learning should be that of a guide who promotes independence of thought, the free flow of information, focuses on group—not individual—learning, and is concerned with successful completion of the task at hand. As opposed to seeking harmony and interdependence, the teacher may want to engender independence of thought and (some) discordance among group members (see Ellis, Hollenbeck, Ilgen, Porter, West, & Moon, 2003). Technologies should be designed or selected that will facilitate the teacher by inducing these processes and keeping the group focused on the task.

Summary

Thus far, this chapter has drawn distinctions between cooperative and collaborative learning, showed how cooperative learning has been conflated with CSCL, and highlighted the need to better conceptualize "group-mind"-like constructs. It was shown that cooperative and collaborative learning and CSCL are all social processes that in some way are related to learning, knowledge construction, and/or problem solving. However, it was also shown that these social processes are distinct and have different goals, units of analysis, and social dynamics. Cooperative learning has the primary goal of student learning and social skill development; it is a structured group process where interdependence and promotional interaction is sought, the role of the instructor is hands-on, and the instructor is heavily involved in monitoring the social process, providing feedback, and fostering individual learning. Collaborative learning has the primary goal of knowledge construction and/or problem solving.

Within the collaborative learning environment, the group is *not* highly structured; rather, it is more laissez-faire—which is consistent with the desire to have a free flow of information—discordance among group members may serve to enhance knowledge construction, and the role of the instructor is a guide, or facilitator of the social process. CSCL is not concerned with individual learning, like cooperative learning, but group cognition or shared meaning-making—that is, CSCL is concerned with the creation of "group mind"-like constructs. Once the collaborative environment moves away from the goal of individual learning or problem solving, and into the realm of creating shared cognitions or meaning-making, then new and different technologies are needed to foster the development of collaborative group cognition. Future research efforts should seek to better understand the notion of a shared reality and "group mind"-like construct.

The Role of the Instructor in a CSCL Environment

CSCL borrows from Vygotsky's (1978) view that human learning is a social activity that is mediated by various tools. The most important of these tools is language. Learning is derived from the social environment, and language is used to communicate those experiences (Assaf, 2005). Today, the instructor is able to use the computer and associated technologies to create the social-communicative environment in which learning takes place. The environment the instructor creates is a function of what the instructor hopes to achieve. Put differently, the role of the instructor is predicated on the instructor's classroom goal(s). In general, however, instructors within a CSCL environment will use technology to enhance interactivity and induce or facilitate group learning.

As previously discussed, cooperative and collaborative learning and CSCL are related—but distinct—constructs. The role of the instructor in a cooperative learning environment is not the same as in a collaborative learning environment (see Table 1). CSCL can take on characteristics of both cooperative and collaborative learning—for example, joint activity (cooperative) within a social framework (cooperative and collaborative). Defining the role of the instructor within a CSCL environment is further complicated by the fact that few studies have evaluated the effectiveness of different teaching strategies and technologies within this environment (Schulte, 2004). Teaching strategies that have been evaluated have resulted in *inconsistent* findings.

Kroonenberg (1994, 1995), for example, had students work in pairs to discuss and debate ideas in a computer-mediated synchronous chat mode. The synchronous mode allowed students to practice rapid interaction. Within this iterative process, students were allowed to reflect on what was said, and to focus on expressive written expression. Kroonenberg claimed that the quality of oral arguments and level of creative thinking was enhanced by prior e-mail interaction.

Instead of using free chat, Van der Puil, Andriessen, and Kanselaar (2004) used a structured dialogue system (via roles and sentence openers) to promote a shared task focus, and enhance collaboration. Van der Puil et al. found that the structured dialogue system served to undermine the collaborative process by promoting argumentative interaction. The authors claimed that the structured dialogue system created relational stress, and that auto-regulation proved to be quite resistant to chat interaction.

The contrasting examples of Kroonenberg and Van der Puil et al. highlight the inconsistencies in the literature regarding the effectiveness of computer-mediated collaboration. Warschauer (1997) discusses many of the advantages of computer-mediated collaboration; yet, Weisband (1992) found that it was more difficult to achieve consensus in an online discussion than face-to-face interaction. Sproull and Kiesler (1991) found that electronic discussion reduced conformity and hindered cooperative learning by encouraging free discussion and enhancing the prevalence of hostile language known as "flaming."

Even though the CSCL literature may be fraught with conflicting findings regarding effective teaching strategies, we do know the following: (a) In the cooperative and collaborative learning environments, there is some guidance as to the role of the teacher, (b) the CSCL literature provides us with some guidance regarding the role of the teacher, and (c) we know that there are some basic roles that a teacher should occupy in most any teaching environment.

As such, the teacher in a CSCL environment should occupy the following roles: (1) regulator (Jaffee, 1997), (2) monitor (Schulte, 2004), and (3) guide (Dewey, 1916). These roles should be considered related, but distinct. Each role will be briefly discussed.

One role of the teacher within the CSCL environment is to regulate the interaction between the student and the teacher, among students, and between the students and technology, or learning environment (Jaffee, 1997). Regulating interactivity may be accomplished a number of ways; yet, the amount and type of interactivity should be guided by the goals or objectives of the class. For example, since I teach at a predominantly commuter campus, one goal I have is to get students acquainted so they feel that they are part of the academic community. Accordingly, I ask students introduce themselves via Blackboard. On the first day of class, I ask students to post some general information about themselves on the class e-bulletin board. This information includes: name, commuter or not, if a commuter—from where do you commute, major, city/state of origin, goal(s) upon graduation, and hobbies. Students have reported finding commuting partners, study partners, and friends. Another strategy for regulating interaction is to have students form e-dyads and respond to discussion questions. Yet another strategy is to have students independently post their comments to discussion questions. Class assignments or tasks can be used to regulate the amount and level of interaction. Another aspect of the regulation function is to assess and seek to understand how familiar and comfortable students are with technology. If students do not understand how to interact with the technology, then there will be no communication to regulate.

A second role that the teacher occupies within the CSCL environment is the e-monitor. The instructor should play an active role in monitoring and maintaining student discussions. The teacher should monitor the amount of chat that takes place regarding assignments and tasks. Brookfield and Preskill (1999) suggest that the teacher should engage in three critical elements of monitoring: questioning, listening, and responding. The use of these elements should engage the student in the learning process. Students may, for example, respond to discussion questions in a haphazard way with little concern for evidence or thought. The teacher may then ask for the student to clarify his/her response using supporting evidence and a logical argument.

A product of the monitoring process is guiding the student in discussion and through the process of discovery. Central to guidance is feedback. If the student fails to respond to e-discussions or tasks, then the teacher should prompt the student to respond to ensure that the student is paying attention. If the student responds, but in a manner that is inconsistent with teacher expectations, then the teacher should take the opportunity to clarify concepts and seek to understand the reasons for the misunderstanding. Another type of feedback that may be provided to the student is graded assignments. Graded assignments provide a mechanism for letting students know "where they stand," and a guide for what they may need to do to improve their class standing. Hawisher and Pemberton (1997), in a study of asynchronous discussions in a *Writing Across the Curriculum* program, found that grades were important in motivating students to participate in online conference assignments. The authors noted that "[m]ere instructor encouragement and good will are generally not enough . . ." (p. 70).

The teacher's guidance role is not limited to the cognitive aspects of learning. The teacher also should mediate the social dynamics of the class. One way to do this is to monitor the prevalence of inappropriate language (e.g., Sproull & Kiesler, 1991) and respond to it immediately. Another way is to provide students with a syllabus that outlines the kind of language that is considered unacceptable to online discussion. Course syllabi may also provide guidance regarding how to deal with social loafing and gold bricking.

In sum, instructors within the CSCL environment occupy three roles:

- Regulator
- Monitor
- Guide

As the field of CSCL evolves, these roles should be revisited and reevaluated. At present, however, it is hoped that this framework will provide some guidance about the role of the teachers within a CSCL environment.

A central theme of this chapter has been that, in order to understand the role of the teacher in a CSCL environment, it is essential to better conceptualize the construct in question. Much of the extant literature has conceptualized CSCL within an individual learning paradigm. More recently, however, CSCL has been conceptualized as building mutually-shared cognition (Van den Bossche, Gijselaers, Segers, & Kirschner, 2006), collaborative group cognition (Stahl, 2005), or joint meaning-making (Koschmann, 2002). Going forward, if CSCL is indeed conceptualized as building mutually shared

cognitions, then the role of the instructor may be expanded to one of negotiator. Negotiation is the process whereby the instructor would help team
members to create mutually-shared cognitions: a common and agreed upon
understanding of meaning and its construction. (Van den Bossche et al., 2006).
The instructor would serve to facilitate those behaviors that lead to mutually-
shared cognitions. How the instructor would satisfy the role of negotiator in
a computer-mediated environment is reserved for future research, although
some researchers have already experienced the difficulty of achieving online
consensus (Weisband, 1992) and constructive argumentation and clarification
(Sproull & Kielser, 1991).

References

Assaf, L. C. (2005). Staying connected: Student teachers' perceptions of computer-mediated discussions. *The Teacher Educator, 40*(4), 221-235.

Brody, C. M. (1995). Collaboration or cooperative learning? Complimentary
practices for instructional reform. *The Journal of Staff, Program &
Organizational Development, 12*(3), 133-143.

Brookfield, S., & Preskill, S. (1999). *Discussion as a way of teaching: Tools and
techniques for democratic classrooms.* San Francisco: Jossey-Bass.

Bruffee, K. A. (1995, January/February). Sharing our toys: Cooperative
learning versus collaborative learning. *Change,* pp. 12-18.

Bruner, J. S. (1996). *The culture of education.* Cambridge, MA: Harvard
University Press.

Cannon-Bowers, J. A., Salas, E., & Converse, S. A. (1990). Cognitive psychology and team training: Shared mental models in complex systems.
Human Factors Bulletin, 33, 1-4.

Carlsmith, K. C., & Cooper, J. (2002). A persuasive example of cooperative
learning. *Teaching of Psychology, 29,* 132-135.

Deatz, R. C., & Campbell, C. H. (2001). *Applications of cognitive principles
in distributed computer-based training* (Research Product 20-01-03).
Alexandria, VA: U.S. Army Research Institute for the Social and Behavioral Sciences.

Dewey, J. (1916). *Democracy and education.* New York: The Free Press.

Ellis, P. J., Hollenbeck, J. R., Ilgen, D. R., Porter, C., West, B., & Moon, H. (2003). Team learning: Collectively connecting the dots. *Journal of Applied Psychology, 5*, 821-835.

Gokhale, A. A. (1995). Collaborative learning enhances critical thinking. *Journal of Educational Technology, 7*(1), Retrieved October 18, 2007, from http://scholar.lib.vt.edu/ejournals/JTE/jte-v7n1/gokhale.jte-v7n1.html

Hawisher, G. E., & Pemberton, M. A. (1997). Writing across the curriculum encounters asynchronous learning networks or WAC meets up with ALN. *Journal of Asynchronous Learning Networks, 1*, 52-72.

Hinsz, V. B., Tindale, R. S., & Vollrath, D. A. (1997). The emerging conceptualization of groups as information processors. *Psychological Bulletin, 121*, 43-64.

Jaffee, D. (1997). Asychronous learning: Technology and pedagogical strategy in a distance learning course. *Teaching Sociology, 25*, 262-277.

Johnson, D. W., & Johnson, P. (1991). *Joining together: Group theory and group skills* (4th ed.). Englewood Cliffs, NJ: Prentice Hall.

Johnson, R. T., & Johnson, D. W. (1986). Action research: Cooperative learning in the science classroom. *Science and Children, 24*, 32-32.

Johnson, D. W., Johnson, R., & Holubec, E. (1998). *Cooperation in the college classroom.* Boston: Allyn and Bacon.

Johnson, D. W., Johnson, R., & Smith, K. A. (1991). *Active learning: Cooperation in the college classroom.* Edina, MN: Interaction Book Company.

Kaptelinin, V., & Cole, M. (2002). Individual and collective activities in educational computer game playing. In T. Koschman, R. Hall, & N. Miyake (Eds.), *CSCL2: Carrying forward the conversation* (pp. 297-310). Mahwah, NJ: Lawrence Erlbaum Associates.

Klimoski, R., & Mohammed, S. (1994). Team mental model: Construct or metaphor? *Journal of Management, 20*(2), 403-437.

Koschmann, T. (1996). Paradigm shifts and instructional technology. In T. Koschmann (Ed.), *CSCL: Theory and practice of an emerging paradigm* (pp. 1-23). Mahwah, NJ: Lawrence Erlbaum Associates.

Koschmann, T. (2002). Dewey's contribution to the foundations of CSCL research. In G. Stahl (Ed.), *Computer support for collaborative learn-*

ing: Foundations for a CSCL community: Proceedings of CSCL 2002 (pp. 17-22). Mahwah, NJ: Lawrence Erlbaum Associates.

Kronnenberg, K. (1994; 1995). Developing communicative thinking skills via electronic mail. *TESOL Journal, 4*, 24-27.

Matthews, R. S., Cooper, J., Davidson, N., & Hawkes, P. (1995). Building bridges between cooperative and collaborative learning. *Change, July/August*, 35-40.

Meyers, S. A. (1997). Increasing student participation and productivity in small-group activities for college classes. *Teaching of Psychology, 24*, 105-115.

Office of Instructional Consultation, UC, Santa Barabara. (2006). *Differences between collaborative and cooperative learning.* Retrieved October 18, 2007, from http://www.id.ucsb.edu/IC/Resources/Collab-L/Differences. html

Olivares, O. J. (2005). Collaborative critical thinking: Conceptualizing a new construct from known constructs. *Issues in Educational Research, 15*(1), 86-100.

Ornstein, A. C., & Hunkins, F. P. (1998). *Curriculum: Foundations, principles, and issues* (3rd Ed.). Needham Heights: Allyn & Bacon.

Orvis, K. L., & Lassiter, A. L. R. (2006). Computer-supported collaborative learning: The role of the instructor. In S. P. Ferris & S. H. Goodard (Eds.), *Teaching and learning with virtual teams* (pp. 158-179). Hershey, PA: Information Science Publishing.

Piaget, J. (1973). *To understand is to invent: The future of education.* New York, NY: Grossman.

Schulte, A. (2004). The development of an asynchronous computer-mediated course: Observations on how to promote interactivity. *College Teaching, 52*(1), 6-10.

Shell, D., Husman, J., Turner, J. E., Cliffel, D., Nath, I., Sweany, N. (2005). The impact of computer supported collaborative learning communities on high school students' knowledge building, strategic learning, and perceptions of the classroom. *Journal Educational Computing Research, 33*(3), 327-349.

Slavin, R. E. (1985). An introduction to cooperative learning research. In R. Slavin, S. Sharan, S. Kagan, R. Hertz-Lazarowitz, C. Webb, & R. Schmuck (Eds.), *Learning to cooperate, cooperating to learn* (pp. 5-16). New York: Plenum.

Slavin, R. E. (1991). Synthesis of research on cooperative learning. *Educational Leadership*, *48*(5), 71-82.

Sproull, L., & Kiesler, S. (1991). *Connections: New ways of working in the networked organization*. Cambridge, MA: MIT Press.

Stahl, G. (2005). Group cognition in computer-assisted collaborative learning. *Journal of Computer Assisted Learning*, *21*, 79-90.

Stahl, G., Koschmann, T., & Suthers, D. D. (2006). Computer supported collaborative learning. In R. Keith, Sawyer (Ed.), *The Cambridge handbook of the learning sciences* (pp. 409-425). Cambridge, England: Cambridge University Press.

Van den Bossche, P., Gijselaers, W. H., Segers, M., & Kirschner, P.A. (2006.) Social and cognitive factors driving teamwork in collaborative learning environments. *Small Group Research, 37*(5), 490-521.

Van der Puil, C., Andriessen, J., & Kanselaar, G. (2004). Exploring relational regulation in computer-mediated (collaborative) learning interaction: A developmental perspective. *Cyberpsychology & Behavior*, *7*(2), 183-195.

Vygotsky, L. S. (1978). *Mind in society*. Cambridge, MA: Harvard University Press.

Warschauer, M. (1997). Computer-mediated collaborative learning: Theory and practice. *The Modern Language Journal*, *81*, 470-481.

Weisband, S. P. (1992). Group discussion and first advocacy effects in computer-mediated and face-to-face decision making groups. *Organizational Behavior and Human Decision Processes*, *53*, 352-380.

Zaccaro, S. J., Ardison, S. D., & Orvis, K. L. (2004). Leadership in virtual teams. In D. Day, S. Zaccaro, & S. Halpin (Eds.), *Leader development for transforming organizations* (pp. 267-292). Mahway, NJ: Lawrence Erlbaum.

Endnote

[1]   The following two sections borrow from Olivares (2005).

Section II

Student Development
Case Studies

Chapter III

Developing a Community of Practice in an Online Research Lab

Stephanie W. Cawthon, The University of Texas at Austin, USA

Alycia L. Harris, Walden University, USA

Abstact

The goal of this chapter is to present instructor and student perspectives on the development of a Community of Practice within an online research laboratory for graduate students in psychology. A computer-facilitated learning environment was set up meet two goals: (1) to encourage individuals to work as a team on a live research project, and (2) to give students research skills needed to further their development as scholar-practitioners. The objective of this chapter is to identify, from the perspectives of the students and the instructor, how social factors influenced learning outcomes and how the group formed into a research team. This chapter begins with a brief overview of the Community of Practice literature and the context of the Online Research Lab in the School of Psychology at Walden University. The second section addresses strategies the instructor used to facilitate the sense of community in the Online Research Lab. The chapter concludes with a summary of challenges in developing a Community of Practice, as well as strategies instructors can use to overcome these obstacles.

Theoretical Framework

Community of Practice

The Online Research Lab discussed in this chapter is conceptualized as a kind of Community of Practice (CoP). A Community of Practice is made up of a group of individuals working together toward a common goal. Essential to the development of a CoP are the practices, activities, and rituals that set the group apart from other groups or organizations (Wenger, 1998). There are four important processes in addition to learning itself that must be in place for a successful CoP: (1) a practice to be learned, (2) a community within which to learn it, (3) meaning developed as part of learning the practice with a group of individuals, and (4) an identity formed as part of membership in that community (Wenger, 1998). As group membership shifts over time, the CoP must also balance the practices of the established community with the learning curve of new members.

Most individuals will belong to a number of different Communities of Practice throughout their lifetimes (Merriam, Courtenay, & Baumgartner, 2003; Stacey, Smith, & Barty, 2004; Wenger, 1998). For example, individuals may participate in a cohort of professional peers, play on a recreational sports team, or perform in a musical production. Membership in one community may influence the development of membership and identity in another CoP (Stacey et al., 2004). For example, by pursuing a higher degree, membership in an academic CoP may provide a person with resources that increases her contributions to a work-based CoP. However, although individuals may overlap in their CoP membership, the activities and contribution of group members must be coherent to constitute a separately functioning CoP.

In Wenger's (1998) CoP model, a meaningful life stems from the practice of a purposeful activity. In this view, learning happens best when it is relevant to the individual's goals and interests (Collins, Brown, & Newman, 1989). In the present discussion, both formal learning activities and "extracurricular" social interaction are assumed to foster the development of a sense of community in the classroom (Browne, 2003; Johnson, 2001; Johnson & Aragon, 2003). Within a CoP, the community members draw from each other, collaborating to develop and validate shared understanding (Browne, 2003; Collins et al., 1989; Johnson, 2001; Johnson & Aragon, 2003; Richardson, 2003). The interactions of most CoP involve members with varying amounts of expertise (Wenger, 1998), but can also include novice-novice relationships (Hertzog, 2000). When applied to a formal education setting, both the instructor and the students contribute to the activity of the classroom. In the Online Research Lab discussed in this chapter, the focus is both on the relationships between students and on the relationship between the instructor and the students as a research team.

Cognitive Apprenticeship

Cognitive apprenticeship was the motivating theoretical framework for the Online Research Lab design and pedagogy (Collins, Brown, & Holum, 1991). Apprenticeships, in the traditional sense, are an opportunity for the novice to acquire a skill by working alongside an expert in his or her work environment. The expert models a skill within his or her own workplace, office, or laboratory. What each apprenticeship has in common is the "real world" context, or situated learning, in which the skill is developed (Brown, Collins, & Danguid, 1989). *Cognitive apprenticeship* is an effort to combine the best of the classroom experience with the applied learning opportunities of apprenticeship (Collins et al.). In traditional graduate education, this model is most closely manifest in the way faculty mentor graduate students by including them as members of a research team. Some online graduate programs in psychology provide research experiences as an independent study or research practicum, where a student works individually with a faculty member (Jones & Wilson, personal communication, 2006). To our knowledge, the Online Research Lab discussed in this chapter is the first example of a research cognitive apprenticeship course in an online, Web-based graduate program in psychology.

Online Learning and Graduate Studies in Psychology

The number of students pursuing online higher education continues to grow (Allen & Seaman, 2004). At the same time, the role of research in training professional psychologists has experienced a lively and sustained debate (e.g. Kahn, 2001; Lejuez, Read, Gollan, & Zvolensky, 2001; Mallinckrodt & Gelso, 2002; Schlosser & Gelso, 2001). Most professional psychology programs require statistics and research design coursework, and allow students to work with a faculty mentor on research projects (Gelso, 1993; Hill, Hall, & Pike, 2004; Krumboltz, 2002; Shivy, Worthington, Wallis, & Hogan, 2003). As graduate training moves into electronically distributed formats, including online graduate programs, what opportunities are available for online research mentorship for professional psychologists (Howell, Williams, & Lindsay, 2003; Rudestam, 2004)?

The Online Research Lab

In Fall of 2004, the first author began an Online Research Lab for graduate students in the School of Psychology at a distance-based online institution. The purpose of the Online Research Lab (Lab) was to provide psychology graduate students with hands-on experience in research design, study implementation, and data analysis. The Lab was similar in intent to research laboratories in traditional settings where graduate students assist a faculty principal investigator on his or her project. In this online setting, the researcher acted both as the principal investigator of the project and the instructor for the Lab course. A Blackboard 5.5 shell (and later, e-College) at the host university provided the "space" for instruction and collaboration. This was not a hybrid course, and did not include any face-to-face components.

The focus of the Online Research Lab was the development and implementation of a national online survey of educational professionals who serve students who are deaf or hard of hearing. The purpose of the survey was to gather data on the use of testing accommodations for students participating in large-scale, standardized assessments used for state accountability purposes (Cawthon & the Online Research Lab, 2006). The Lab participants conducted literature reviews, developed survey items, piloted the measure, recruited participants, analyzed data, and assisted in drafting manuscripts for publication. The Lab was an ongoing course for three years; the activities reported in this chapter occurred over the course of five quarters (one year and three months) during the 2004-2005 academic year.

One goal of the Lab was to invite the students to think about their role on the team as distinct from what they typically experience in graduate school.

Students in this online graduate program took courses and worked on a thesis or dissertation, but usually did not have the opportunity to act as a research assistant or teaching assistant alongside a department faculty member. Instead of thinking of their role as consumers of information, and the instructor as the primary source of information, the goal was to help students take on their own identity as researchers. Furthermore, the goal was for them to see the group as a team, as a community of researchers working together towards project completion.

At the close of the Lab, the instructor and two student participants sought to understand more about the learning process that had occurred. Using a case study approach, the research team gathered data about the Lab from a variety of sources. First, Lab alumni were invited to participate in a survey about their academic background and basic demographic information. Alumni also participated in structured interviews about their learning experience. These interviews included questions about student expectations about the Lab, how they learned, their interactions with the instructor and colleagues, and recommendations for future online research opportunities. Finally, the research team analyzed the online transcripts of discussion board postings and announcements in the Web-based classroom format. Examples from each of these data sources will be used to illustrate the emergence of a community of practice in this online learning environment.

The chapter will discuss key components in the development of a sense of community in the Online Research Lab. This discussion will look specifically at three key goals: (a) inviting the students into a community of researchers, (b) providing opportunities for collaboration, and (c) encouraging the development of nonactivity-related social interaction. Student perception of the role of communication tools such as discussion board posts, instant message chats, and e-mail will also be addressed. Finally, the authors will discuss challenges to developing a community of practice in an online setting and offer recommendations for future research training formats.

Developing a Community of Practice

When facilitating a research training environment, two leading roles emerge: principal investigator, and course instructor. If the research endeavor is to be successful, there must be an effective principal investigator whose role it is to initiate the research idea, and ensure that the project comes to completion. In addition, if the learning process for students is to be successful, there must be an instructor who is attentive to the needs of students. The project-based learning environment thus required the faculty member to balance these two roles. As a result, both the principal investigator and course instructor roles were important to the development of a sense of community.

Data analysis yielded a total of five strategies for developing a CoP, and two obstacles that, at times, threatened the success of the Lab as a CoP. The five strategies summarized below include: the use of CoP language, providing the big picture of the research project as a whole, providing opportunities for collaboration, creating student-centered assignments, and allowing for social interaction. The two obstacles to a strong CoP were technology issues, and students who were inconsistent in their participation in the Lab.

Community of Practice Language

Research team terminology. The first strategy to facilitate a sense of community was to use specific "research role" terminology in communications with Lab participants. The purpose of this terminology was to give students a sense of feeling like a fellow researcher, as part of a team effort. One of the simplest forms of role terminology was the use of the first-person plurals "we" and "our" in discussion board posts and classroom announcements throughout the course of the Lab. Another strategy was to tie individual student responsibilities to the broader project goals. Here is an example of an announcement from halfway through the project:

Week 9, Winter Term: *Hello! The major thrust of this week (Week 9) will be to email our letters out to those individuals we identified when developing our database of contacts. The directions for what we need to remember as we send out our letters are attached to this post. Your specific assignment is also in this attached document. Please read through this before proceeding with your emails!*

The remaining posts for this week contain your specific resources: Your contact list and your letter. Each of these will be designated by your name and group. Please verify that you have the correct materials before proceeding!

I ask that all emails be sent individually (not in a group email with multiple recipients in the to: line), from your email account. Please send all emails by Friday, February 4th at the very latest.

Thanks so much!

Instructor

(Announcements, Winter Term, 2004)

In addition to weekly (or, at times, daily) announcements, Community of Practice language also appeared throughout the discussion board posts. Unlike a traditional online course that begins a new topic each week, the Lab started a new topic roughly every other week. This was necessary because the topics and tasks were often challenging enough to require two or three weeks to complete. The use of "we" language was used to help motivate students as they started the activity in the topic's first week. The second week of each unit required other kinds of contributions, such as feedback on individual student tasks, and further instruction on how to meet task goals.

Transcript analysis of the first quarter included coding for "we" terminology, denoting a sense of community (see Figure 1). Interestingly, student and instructor usage of CoP-type terminology appears to spike in opposite weeks. Weeks with high student use of "we" terminology happens immediately following weeks with high instructor use of CoP language. This pattern may be because students are reflecting the language modeled by the instructor. It is also possible that the sequence of course activities lent to this alternating use of "we" terminology. Activities spanned over multiple weeks, initiated by the instructor ,and then discussed by students. Finally, the diverse content of activities may also be a factor in the use of "we" terminology. For example, literature review searches may not be conducive to the use of CoP language, because students were more likely to report on an article from the research literature than to discuss the ongoing project as a whole. In contrast, sharing the results of pilot studies and needed changes may facilitate more discussion as a research team.

Progress over time. In the first quarter, the sense of community developed slowly, and was not immediately evident in early activities. During interviews, students discussed difficulty with group activities, especially initially, and were frustrated when their colleagues did not complete their assigned tasks. However, despite early difficulties, they began to get comfortable with the

Figure 1. A line graph showing the percent of posts with CoP related terminology over the course of the twelve week Fall, 2004 term. Terminology included use of "we" and references to the group research activities. The instructor had higher rates of inclusive language in weeks 5, 7, and 9, whereas students had higher rates in weeks 1, 2, 3, 6, 8, and 12. This alternating pattern reflects a "give and take" in CoP language between the instructor and students.

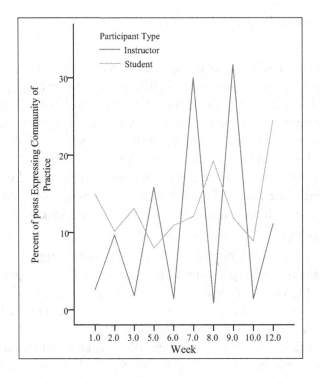

environment, developing a strong sense of community that lasted throughout the duration of the project. Students indicated a strong sense of overall community during the interview process.

Kelly: *Initially I truly believed there wasn't any. [laughs] But it did develop and um It did happen. Um and I personally, my personal thoughts on this because another area I spent a lot of time thinking about was that we were so ...busy perhaps learning new skills that the sense of community took time to develop because we needed to start feeling comfortable with what we were supposed to be doing. And as we learned uh and as we figured out what we* *were supposed to be doing that being able to be more collaborative with our team members...um...was easier.*

Sheila: *I would think um uh percentage-wise something like 99% we were really cohesive.*

Erica: *It was a community. It was very bonded.*
(Student Interviews, 2005)

Students identified with each other as a group, particularly those who participated in the Lab for more than one term. The first student quoted above, Kelly, did not realize at first that working together as a team was as important as completing the assigned research tasks. Reflecting back on the experience, Kelly understood that the assignments were structured to facilitate collaboration, and that teamwork was actually required for the project to be successful.

Establishing a CoP from scratch takes time and a great deal of work. Individuals entering later quarters joined an existing community as newer members, and then aided in the development of community over the course of their participation. Subsequent quarters were easier, in that the community of practice already existed, and new members came in, began working on their own trajectory of membership, and contributed new knowledge and ideas to the community:

Kelly: *Oh I think everyone was extremely supportive...Um when new members came um it was it was a, you know, definitely welcoming. Um I think at that point it was um really um good again to have that new perspective of new people joining even just for one quarter.*
(Student Interviews, 2005)

Kelly was a student who started with the group from the beginning, whereas others started later in the process. The "veterans," or those who were returning each term, were very conscious of the importance of their role of welcoming the new students.

Providing the Big Picture

The second strategy used by the instructor to build a sense of community was to continually update students on the progress of the research project as a whole. The purpose of these updates was to facilitate the transition of the contribution of each individual activity to the big picture of the study (Collins et al., 1989). The "project updates" were similar to what you might find in a regular research staff meeting in traditional settings. Here is one example of these project updates from the class announcements archives:

Week 4, Fall Term: *Hi all. Back in August I submitted a proposal to give a paper at the 2005 AERA (American Educational Research Association) conference in Montreal. The proposal was based on (1) The paper on Schools for the Deaf and No Child Left Behind and, (2) The design and pilot phases of this study.*

I found out today the paper is accepted! This is a big deal. The group only accepted four papers this year. So we actually have a target audience already, and we're still in the development phase! Actually, this is good. They're more interested in how we're doing than having it all finished (remember, pilot data!).

(Announcements, Fall Term, 2004)

These posts touched upon activities the instructor was involved in as the project principal investigator outside of course instruction. They also illustrated for students how research findings are presented in the academic community, and how their activities will eventually be represented with presentations and publications. Finally, the announcements helped to clarify what each person's responsibilities are towards the larger Lab goals, and reminded them of the timeframe for task completion and discussion contributions. Students provided positive feedback regarding these project updates. When interviewed about their experiences in the Lab, and the way the instructor facilitated communication and a sense of community, students said that the announcements and e-mails provided much-needed context and support.

Edward: *Bar none. Um…creating an environment that was both supportive uh…collaborative and uh and yet still had a solid guidance from uh Stephanie the instructor.*

Julie: *In her announcements she also posted a lot of helpful instructions. She would keep us posted all the time of what to expect, um, time frames again reminding us that, you know, she posted or uh put documents out there for us to share, for us to use or look at. Um…reminding us of resources …um… very very helpful.*

Student-Centered Assignments

Soliciting student input on what research activity they were assigned was a third strategy used to enhance student identification within the community of researchers. This strategy is supported by adult learner research literature that encourages instructors to draw up on students' previous experiences (Huang, 2002; Knowles, 1990). In this case, students provided information, both on their skills and knowledge about research, as well as research tasks they wanted to learn. At the start of the Lab, each participant completed the following "mini survey" (Figure 2).

Student information from these intake surveys was used to develop teams, matching those students who were looking to develop skills with those who were proficient and looked to use those skills to help others. This information also helped us to target individuals to take leadership in specific areas related to the project such as advertising and Web site development. One student member continued to be the Web site developer and consultant on the project a full year after her involvement with the project ended:

Maria: *Oh. Well she was giving assignments and everybody would pitch in and do their part and it was divided up. And she tried to make it accommodate um the skills of the people in the class … So that um everybody participate and uh and … succeed. And never stopped looking for the overall goals of what needed to be accomplished.*

(Student interviews, 2005)

This participant recognized that the tasks were divided up in a way that was meaningful for students. These assignments drew on their background, but challenged them to apply previous knowledge to a new area. Her comment reflects a feeling of purpose and of success that arose from deliberate allocation of tasks according to student preferences and strengths. This student

Figure 2. Intake survey given to students when the enrolled in the Online Research Lab. This survey was used to form project teams throughout the course of the research activities.

	I have experience with and am..		In this project, I would like to...	
Task	*Beginning*	*Proficient*	*Develop*	*Help others*
Website publishing				
Desktop publishing				
Statistical analysis				
Report writing				
Project management				
Advertising or marketing				
Survey item development				
Fundraising				
Team-building				
Online project work				
Literature reviews				
Topics	*Beginning*	*Proficient*	*Develop*	*Help others*
Students with disabilities				
Accountability reform (NCLB)				
Assessment practices				
Testing accommodations				
Deafness				

also recognized the challenge of both attending to student needs, and those of the overall project.

Opportunities for Collaboration

The fourth strategy for building community was to provide structured opportunities for collaboration. This also provided students with varying skills within the CoP to assist one another and broaden their understanding of research tasks (Browne, 2003; Collins et al., 1989; Hertzog, 2003; Johnson, 2001; Johnson & Aragon, 2003; Richardson, 2003). This was done mainly through the use of project pairs. The Lab offered many opportunities to engage in team-oriented projects or decision making. There were many factors that led to the decision to place students in teams. First, the Lab enrollment was quite large compared with a traditional research lab, often over 10 students. Large enrollment was due both to the minimum enrollment needed to run the course, as well as the popularity of the course with students. Each student task required a detailed list of instructions and follow up e-mails. It is challenging to individually tailor activities for a large group of students, and teaming students up meant there could be five or six quality activities instead of 10 smaller, less well-defined tasks.

The second reason for pairing students was to provide an embedded structure for peer support. Students were often using research tools for the first time. The intent was to provide a peer safety net by teaming students on projects that could be administered jointly. Learning within the community of practice took place primarily in the form of experiential learning, or learning by doing a portion of the project. Activity-based learning forms the core of any cognitive apprenticeship (Brown et. al., 1989). For example, one task was to randomly select schools from a national database that was disaggregated by state. This task required an advanced knowledge of database tools, including sorting fields and adding a randomized number in an additional field. Students with greater background in database software served as mentors to those who did not have the skills required to complete their tasks. After everyone was trained on the techniques, students completed their state lists individually. Students did not necessarily complete projects together, but could use each another as a support before submission to the larger group.

Gina: *Working with other researchers was um obviously very enlightening because we shared a lot back and forth. And some of us, maybe, had stronger skills in one area and others maybe had stronger skills in another area and we supported each other, and, you know, helped each other, and really kind of taught each other too. And I really liked that.*
(Student Interviews, 2005)

Because the research project relied upon task completion, the teams also provided a safety net for the research project itself. If one student was unable to contribute to the task, or dropped the course midway through the process, there was at least one other person who was familiar with the task, and who could take up the slack where needed. This is an example of how a pedagogical strategy also served as good research practice.

Students collaborated not only in the development of new skills, but in giving feedback on contributions to the research project. Students often provided as much feedback to another as the instructor, and at times, perhaps even more. Student feedback was particularly helpful when a group member struggled with the week's assignment or needed additional help with computer software, locating needed resources, and so on. This collaboration resulted in a strong sense of community identity, as opposed to just an identity as a student in the group. Feedback could be in the form of help in answering a question or in evaluating a fellow student's ideas in the discussion area. During the interview, when asked about forms of feedback, 75 % of students mentioned receiving feedback from fellow Lab members:

Jane: *"It was pretty scary because I entered in the last quarter. And I felt like a fish out of water. And...uh...I was assigned a partner and evidently it's my feelings that she was quite astute to what was going on. And she guided me through figuring out what to do. She gave me examples so that I knew why'd she'd do...she didn't tell me what to do. She gave me examples. And that helped me learn really, really well. Um...it gave me ideas on what I should find out. She was kind of like a mentor towards me and everybody was so wonderful and so understanding and made me feel like I was actually part of a team."*

Joan: *Personal e-mails from either the instructor or from either other uh colleagues, you know, in the class...*

Kelly: *It was like we were, you know, pretty much hand holding even though I'd been in the project longer than she had.*

James: *I found it comfortable. It was enjoyable. Um I thought we had a really good close-knit group, again, supporting each other. It was that type of group where, no matter where you were coming from, no...I don't think anyone felt like it was a bad thing or it was embarrassing to say "Hey I'm stupid here! I don't know what you're talking about."*
(Student Interviews, 2005)

Feedback activities included suggestions for revising a work product, or ways to address problems with the research task. Though less prevalent than helping activities, feedback was particularly strong in the early weeks (up to 15% of the posts). At times, especially towards the end of the term, more feedback came from the students than the instructor. This demonstrates how students grew in their willingness to provide substantive feedback, and to work as a team towards project completion.

Breadth of Communication

The Online Research Lab members used several forms of communication, including discussion boards, email, chat, and telephone calls. The multiple communication formats met the needs of different students. For example, some students had difficulties with the technology or the synchronicity (i.e., finding a time when they could all meet, especially across time zones) of the chats. These students used asynchronous communication—such as the discussion board or e-mail—when they could not access the chats. Students also indicated varying preferences for different forms of communication depending on the content of the task:

Jane: *Some of the things, like when we got into the more complex data analysis, it was nice to be able to go to the message board and see what other people were doing and see how they were doing. And to be able to post so you could get everyone's feedback on where you had gone with it so far. But then smaller tasks like when we were doing the literature review that first term there were three of us who were supposed to do a certain section back-groundwise. And in that instance the e-mail was much more helpful because if we could e-mail each other back and forth and get the list put together and then just post it all as one big list. So I think the one that's most helpful depended on what the task was.*

Edward: *From the uh my peers in the research Lab. Um… e uh even though everything was through e-mail. E-mail I meant from the instructor. Like if I reached out to her or whatever. And then also from my peers in the class. Because you know when you when I posted something, you know people would respond and were really supportive.*
(Student Interviews, 2005)

Students showed different preferences for discussion boards and e-mails depending on the task at hand. Some students preferred e-mail when detailed communication was required, but discussion board postings when input was needed from the entire group. Students indicated that instruction for tasks with multiple steps, such as for data analysis, was more effective in an e-mail format. It was therefore important to use multiple forms of communication in this course, and to supplement discussion board postings with follow-up e-mails to students.

Allowing for Social Interaction

The last strategy for building a community of practice is to allow for social interaction. A successful community is one that works well together—not just on the task at hand, but as members of a social group. An effort was made by the instructor to contribute to social interaction by purposefully setting the stage for such activity, allowing its natural occurrence, and participating where appropriate. The first place where this is done in an online setting is through the "Class Café." The Class Café in Blackboard and e-College is set up as a place for social interaction that is not necessarily tied to the content of the course.

The Class Café functioned in a similar manner in the Lab. One strategy was to intertwine more informal requests for student perspectives with social interaction. For example, at the start of the second (Winter) term, the instructor made the following post early on in the Class Café:

Please check in here! Some of us are continuing on from last term, others are joining us for the first time. Please do welcome each other and share a bit about yourselves. For those of you who are returning, if you could answer the following:

What resource/reading/activity did you find most helpful getting going last term? How can we help our new folks get revved up?

Thanks!

Instructor
(Course Transcripts, 2004)

Personal events often made their way into the conversation in the Class Café and on the main discussion boards. For example, the Lab was held during the

2004-05 hurricane season. Participants often expressed concern when there were major weather events occurring in different regions of the country. Students were spread throughout the United States, and there was an awareness of how people in different regions were faring throughout the term.

Stacey,

My goodness! You said it, Florida was really pummeled this last hurricane season. We have friends and relatives who live down in your neck of the woods so we were constantly praying for them!

Glad to have you with us. Welcome aboard! I think you will really enjoy this opportunity!

Jennifer

(Course Transcripts, 2004)

Finally, the online chat was an important place where students connected with each other. After the first term, regular, bi-weekly chats became a fixture of the Lab environment. This was important in gauging student understanding of the research process, providing specific feedback, and demonstrating "live" thinking processes that come up in synchronous conversations. A pleasant side effect of the online chats was the opportunity to connect with each other in a social way. The instructor intentionally allowed the beginning and end of each chat to flow naturally between group members. Participants often checked in with how each person was doing, personally, before delving into the task at hand. Although the instructor certainly had a role in facilitating this process, students were the ones who took ownership of developing community. Here is an excerpt from a "live" chat discussion in the Spring, 2005 term:

Allison > hi
Instructor > How are you today?
Mary > how's allison?
Allison > got my chicken soup and I'm in bed
Instructor > oh no!
Mary > oh no...
Instructor > hey, in answer to your question allison, filter then categorize
Allison > okee doke that is what I have been doing

Mary > allison...flu?
Allison > I don't know
Allison > I could not get warm at all today at work
Instructor > oh dear!
Mary > aches from head to toe, yet?
Allison > Oh yea. I came home yesterday and went to bed and felt better this am. So tomorrow's lookin good
Instructor > oh good How is the new job going this week?
Mary > sounds like what i had last week
Allison > I'm just bein a baby
Mary > nah.... if it's what i had, you have a right to flat-out whine
Instructor > tee hee
Allison > How is the thesis going?
Mary > gettin' there dr. keeps coming up with something else he needs for my file . i keep giving it to him
(Chat, Spring, 2005)

Students frequently brought up whatever issues were on their plate at the time of the chats, be it thunderstorms in the neighborhood, thesis woes, their children, or the latest flu bug going around. The chats gave participants an opportunity to share their life experiences in a natural way. For example, one student experienced this camaraderie during the later phases of the project (personal communication, "Allison," 2006). She was assigned to assist a new member who preferred communication via phone over e-mail exchanges. During their nearly two-hour phone conversation, they discussed many aspects of the Lab, but also discussed each other's families, interests, and so on. This and other such personal communication enabled them to feel more comfortable in interacting within the practices of their CoP. That is, the more they knew each other—especially given the fact that this was done online—the easier it was to offer suggestions, critique one another's work, and work together as fellow researchers.

Challenges to Community of Practice

As with any learning environment, there are sometimes challenges to communication among group members. Working within an online environment resulted in some unique challenges, and required proactive attention from all members, especially from the instructor. There were two main sources of communication breakdowns in the Lab: technology problems, and nonresponsive students. Technology breakdowns were typically temporary, and usually overcome with alternative strategies for task completion. Nonresponsive students, however, proved to be a persistent problem, and quite difficult to remedy in the context of a group project.

Technology

Online education is wholly dependent on functioning technology for the environment to run smoothly. Because the Lab was interaction-intensive, intermittent technology outages were perhaps even more disruptive than in a typical online course. For example, when the classroom servers were running slowly, or the online chat mechanism failed to launch, the students could not access the course materials, post their feedback, or participate in the synchronous discussions. As the Lab progressed, access to the online chats proved to be an increasingly important source of feedback and troubleshooting for students, particularly in statistics and data analysis. Students also expressed their frustration with failed technology during the online chats. When both e-mail and the classroom servers were down (once, for about two weeks, at the start of a term), research activities ground to a halt.

Using e-mail to convey information and answer questions usually led to more intense communication between the instructor and the Lab participants. In the classroom, students often read announcements and posts without posting a response or comment. In e-mail, however, it was not uncommon to receive separate messages from many students about the activities of the week. In an e-mail communication format, students treated the Lab as a one-on-one independent study instead of a group project. This changes the nature of a community of practice by shifting the emphasis away from collective knowledge to a more comfortable—but at times less productive—individual learning experience. E-Mail communications were welcomed, but the questions were often redirected back to the group discussion board for further consideration.

Nonresponders

There were a handful of students throughout the year who did not participate as fully as was needed to be successful in the Online Research Lab environment. In all cases, students expressed a desire to participate in their introductions and e-mail communications, but underestimated the time required to participate in research, given the other demands in their lives. Students in face-to-face research training environments also face this kind of challenge in allocating enough time for research activities (Shivy et al., 2003). This is partly an artifact of the kinds of students that attend this online program. As adult learners, Lab participants frequently worked, in addition to working towards their degrees. The majority worked outside of the home, mostly in the education field. Participants were mostly employed full-time, with an average workload of 37 hours per week.

However, it was lack of communication with team partners that had the most significant impact on the sense of community, not the task noncompletion itself. There were often ways to rearrange the work so that the research project continued as needed. It was much more difficult to repair damage to the social network when a Lab member chose not to respond to e-mail communications or telephone calls to maintain contact. Students often took it personally when their partner would not respond to attempts to work on their team project. In their interviews about their experience in the Lab, several participants noted the frustration they felt when the person they were teamed with let them down.

The instructor took some proactive steps to remedying or at least preventing future issues. When a team member became "missing in action," the first strategy to support the student who now had the team's project on his or her own plate. As the Lab continued, we were able to employ a teaching assistant (a Lab alumnus). The teaching assistant proved invaluable in both supporting the remaining participant emotionally, and with the work that was left to be done. The priority was to ensure that the remaining participant did not have to do double the work, and to mitigate feelings of abandonment they often expressed.

However, communicating with and supporting the nonresponder was often a more challenging task. In the case of students with significant personal life and health issues, frequently the discussion surrounded the wisdom of continuing in the Lab. At other times, students were struggling with time management. In these cases, structured work timeframes were useful tools in bringing students back on track. These strategies were challenging at times, because the research project deadlines sometimes meant that the student needed to start on a new or alternative task, instead of completing the original assignment. The realities of the timeframe in "live" research sometimes meant that nonresponders could not be fully reintegrated where they left off.

Conclusion and Recommendations

This chapter presented components of Community of Practice as they evolved in an Online Research Lab. Strategies for developing a sense of community in this setting included deliberate use of "we" language by the instructor, student-centered assignments, collaborative tasks, feedback among students, and encouraging social interaction. There were, however, many obstacles to a community of practice in an online research setting, especially technology breakdowns, and nonresponsive students.

There are several key points that we hope the reader will take from this discussion:

1. The purpose of the Online Research Lab was to have students learn about research by participating in a live project. For this to be successful, members of the class must work well together and be involved in constructive communication. Without strong, consistent communication among participants, it is challenging for the instructor to both meet the needs of students and the demands of an ongoing research project.

2. The structure of the class, using larger two- and three- week units, resulted in mirrored patterns of dialogue from both the instructor and the students. We saw communication strategies used by the instructor later integrated by the students. Instruction and feedback cycles were also paced by the structure of classroom activity. Instructors can use these cycles to model research tasks, and to allow students to provide feedback to their peers.

3. It is important to use multiple forms of communication (discussion board, e-mails, chats) for instruction, feedback, helping, and other community of practice activities. Some students prefer e-mail communication over discussion board postings when they find the material challenging, or

have questions about the activity. However, the community of practice may be enhanced by having these discussions as a group. Careful thought should be given to the amount of support offered to an individual outside of the format of the online classroom.

4.   Nonresponding students are a significant obstacle to a successful Community of Practice. One way to be proactive is to provide interested students with information about the expectations and time commitment required for participation. These expectations should include communication with peers. Even if grading is pass/fail, frequent opportunities for graded evaluations of communication with peers may also be helpful in reinforcing the importance of dialogue within the classroom.

5.   Technology failures were often beyond the control of the Lab participants, but could be remedied by having back up plans and using other communication strategies to cover the gaps of a failed e-mail or online discussion board system. For example, provide essential information in course announcements, discussion boards, and e-mail to ensure that students are aware of key issues, particularly those that are time-sensitive.

6.   Veterans of the project—those who participated in the Lab for more than one term—played an important role in bringing new students on board each term. While it is challenging to have research assistants at different skill levels, the project benefits from having students with previous experience available to apprentice the new students on specific Lab-related tasks. Instructors of research labs may want to consider how best to structure activities for new team members.

7.   Instructors of research labs should be aware that it takes a considerable amount of time investment for outcomes to be successful for both the students, and the research project. Part of this time investment is required to develop one's role as both an instructor of research, and principal investigator of a research project. There will be times when the need to provide additional instruction may draw one away from pressing administrative issues that arise. Likewise, research timeframes did not always fit neatly within the schedule of the academic year. In each, keeping students informed about the larger research activities helped to illustrate where their work fit into the broader project.

An Online Research Lab contributes in unique and significant ways to the development of research skills for online graduate students in psychology.

Through deliberate scaffolding of student participation in research activities, and conscious facilitation of both the academic and social environment, students can grow into a thriving Community of Practice. Students noted that this community was an important part of their enjoyment of the process, and that research experience in isolation would not have generated a similar level of learning outcomes. Although they were frustrated when peers did not contribute as expected, students appreciated the interaction with their colleagues on both a personal and professional level. Strategies for integrating students into faculty research may also be considered for other programs and fields of study, especially those that allow students to apply the literature review, statistics, and research design skills they have learned through their coursework. In light of the increased enrollment of students in online graduate programs, particularly those at the doctoral level, universities will be challenged to structure research experiences for aspiring academics. Experiences such as the Online Research Lab maybe a way that both faculty and students can participate in joint scholarship activities, while maintaining the flexibility of the online learning environment.

References

Allen, I. E., & Seaman, J. (2004). *Entering the mainstream: The quality and extent of online education in the United States, 2003 and 2004.* Retrieved October 19, 2007, from http://www.sloan-c.org/resources/entering_mainstream.pdf

Brown, J., Collins, A., & Duguid, P. (1989). Situated cognition and the culture of learning. *Educational Researcher, 18*(1), 32-42.

Browne, E. (2003). Conversations in cyberspace: A study of online learning. *Open Learning, 18,* 245-259.

Cawthon, S., & the Online Research Lab. (2006). Accommodations use for statewide standardized assessments: Prevalence and recommendations for students who are deaf or hard of hearing. *Journal of Deaf Studies and Deaf Education, 11*(3), 337-359.

Collins, A., Brown, J.S., & Holum, A. (1991). Cognitive apprenticeship: Making thinking visible. *American Educator, 15,* 6-46.

Collins, A., Brown, J. S., & Newman, S. E. (1989). Cognitive apprenticeship: Teaching the crafts of reading, writing, and mathematics. In L. B. Resnick (Ed.), *Knowing, learning, and instruction: Essays in honor of Robert Glaser* (pp. 453-494). Hillsdale, NJ: Lawrence Erlbaum.

Gelso, C. J. (1993). On the making of a scientist-practitioner: A theory of research training in professional psychology. *Professional Psychology: Research and Practice, 24,* 468-476.

Hertzog, H. S. (2000). *When, how and who do I ask for help? Novice perceptions of learning and assistance.* Paper presented at the Annual Meeting of the AERA. New Orleans, LA. Retrieved October 19, 2007, from ERIC database.

Hill, P. C., Hall, T. W., & Pike, P. L. (2004). Research at an explicitly integrative program: Rosemead school of psychology. *Journal of Psychology and Christianity, 23,* 338-344.

Howell, S., Williams, P., & Lindsay, N. (2003). Thirty-two trends affecting distance education: An informed foundation for strategic planning. *Online Journal of Distance Learning Administration, 6*(3), 19.

Huang, H. (2002). Toward constructivism for adult learners in online learning environments. *British Journal of Educational Technology, 33,* 27-37.

Johnson, C. M. (2001). A survey of current research on online communities of practice. *Internet and Higher Education, 4,* 45-60. Retrieved October 19, 2007, from http://www.learnloop.org/olc/johnsonOnlineCoP.pdf

Johnson, S. D., & Aragon, S. R. (2003). An instructional strategy framework for online learning environments. *New Directions for Adult & Continuing Education, 100,* 31-43.

Kahn, J. H. (2001). Predicting the scholarly activity of counseling psychology students: A refinement and extension. *Journal of Counseling Psychology, 48,* 344-354.

Knowles, M. S. (1990). *The adult learner: A neglected species* (4th ed.). Houston: Gulf.

Krumboltz, J. D. (2002). Encouraging research: Making it collegial, enjoyable, and relevant. *American Psychologist, 57,* 931-940.

Lejuez, C. W., Read, J. P., Gollan, J. K., & Zvolensky, M. J. (2001). Research considerations for obtaining a predoctoral clinical psychology internship. *Professional Psychology: Research and Practice, 32,* 650-654.

Maillinckrodt, B., & Gelso, C. J. (2002). Impact of research training environment and Holland personality type: A 15-year follow up study of research productivity. *Journal of Counseling Psychology, 49*(1), 60-70.

Merriam, S. B., Courtenay, B., & Baumgartner, L. (2003). On becoming a witch: Learning in a marginalized community of practice. *Adult Education Quarterly, 53*, 170-188.

Richardson, V. (2003). Constructivist pedagogy. *Teachers College Record, 105*, 1623-1640.

Rudestam, K.E. (2004). Distributed education and the role of online learning in training professional psychologists. *Professional Psychology: Research and Practice, 35,* 427-432.

Schlosser, L., & Gelso, C. (2001). Measuring the working alliance in advisor-advisee relationships in graduate school. *Journal of Counseling Psychology, 48*(2), 157-167.

Shivy, V. A., Worthington, E. L., Wallis, A. B., & Hogan, C. (2003). Doctoral research training environments (RTEs): Implications for the teaching of psychology. *Teaching of Psychology, 30,* 297-302.

Stacey, E., Smith, P. J., & Barty, K. (2004). Adult learners in the workplace: Online learning and communities of practice. *Distance Education, 25,* 107-123.

Wenger, E. (1998). *Communities of practice: Learning, meaning, and identity.* Cambridge: Cambridge University.

Chapter IV

The Case Method and Collaborative Learning

Stephanie L. Brooke, University of Phoenix, USA

Abstract

With increasing interest in online education, instructors must have a repertoire of tools available to promote the critical thinking skills of their students. This chapter will present the case method as one pedagogical approach for teaching online courses. Example cases are provided. Pedagogical approaches to working with new and seasoned online students are addressed. Further, the benefits of using the case method to promote learning in the virtual classroom are explained. The case studies presented for online classes present concrete situations that can be used to stimulate analysis, requiring students to project how they might respond to a set of circumstances. The case studies promote Socratic dialogue and higher order thinking skills. Further, the case method can be a good vehicle for stimulating students' thoughts about step-by-step planning.

Introduction

With increasing interest of students, educators, and administrators in online education, instructors must have a repertoire of tools available to promote the critical thinking skills of their students (Bloom, 1956; Krathwhol, Bloom, & Bertram, 1973). This chapter presents the case method as one pedagogical approach for teaching online courses, one which can promote collaborative learning. Research shows that students are satisfied with opportunities for collaborative learning in asynchronous, computer-supported environments (Dewiyanti, 2007). Example cases for beginning and experienced—or seasoned—online students are provided. Further, the benefits of using the case method to promote problem-based learning in the virtual classroom are explained. The virtual classroom refers to classes taught online. The case studies presented for online classes present concrete situations that can be used to stimulate analysis, requiring students to project how they might respond to a set of circumstances. The case studies promote higher order thinking skills. Further, the case method can be a good vehicle for stimulating students' thought about step-by-step planning. Using the cases with groups of students promotes opportunities for collaborative learning. Finally, cases promote learner-learner interaction through Socratic dialogue and cooperative learning.

The use of the case method to teach is not particularly novel. It has been used for some time in face-to-face classes. Conant (1949) of Harvard University was the first professor to center his entire course on the use of the case method. As colleges and universities go through technological innovations, such as offering classes online, the case method can be adapted to the virtual classroom to promote critical thinking skills, and promote collaborative learning. One critical challenge is to engage the online learner in the material presented, and to foster higher order thinking. The case method is an active learning strategy that engages students and fosters higher order thinking. Also, the case method facilitates problem-solving skills (Levine, 1994).

Problem-Based Learning

Problem-based learning (PBL) is an instructional method that challenges students to actively learn by working cooperatively in groups to seek solutions to real world problems. "The ideas embodied in problem-based learn-ing have a long history, ranging back at least to the use of cases in Harvard Medical School in the nineteenth century and extending through John Dewey's philosophy, Jerry Bruner's discovery learning, and the development of simulations in the 1960s" (McKeachie, 1999, p. 175). The case method, like other problem-based learning strategies, "are intended to develop student ability to solve problems using knowledge, concepts, and skills relevant to a course. Cases provide contextualized learning, as contrasted with learning disassociated from meaningful context" (McKeachie, 1999, p. 177). Cases provide a framework for applied knowledge, as opposed to learning informa-tion outside of a meaningful framework. Problems embedded in cases are used to engage students' curiosity and initiate learning the subject matter. PBL prepares students to think critically and analytically, and to find and use appropriate learning resources. Problem-based learning can be set up in a variety of formats. The next section will describe such formats, as well as define the case method approach.

According to Levine (1994), effective problem solving happens in groups. For instance, Levine talks about functional blindness as a block to effective problem solving. With functional blindness, a person uses habitual modes of responding while being blind to other options. One way around functional blindness is to collaborate or brainstorm in groups. Brainstorming facilitates flexibility in problem solving and can be used with the case method.

Collaborative Learning

In the collaborative model, learning teams assume almost total responsibility for answering a case question. The students determine if they have enough information for answering the case question. If not, they identify other sources, such as journals, books, videos, or the Internet. Students are encouraged to use references to support their work on the cases. The work of obtaining the extra source information should be distributed among the learning team by the group members. This helps to develop research skills, and to promote effective utilization of the Internet. Together, the learning group drafts a response to the case question. The instructor assesses the progress of each group, and provides suggestions about each group's approach. In addition, the instructor should be available for consultations, and would facilitate the process by asking for frequent progress reports from the groups, facilitate group discussions about group dynamics, and help with conflict resolution. The final case answer is determined by each group, after consultation with the instructor.

Consider the following example, which uses a learning team charter developed by the University of Phoenix to guide group work. Peer evaluations are used at the end of the class. Students are rated by their peers on a scale of 1-10, with 10 being a highly-valued and functioning team member, and 1 as a team member offering little assistance and support to the group. The scores are totaled. For example, suppose a student's score is 80 points. That individual would earn 80% of the group's final score. This usually ensures that all members of the learning team are active in helping find resources for the case and developing the final answer.

The process is open-ended while maintaining a focus on the overall goal. The students develop a strong ownership for the process, and respond very positively to the fact that they are given almost complete responsibility to deal with the problem posed to them. Further, they have significant input into their assessment. The instructor sets the tone for the group, and this tone or climate is the one students will follow. "The facilitator helps elicit and clarify the purposes of the individuals in the class as well as the more general purposes of the group" (White & Weight, 2000, p. 115). Expectations for the group exercise can be clarified. As the group works together more, the instructor can become a model for the class—a participant learner, member of the group—and can express views as an individual. It is the instructor's job to remain alert to strong expressions or emotional indicators. McKeachie (1999) provides a good chapter advising on how to deal with difficult or emotional students. Overall, the instructor helps students connect ideas to experiences, integrate material, empower and motivate others, and maintain a group learning environment (White & Weight, 2000). Kaplan (2002, para. 15) makes the following suggestions for building a strong online community that can be applied to groups in the virtual classroom:

People Approaches:

* **Clearly define roles:** Describe the relationship between the different roles in the community, including the instructor, subgroups, group leaders or facilitators, and individual learners. Be sure to detail responsibilities and interdependencies.

* **Create subgroups:** Create a breakout group of learners that has its own online space for small group learning activities and group project collaboration.

- **Support individuality:** Provide a way for learners to create personal profiles that include photos and salient information to the topic. For example, a course on marketing might ask participants to identify their favorite innovative television commercial.

Process Approaches:

- **Establish operating norms:** Include guidelines for online and offline etiquette, and obtain agreement on the behavior that will lead to successful group and individual learning outcomes. For instance, ask each community member to log in three times per week, and post one question and one response on the discussion board.

- **Foster trust:** Establishing and aligning learners' expectations around shared objectives, including how individual contributions tie in to the broader success of the group, helps create an open and sharing environment. Using the entire group, explicitly define the common values and behavior that will help the community achieve a shared goal, and also build trust.

- **Create a buddy system:** Keeping learners engaged in an online environment can be challenging. Create a support structure to keep people involved by employing a system in which pairs or groups of learners are responsible for joint participation and contribution, such as codevelopment of a case study, or alternating postings in the discussion area.

Kaplan (2002) also suggests technology approaches. Specifically, it helps the students if the learning environment is user-friendly: Some platforms are difficult for students to utilize, which creates technical issues that interfere with collaborative learning.

Case Method Defined

What is meant by the term, case method? "Cases are often actual descriptions of problem situations in the field in which the case is being used; sometimes, they are syntheses constructed to represent a particular principle or type of problem" (McKeachie, 1999, p. 177). The case method is an inductive process by which students learn through their joint, cooperative effort, as opposed to the professor conveying views to students (Herreid, 1994). This is in direct opposition to what Friere (1971) termed the banking method of education. With the banking method of education, students are repositories for the instructor's information. According to Friere (1971), students then "spit back" the facts that the instructor has provided—there is no critical thinking involved in this practice. With the case method, students and the professor engage in a Socratic dialogue. This fosters critical thinking skills, thereby eradicating the banking method of education in the virtual classroom. The case method is designed to enhance student understanding of core concepts of the course, as well as to encourage critical thinking.

In using cases, students become active, similar to the Bau Hause method, which is "learning by doing"—it is an active learning strategy. The case method follows this line of philosophy. Cases provide students with the opportunity to exercise decision making, whether individually or as a team. This is done through presentation of a dilemma case, and through the series of questions designed to accompany the case. For the disciplined student, cases help increase motivation (Washull, 2005). Further, it provides them with real life examples (Brooke, 2005). Some students have difficulty connecting the theory to real life, practical examples. The case approach alleviates this problem.

The method is easy to implement. The following sections will describe short case scenarios that were created and integrated in the presentation of the course material. The difference between face to face classes and online classes is in the length of the case study. Shorter, abbreviated, problem-based cases are used to effectively teach online classes (Brooke, 2005). The reason that shorter cases work is that many online classes only meet for a short period of time. For instance, at the University of Phoenix, the average class is five weeks long. The following section examines several types of cases that instructors can utilize in the online classroom to motivate students to learn.

Types of Cases

There are a variety of tools or learning activities for presenting cases, such as discussion, debates, trials, and public hearings. I regularly use discussion, debates, and trials. The public hearings can be quite complex for a face-to-face classe, and may be very difficult to implement in an online environment; therefore, public hearings will not be discussed here.

Discussion Approach

The discussion approach is perhaps the best known for presenting cases (Herreid, 1998), and is one utilized most often in the online classroom. For this approach, instructors present a case that requires students to make an evaluation. In an online abnormal psychology class, cases were presented in which a person may or may not be suffering from a mental disorder. Students try to diagnose the case according to Diagnostic Statistical Manual (DSM) criteria. Here is an example:

How would you diagnose the following case and what treatment approach would you use? Use theory to support your response: This is a case of a woman who is quiet, reclusive, and withdrawn. She has no close friends and resents it when people try to intrude on her solitude. She works in a library in the stacks and prefers not to deal with the public. Her coworkers find her to be unresponsive, unemotional, and she does not seem to be interested in interacting with them. She reads at night and rarely goes out. She is often described as a loner.

This brief version has worked well for online cases that utilize discussion questions where classes meet for only five weeks. For online classes which meet for 14 weeks, similar to the length of time of traditional classrooms, more extensive cases can be used, such as the case of Maria (Brooke & Martin, 2004). Briefly, this case is about a Latina woman represented as depressed and suicidal, working with a Caucasian therapist who is not culturally sensitive to her client. To view the case, please see the following Web site: http://www.sciencecases.org/therapeutic_relationship/therapeutic_relationship.asp. The teaching notes explain how to present the case, list questions to ask, and breaks down the activities by time. To see the teaching notes, see this Web site: http://www.sciencecases.org/therapeutic_relationship/therapeutic_relationship_notes.asp

This discussion approach can be used with online classes that have 25 students or less. For this approach, the instructor should be sure that students stay on track with the discussion. Reiterating questions, asking thought-provoking questions, and providing brief summaries are ways the instructor can keep students on task.

Debates

Debates are an interesting way to deal with subjects that have two extremes or opposing views. For instance, when teaching child development online, the class is split into two teams for debates: those who support cosleeping with infants, and those who do not support co-sleeping with infants. Such a topic is a good way to bring up cultural variations in the way children are raised. Students have the opportunity to see evidence on both sides of the debate through their research and evidence provided. Additionally, students who have had one point of view at the beginning of the class may change to the other point of view after the presentation of evidence in the debates.

Trial Method

For online teaching, instructors can also use the trial method. The trial should be focused on the material in the lecture. To begin, both teams write an introductory statement. Individuals should write this introduction as a team, using references to support their work. One recommendation is to assign members to teams, and create a work area for each team. After the posting of the introductory statement, each team creates a rebuttal in direct response to the opposing team's introductory statement. Next, they pose one question to the opposing team. The question is designed to challenge the team's point of view, and require that they back up their point with research and references that support their point of view. Time permitting, more questions can be added. Each team ends with the closing argument or statement. The debate format works well with a smaller group of students, 15 or less. The following case study is an example of a scenario that has been used in introductory psychology courses:

Case: *A woman's twelve-year-old daughter had been approached sexually by her grandfather, the woman's father. The grandfather, as is often the case, was a responsible member of the community, a proverbial "pillar" of family rectitude. The child's experience had triggered a memory that the mother had long repressed: when she was the same age as her daughter, her father had* *sexually molested her. As a young teenager, she had dealt with it fairly well, told no one, and repressed the incident altogether. Though she had managed reasonably well to overcome her feelings of fear and guilt, in retrospect she realized that it had inhibited her sexual responsiveness and healthy adjust-ment to adulthood. When she confronted her father with the truth, he denied it absolutely and acted as if she had imagined the whole thing. Her own mother accused her of hating her father and plotting to destroy the family. Now she wants to bring her father to trial for sexually abusing her as a child.*

Students can be quite dramatic with this approach, and find it a beneficial learning experience. The instructor may assign the roles of lawyers, grand-father, grandmother, mother, and daughter. The lawyers ask a question of their witnesses, and the witnesses respond. The trial ends with the lawyers making their closing statements. "Whatever the case, it typically involves the possibility of several alternative approaches or actions and some evaluation of values and costs of different solutions to the problem posed" (McKeachie, 1999, p. 177).

Beginning Online Students

The pedagogy of teaching beginning online students differs greatly from that of teaching experienced online students. In some senses, there is a great deal more hand-holding and direction from the instructor. Students are challenged to acclimatize to the online environment in addition to learning the course content. Some online institutions require that students work in virtual teams, so the instructor needs to facilitate their experience in working in groups online. In addition, many students are new to this format, so instruction in communicating online and netiquette are essential. Please see Appendix A for the Communicating Online Tips sheet that has been used to teach online classes.

Tone

New students will need assistance with tone. When we meet people face-to-face, we usually have a clear sense of what is appropriate in the way we act and communicate. Meeting people over the Internet similarly requires a certain level of awareness. On the Internet, we cannot read body language such as smiles, nods of the head, or looks of disapproval. We cannot hear the tone of another person's voice. Tone is conveyed through word choice in the virtual classroom. Sarcasm in particular comes across poorly in Internet communication. For example: Think of a simple question such as, "Are you serious?" In a friendly situation, this could be sincere. In a loud and aggressive tone, it could mean something quite different, perhaps "Have you lost your mind?" When using electronic communications, it may be difficult for others to know what you really intended to convey. Students must be guided into communicating carefully and effectively, particularly at the start of a course.

Dealing with Conflict

Conflict between students, when working in online teams, is an issue with beginning students. It is important for the facilitator to guide the groups from destructive conflict to constructive conflict or criticism. For instance, destructive conflict involves disagreements centered on personality, whereas constructive conflict involves substantive conflict or disagreement with ideas and group issues (Tannen, 1998). Conflict arises from communication failure, personality clashes, value and goal differences, substandard performance, and responsibility issues (White & Weight, 2000). The key is teaching students to respond constructively to conflict, rather than react to conflict. The case method ameliorates destructive group conflicts by building cohesion, and promoting positive group interaction skills such as brainstorming and conflict management. Instructors can teach beginning students conflict management skills, and can provide references for more experienced online students. For more information on promoting positive team decision making, see Porter's (2003) article. Beginning students and experienced students can benefit from conflict by opening up hidden issues, clarifying subject matter, improving the quality of problem solving, increase involvement in learning, and increase cooperation and interaction (White & Weight, 2000).

Beginning students also will need opportunities for proactive problem solving. Working in teams seems to be the most troublesome area for students. The following case vignettes were developed to teach beginning students how to resolve team issues before they start working in learning teams:

Case: *Learning Team A is made up of Frank, Omar, Lisa, Jackie, and Shawn. Frank volunteers to be the team leader and takes control rather easily. He notices Lisa is the last person to make comments and suggestions. Also, she shows up in the main folder but not the group folder. The deadline for the first project is in two days and Lisa has not contributed much. If you were in Learning Team A, how would you first define the problem?*

Not only does this case study show students ways to deal with problems before they may arise in the team, it gives them the chance to exercise critical thinking skills. In this case, students are asked to first think of the possible reasons why Lisa might be inactive, prior to jumping in to problem solving. Students are exposed to different points of view on the possible reasons for Lisa's behaviors. After this, they are asked how to resolve the dilemma. Here is one beginning student's response to the cases developed for beginning online students:

I thought that the case studies were interesting. I learned a lot from them because I had to perform more research to understand what the studies were about before I could reply on them. They opened my eyes up to topics that I would not ordinarily had been interested in, sought after on my own, or been aware of. They also made me aware of how much I do and do not agree with certain aspects of a topic. Also, they corrected my perception on certain aspects of subjects. All in all, the cases are very informative, prompt an awareness, and was good practice for enhancing my research skills.

Teaching students how to create substantial discussion responses to the cases is the critical task of the instructor. This holds true for beginning as well as experienced online students. Writing, "I agree with you," or "Good point," is not enough, and certainly not a substantial response. Instructors should require that students build on their peer's response, and use references and theory to support their work. This can provide them with an opportunity for reflective feedback. Please see Appendix B for an example post to students on creating substantial responses.

Seasoned or Experienced Online Students

The principles for teaching the case method for new students will occasionally have to be reinforced with seasoned students. With seasoned students, cases can be taken a bit further by having them actively apply the course material to the case. The cases can be more complex, challenging students to spend more time analyzing the problems and issues of the case. This promotes a highly interactive discussion. For seasoned students, instructors should try to find real-life cases to which they can apply the theory from the course, and exercise their critical thinking skills. Here is an example used for an online philosophy class:

Case: *Cities around the country are preventing Wal-Mart from opening new stores on the grounds that these stores would "threaten" other businesses and replace higher paying jobs with lower paying ones. Develop a logical argument which presents your support or lack of support of this idea.*

Students have a variety of stances on this particular case, sometimes challenging one another because their views are diametrically opposed. In this case, instructors can also teach about the logical fallacies, such as ad hominem. It is important that they logically respond to the ideas of a post, and not attack other students. The Minoa Writing Program (2005) provides some good suggestions for students when they respond to a peer's post (See Appendix C).

The Wal-Mart case is quite controversial. This case can promote a great deal more interaction between the students, and can also increase attendance in the online classroom. Here is what a previous student said about the Wal-Mart case:

Case One regarding Wal-Mart was one of the most growing experiences I have had of the four cases posted. I think the controversy of that topic had the most passion of all the discussion questions we had. It really made me see how divided people can be over an issue and made me more aware of how references can really help drive your side of the argument home. It also opened my eyes more of how the other side feels on this issue. I still don't agree with them but I know in this class I was highly out numbered and I started wondering if the odds are the same outside of this class.

Overall, students tend to enjoy this case. Although the cases can be used individually in the classroom, they can also be use to help promote collaborative learning by assigning cases to teams or groups.

Benefits of Using the Case Method

According to Herreid (1994), traditional lectures have only 50-65% student attendance. On other hand, when using the case method, Herreid (1994) reports 95% student attendance. I have experienced an increase in student participation with the cases online. Specifically, there were more postings related to the cases which took students beyond the school's required minimum number of postings per week. An evaluation form (see Appendix D) has been used to gather student feedback on the case method, from which the student comments were derived for this article.

There are several benefits to using the case method to teach online classes. The goal of the case approach is to develop students' analytical and decision-making skills (Erkine, Michiel, & Mauffette-Leenders, 1981; Gragg, 1953). In addition to these skills, other learning outcomes include application of theory, synthesizing material, and making evaluations. By providing opportunities for application, analysis, synthesis, and evaluation, the case method goes beyond the recall and recognition tasks that are associating with the banking method of education (Friere, 1971; Gross, 1999).

Problem-based learning is one method instructors can use to help students learn. The case approach is one form of problem-based learning that activates the student's prior knowledge base. According to Barrows and Kelson (2005), problem-based learning (PBL) is:

both a curriculum and a process. The curriculum consists of carefully selected and designed problems that demand from the learner acquisition of critical knowledge, problem solving proficiency, self-directed learning strategies, and team participation skills. The process replicates the commonly used systemic approach to resolving problems or meeting challenges that are encountered in life and career. (par. 1)

Through the use of the case method and thought questions, the instructor can promote active engagement in the virtual classroom. Since many cases focus on real-life problems and dilemmas, the students will be able to transfer this information to other settings, such as their work environment. Many online students already have careers, so the practical applications of the case method approach are immediately applicable.

Learning teams also can promote online community. According to Werapitiya and Altman (2004), an online community is a group of people "brought together by shared goals and interests, bound by mutual trust, respect and a sense of belonging, committed to supporting each other in pursuit of achieving their common goals" (p. 1). Building an online community is important for several reasons: student satisfaction, student retention, and student learning. Students are more satisfied with their classes/instructor, and therefore less likely to drop the course. Further, it is important for student learning, as it takes the student to higher levels of reasoning, moving beyond comprehension and application, to analysis, synthesis, and evaluation of knowledge (Bloom, 1956; Krathwhol et al., 1973).

Through the case method, students gain a great sense of meaning, and can actively apply theory to support the solution to a problem presented in a case. In some ways, this is a proactive approach to problem solving, particularly with beginning students first learning how to work in virtual teams. Enhancing intrinsic learning, combating retroactive inhibition, increasing encoding specificity, and developing more diverse schemes are other benefits of using the case approach to teach online courses (Brooke, 2005). In summary, the case approach promotes social change, in that students reflectively and critically examine their own thoughts in relation to the course material and other students' responses.

Discussion

A common challenge facing faculty is how to encourage students who are not using their critical-thinking skills to reach their fullest potential. The reason for this lack of use could be cognitive, effective, or a mix of both areas. There are some disadvantages to using cases, particularly in a collaborative fashion. There may be some difficulty monitoring instruction practice when using learning teams. Corrective feedback is not always instantaneous with groups. The instructor may also be challenged to make sure the learning teams are operating effectively and applying material from the course appropriately to the case. Failure to address any one of the aspects of cooperative learning processes can make the use of learning teams both frustrating and educationally unproductive. To prevent failure when using a collaborative approach, the instructor should assign individuals to the teams, and make sure there are roughly six members per team; having eight or more members may be too large. Additionally, instructors should have the groups stay together for the duration of the classes. Granted, these cases are meant for five-week classes; if the class meets for a semester, using the same learning teams would be beneficial. Instructors should ensure peer evaluations are part of the process, and should try to assess the progress of the group frequently. Instructors should also get feedback on the cases being used. An example feedback form is included in Appendix D. Student feedback can then be used to support continued use of cases, to indicate areas for revision, or to identify cases that should be deleted from the discussion.

Conclusion

Using the case method to teach online classes promotes a learner-centered culture (Brooke, 2004, 2005), and provides an opportunity for collaborative learning. "Learning-centered" refers to students developing responsibility for their own learning, whether individually or as a member of a learning team. The instructor is the facilitator, and further helps to refine critical-thinking skills and analysis. Using the case method allows for a balance of power between teachers and students. Additionally, cases are highly motivating, as demonstrated by increased attendance (Herreid, 1998) and discussion online. Instructors have a wealth of information for creating cases. For short, five-week classes, case vignettes are appropriate. For beginning students, instructors can use past student problems to help current students engage in proactive problem-solving. Seasoned students can be challenged to view another side to a topic, thereby allowing further refinement of their thoughts on the matter. The case method is a didactic, pedagogical approach for promoting learning in the virtual classroom. Given that most online schools set a large percentage of the grade on discussions, the case method is a useful way of promoting Socratic dialogue.

References

Barrows, H., & Kelson, A. (2005). *Overview of PBL*. Retrieved October 25, 2007, from http://www.mcli.dist.maricopa.edu/pbl/info.html

Bloom, B.S. (1956). Taxonomy of educational objectives. In *Handbook I: The cognitive domain*. New York: David McKay Co. Inc.

Brooke, S.L. (2004, October). The use of the case method in the virtual classroom. In *Proceedings of the 5th Annual Case Studies in Science Conference,* Buffalo, NY.

Brooke, S.L. (2005, October 13-15). The use of the case method to teach online classes. In Proceedings of the *2005 Annual Conference of the International Society for Exploring Teaching and Learning,* Cocoa Beach, FL.

Brooke, S.L., & Martin, J. (2004). *The case of Maria*. University of Buffalo, NY: National Center for Case Study Teaching in Science.

Conant, J.B. (1949). *The growth of the experimental sciences: An experiment in general education*. New Haven, CT: Yale University Press.

Dewiyanti, S. (2007). Students' experiences with collaborative learning in asynchronous computer-supported *collaborative learning* environments. *Computers in Human Behavior, 23*(1), 496-514.

Erskine, J.A., Michiel, R.L., & Mauffette-Leenders, L.A. (1981). *Teaching with cases*. Waterloo, Canada: Davis and Hedersen, Ltd.

Friere, P. (1971). *Pedagogy of the oppressed*. New York: Herder and Herder.

Gragg, C.I. (1953). Because wisdom can't be told. In K.R. Andrews (Ed.), *The case method of teaching human relations and administration* (pp. 3-12). Cambridge: Harvard University Press.

Gross, R. (1999). *Peak learning*. New York: Pearson Custom Publishing.

Herreid, C.F. (1994, February). Case studies in science: A novel method of science education. *Journal of Computer Science and Technology*, pp. 221-229.

Herreid, C.F. (1998, February). Sorting potatoes for Miss Bonner: Bringing order to case-study methodology through a classification scheme. *Journal of Computer Science and Technology*, pp. 236-240.

Kaplan, S. (2002). *Building communities: Strategies for collaborative learning.* Retrieved October 25, 2007, from http://www.learningcircuits. org/2002/aug2002/kaplan.html

Krathwohl, D.R., Bloom, B.S., & Bertram, B.M. (1973). Taxonomy of educational objectives, the classification of educational goals. In *Handbook II: Affective domain.* New York: David McKay Co. Inc.

Levine, M. (1994). *Effective problem solving.* Upper Saddle River, NJ: Prentice Hall Publishers.

Manoa Writing Program. (2005). *Peer review.* University of Hawaii at Manoa. Retrieved October 25, 2007, from http://mwp01.mwp.hawaii. edu/resources/peer_review.htm

McKeachie, W.J. (1999). *McKeachie's teaching tips: Strategies, research, and theory for college and university teachers.* New York: Houghton Mifflin Co.

Porter, S. (2003). *Team decision-making.* Arizona: University of Phoenix.

Tannen, D. (1998). *The argument culture: Moving from debate to dialogue.* New York: Random House.

Washull, S.B. (2005). Predicting success in online psychology courses: Self-discipline   and motivation. *Teaching of Psychology, 32*(3), 190-192.

Werapitiya, D., & Altman, T. (2004, July 11-15). Building community in online courses: Poster summary. In *Proceedings of the 6th Annnual WebCT User Conference.*

White, K.W., & Weight, B.H. (2000). *The online teaching guide.* Boston: Allyn and Bacon.

Appendix A

Communicating Online Tips

Hello Everyone!

Remember that conveying meaning is extremely important since there are no facial, voice or body clues that are transmitted with your message. In class you may be able to say *No* in a sarcastic tone, and everyone will know that you do not really mean it. Online, you must make sure that the words that you use to communicate your message are accurate and appropriate. In no time at all, you will feel **techno-savvy** and completely comfortable with online communication!

Netiquette:

Many members of the electronic community have contributed to these guidelines. A couple of URLs are included below that may be helpful as you learn to communicate in the online world.

Arlene Rinaldi, Florida Atlantic University wrote *The Net: User Guidelines and Netiquette*:

http://www.fau.edu/netiquette/net/index.html

Delaware Technical Community College posts this web page about Netiquette:

http://www.dtcc.edu/cs/rfc1855.html

Albion.com (a San Francisco-based Internet reference publishing firm) publishes a web page labeled *The Core Rules Of Netiquette* excerpted from the book *Netiquette* by Virginia Shea:

http://www.albion.com/netiquette/corerules.html

An unknown author has posted a web page on GeoCities that provides the reader with etiquette for chat rooms:

http://www.geocities.com/SouthBeach/Breakers/5257/Chatet.htm

Emoticons:

It is often difficult to express emotion or humor when communicating online. Adding *Emoticons (Smileys)* to your e-mail or chat message may help you to convey more clearly the meaning of your message. Remember, though, you are in an academic setting – too much humor is probably not wise!

From MIT, this web page has been posted:

http://www.mit.edu:8001/people/cordelia/smileys.html

A professor from Tokyo International University of America posted this web page with emoticons:

http://www.mit.edu:8001/people/cordelia/smileys.html

About.com provides this web page of smileys:

http://netforbeginners.about.com/internet/netforbeginners/gi/dynamic/offsite. htm?site=http://rcswww.urz.tu-dresden.de/~jloeffle/smiley_dict.html

Appendix B

Creating Substantial Discussion Responses

Discussion Responses:

- A good response to the question should be one or two paragraphs, and address all of the issues that are raised.

- A good response to others is not something like "I agree." Please find something that you can analyze, add to, critique, explain, disagree with, or something. It should be a few cogent sentences. It should contain something that shows your knowledge of the book, as well as additional materials you might bring to class from the web and elsewhere.

- A good response to a written question should be one to two pages in length, and address all of the issues that are raised.

- You must use references to support your work. You **CANNOT** copy a Web site and paste it as your response. If you want to use a Web site, summarize it, outline the pertinent information, and then cite the webpage. If you copy a webpage as your response, you will earn a 0 points for the module.

- Think of this as your opportunity to teach. Create substantial responses which expand on a point and present information on the topic. Your responses should demonstrate your critical thinking on the topic.

Appendix C

Ground Rules/Guidelines for Peer Review

From the Manoa Writing Program (2005):

- Read a draft all the way through **before** you begin to comment on it.
- Give yourself **enough time** to read and respond.
- If something on the feedback form is unclear, **ask the instructor**.
- Point out the **strengths** of the draft.
- When discussing areas that need improvement, be nice. Offer **appropriate, constructive comments** from a reader's point of view.
- Make comments **text-specific**, referring specifically to the writer's draft (NO "rubber stamps" such as "awkward" or "unclear" or "vague," which are too general to be helpful).
- **Do not overwhelm the writer** with too much commentary. Stick to the major issues on the feedback form that are problematic.
- Make sure your suggestions are **reasonable** (i.e., do not suggest that they totally rewrite the paper because you did not agree with the author's point of view or did not like the topic).
- If something appears too complicated to write in the commentary, just mention that you have something that you would like to talk to the writer about when you discuss the draft afterwards.
- Before giving your written comments to the author, **reread your comments to make sure they are clear and make sense**.

"As a peer reviewer, your job is not to provide answers. You raise questions; the writer makes the choices. You act as a mirror, showing the writer how the draft looks to you and pointing our areas which need attention." - Sharon Williams

Appropriate, Constructive Comments:

- **Be respectful and considerate** of the writer's feelings.
- **Use "I" statements**.

- **Offer suggestions, not commands.**

- **Raise questions** from a reader's point of view, points that may not have occurred to the writer.

- Phrase comments **clearly and carefully** so that the writer can easily understand what needs to be improved.

- Make sure comments are **constructive and specific** (not "This paper is confusing. It keeps saying the same things over and over again" but rather "It sounds like paragraph five makes the same point as paragraphs 2 and 3.").

Appendix D

Case Evaluation Form

Name: (optional)_____

Class: _____   **Date:** _____

Content and Organization	Points Earned	Comments:
Please rate with a 1 (strongly disagree) to 4 (strongly agree) Scale in the Points Earned Column		
All key elements of the cases were covered in a substantive way.		
The cases were comprehensive, accurate, and /or persuasive.		
The cases developed a central theme or idea, directed toward the appropriate audience.		
The cases helped me link theory to relevant examples of current experience and industry practice and uses the vocabulary of the theory correctly.		
Cases were stated clearly; are supported by specific details, examples, or analysis; and are organized logically.		
I learned more about the course topic through the use of the cases.		
The cases allowed me to develop new perspectives with respect to the course content.		
Add your own criterion here:		
This section will be tallied by me.	*Points Earned*	Comments:

Chapter V

Preparing Online Instructors:
Beyond Using the Technology

Evelyn S. Johnson, Boise State Univesity, USA

Jane Pitcock, Walden University, USA

Abstract

This chapter discusses methods for supporting the instructor in the development of strong learner-learner interactions. In this chapter, we present a brief overview of the importance of social learning theories and existing research that support learner-learner interaction as an important aspect of learning. Next, we discuss the multiple factors, and their complex interaction on the instructor's ability to support learner-learner interaction. Additionally, we report and discuss findings from a qualitative study examining the use of an ecological assessment tool to evaluate an online course's ability to support learner-learner interaction. The chapter concludes with suggestions for improved approaches to faculty development to support learner-learner interaction.

Introduction

As the number of learners engaging in online education increases, a growing body of literature is developing to recommend best practices for instructors. As online education was developing, the focus for instructors was on how to use the technology to transition traditional courses to the online format. Increasingly, best practices for instructors of online courses focus on sets of recommendations to enhance learner outcomes. Typically, these recommendations are oriented to a particular aspect of interaction based on Moore's (1989) extended framework to include learner-instructor, learner-learner, learner-content, and learner-interface interactions.

Any educational experience, to include online learning, seeks to achieve defined learning outcomes, and does so largely through adopting instructional models based on theories of learning integrated with the unique demands of the content and intended audience. However, online instructors and learners operate within a complex environment in which many aspects can have a direct impact on the instructor's ability to facilitate learner-learner interactions. Although specific recommendations are important, in that they provide guidance to direct the actions of an instructor based on research, we know that distance education programs vary a great deal in content, delivery methods, and learner characteristics (Zhao, Lei, Yan, Lai, & Tan, 2005). By examining these variables in context, we may incorporate an integrated approach to evaluating the learning context as a fundamental part of faculty development, so that the instructor can make appropriate decisions about how to increase learner-learner interaction (Roblyer & Wiencke, 2003; Zhao et al., 2005).

Objectives of the Chapter

*   Provide a brief overview of the importance of social learning theories and existing research that support learner-learner interaction as an important aspect of learning.
*   Discuss the multiple factors and their complex interaction on the instructor's ability to support learner-learner interaction.
*   Report and discuss findings from a qualitative study examining the use of an ecological assessment tool to evaluate an online course's ability to support learner-learner interaction.

- Suggest improved approaches to faculty development to support learner-learner interaction.

Background

Many current theories of adult learning maintain that knowledge is actively constructed through interactions with other learners. Such theories contend that an important element in the learning process is the level and quality of interaction that occurs within a learning community (Garrison & Anderson, 2003; Moore, 1989). Through discourse, learners create meanings and understandings, critically reflect on stated assumptions, and negotiate new learning through consensus (Mezirow, 1998). These concepts of learning are grounded in social learning theory, which contends that cognitive processes experienced and observed in social settings are then internalized by individuals (Bandura, 1977; Glaser, 1990). Social learning occurs when a group exposes a learner to new understandings that challenge, extend, and complement their current conceptualizations (Glaser, 1990). Examples of instructional models based on social learning theories include collaborative learning (Slavin, 1991) and reciprocal teaching (Brown & Palinscar, 1989). A key requirement to support learning, according to such models, is a high level of learner-learner interaction within the instructional environment.

At the same time, an increasing number of adult learners are turning to online institutions of higher education (IHE) for advanced degrees and continued professional development. Over 2.5 million people engaged in some form of online learning in the last few years (U.S. Distance Learning Association, 2004). Recent meta-analyses on the effectiveness of distance, as compared with face-to-face education, have confirmed what has been called the "no significant difference" finding (Zhao et al., 2005). This finding implies that when other variables—such as the quality of instructor, content materials, and course design—are held constant, online learning can be as effective as face-to-face education. Despite this finding, there has long been recognition that online learning is subject to one significant, potential shortcoming: the lack of face-to-face interaction, "real-time" dialogue, and opportunities for discussion, which may limit the development of true learning communities.

To that end, significant effort has been invested in researching the role of interaction in the online environment. Consistent with social theories of learning and research on interactive learning, research in online learning yields evidence that increased interaction is associated with improved learner outcomes and overall satisfaction (Fulford & Zhang, 1993; Hillman, Willis, & Gunawardena, 1994). Students express concern and dissatisfaction when there is a lack of interaction with the instructor and other online students (LaRose & Whitten, 2000; Russo & Campbell, 2004). However, while many educators believe that the advent of online learning can actually promote and increase opportunities for interaction, instructors and course developers often operate under the mistaken assumption that interaction will occur if the technology supports it (Orvis & Lassiter, 2006), while ignoring the critical role the instructor plays in supporting this process. The focus of many instructor training programs for online learning IHEs reflects this mistaken assumption, in that most concentrate on how to use the technology, as opposed to developing the pedagogical skills to operate effectively in an online environment (Johnson, in press). Despite the need to promote and sustain quality learner-learner interactions, and an increasingly substantial literature reflecting best practices by which to do so, instructors new to online learning require training in pedagogical aspects of technology (Johnson, in press; McCauley, Jugovich, & Reeves, 2006).

Online learning programs differ a great deal in content, learner characteristics, and delivery design structure (Zhao et al., 2005). The growth of such a myriad of offerings reflects not only advances in technology, but also the increased need for adults to have more flexibility over the learning process. Online universities are generally populated by non-traditional learners who balance professional, family, and social obligations with the requirements of their continuing education. A growing body of literature suggests that some learners highly value the independent and self-directed nature of online learning, and place less value on learner-learner interactions such as collaborative group work (Reisetter & Boris, 2004; Sharp & Huett, 2005). Such findings suggest that a blanket approach to improving online education—such as increasing learner-learner interactions—may not be warranted, and that a more comprehensive, individualized understanding of the factors that contribute to positive online learning experiences is needed.

In summary, both theory and research support the importance of collaborative learning and learner-learner interactions. An increased number of learners are turning to online education for personal and professional development, and the nature of the online environment poses significant challenges to the development of learning communities. Instructors of online courses typically receive little-to-no training in how to engage in practices that promote the development of online learning communities, and for some learners, collaboration with other learners may actually detract from the elements of online education that they most highly value. These conclusions led us to ask and investigate two questions:

1. How can an ecological assessment allow an instructor to examine the online learning environment to determine how to create opportunities for learner-learner interaction?

2. What are the important elements to include in online instructor training programs to support their ability to develop effective learning communities?

Issues, Controversies, Problems

Identifying and understanding problems in education, and developing solutions based on research have typically been the work of researchers. When promising solutions are discovered, the hope is that these practices will find their way to educational institutions through a variety of models for replicating these innovations (Robinson, 1998). However, practices are formed and maintained within the context of constraints, and these constraints must be understood to propose relevant solutions (Robinson, 1998).

Emerging literature identifies some promising practices for instructors to improve the way in which they support learner-learner interaction (see for example, Garrison & Anderson, 2003; Ko & Rossen, 2004; Orvis & Lassiter, 2006). Essentially, these practices focus on the instructor's role in providing feedback, responding to student inquiries, and providing clear expectations for participating in group work. While these practices certainly can help improve the level of learner-learner interaction, and address specific actions that the instructor can take in facilitating this process, instructors work within a broader set of constraints that warrant a more in-depth examination of the environment to develop solutions that more accurately address the unique issues that instructors face.

An instructor may improve the level of facilitation by incorporating a more global review of the context in which they operate, so they can tailor their actions in ways that address their unique situations. This implies that instructors need to be more reflective about the environment in which they teach, if their attempts to facilitate increased learner-learner interactions are to be successful. The constraints that influence an instructor's ability to effectively facilitate learner-learner interactions may be viewed as a two-tiered system that includes the initial and ongoing faculty development and training the instructor receives, followed by the subsequent course delivery and online environment in which the instructor works.

Tier One: Faculty Training/Professional Development

Online universities have grown significantly in recent years at all degree and program levels. This growth is seen at all levels across many institutions of higher education (IHE) and professional training, from the community college to doctoral level. The theory that technology changes the role of the instructor to that of facilitator has been generally accepted (Orvis & Lassiter, 2006). However, training for faculty who deliver online courses typically includes training in the software platform used, but rarely does it include systematic guidance on pedagogical issues and challenges. There are several guides for teaching online that detail the basic principles for effective communication (see for example, Ko & Rossen, 2004). These principles tend to focus on specific behaviors, such as posting information in more than one place and providing clarity about administrative tasks, such as how often the instructor will log on to the course, how soon she will respond to email, and when students can expect to receive a graded assignment. While these "how to" specifics are essential in online teaching, they do not necessarily focus on pedagogical approaches to facilitate learner-learner interactions, such as designing opportunities for meaningful collaboration, learner-learner discussions, and other opportunities for group work.

In a review of faculty development programs for a variety of online IHEs, Johnson (in press) found that none of the initial instructor development programs presented types and levels of interaction, and none discussed or provided opportunities for instructors to consider how to promote learner-learner interaction. Since the publication of Boyer's (1991) *Scholarship of Teaching,* which emphasized teaching at the college level as a scholarly activity, IHEs have begun to develop resources that improve the teaching abilities of their faculties. The movement to online education presents new challenges to teaching, and given the increased reliance on distance education to provide professional development and higher education opportunities, it is critical that faculty receive training in both the technology and the educational processes used.

If online IHEs hope to reflect current theories and research that support increased learner-learner interactions and the development of learning communities, they need to provide instructors with the professional development opportunities with which to do so. While instructors are typically content area experts, few have backgrounds in theories and practices of effective adult education. New instructors, however, have little control over the initial faculty development provided by an institution. We offer the problem here for programmatic and systemic consideration, as institutions of higher education (IHEs) continue to expand and develop the opportunities for engaging in professional development.

Tier Two: Evaluating the Online Learning Environment

As stated previously in this chapter, instructors operate within complex systems that place different types of constraints on their actions, and require a broad lens through which they can thoroughly represent the particular constraints under which they operate. When instructors engage in reflective activities that include critical assessments of the learning environment, they can improve their teaching practices in ways that respond to the specific constraints of each course, program, and learning community. These constraints include the following:

1. **Content/objectives/purpose of interaction:** In Moore's seminal writing (1989), the focus on learner-learner interaction was related to a course where the objective was to teach learners how to interact effectively with one another. Similarly, many programs require students to begin with an introductory course that not only teaches them the basics of navigating online courses, but also devotes energy towards promoting collegial relationships. These courses will likely lend themselves well to support learner-learner interaction, and given these objectives, the instructor will come to the course with this orientation. Courses that are focused heavily on content or acquiring a skill, such as a statistics/research methods course, may have less focus on learner-learner interaction, and the instructor may focus more on presenting the content

in ways that support learner understanding. For example, in a research methods course, learner-content and learner-instructor interactions may take precedence over learner-learner interactions.

2. **Course structure:** In general, instructors operate under two different course structures: those with predetermined content, applications, and requirements, and those in which the instructor is responsible for meeting objectives, but is free to design the course as they consider appropriate. An instructor with more latitude over course structure can use the principles for effective learner-learner interaction, and implement these procedures at their discretion. Instructors who operate under existing requirements and procedures will need to evaluate the tools at their disposal, and consider how they might help develop/promote learner-learner interactions.

3. **Program structure:** Learners in an online environment tend to require more time to develop trust, cohesion, and shared cognition than those in face-to-face courses (Orvis & Lassiter, 2006), which can determine both the amount and quality of learner-learner interactions. Programs that are degree-oriented, and assign and maintain cohorts throughout the life of the program will likely have stronger avenues through which learner-learner interactions can be sustained. When online courses occur outside the realm of a program structure (e.g. single professional development courses; students in a degree program not progressing as a cohort), students will not have the benefit of long-term interactions, and the instructor will have to devote more energy to develop trust and cohesion early on for learners.

4. **Technology:** Technological enhancements in online learning delivery systems have greatly increased the potential for promoting strong communications, and specifically, connecting learners with other learners (Garrison & Anderson, 2003). Nevertheless, many distance education programs still rely on few or a single medium (generally text based) for course delivery, thus limiting these potentials (Moore, 1989). An instructor rarely has control over the technology available, although she may have control over the elements of a platform (e.g. discussion board, group chat, audio streaming, video/Web conferencing) if designing her own course. Recognizing that face-to-face components are often not feasible, tools such as video-conferencing and other synchronous communication tools can effectively create social organizations (Levin, Levin, & Chandler, 2001). A recent survey on actual use and preference

for technology found that high percentages of instructors do not always use technological tools that can support stronger social networks (Zhao, Alexander, Perreault, & Waldman, 2003). Even when the technology is present and used, however, this is no guarantee that the instructor uses it effectively (Loeding & Wynn, 1999).

5. **Learner characteristics and needs:** Demographics of online universities typically show that the student population consists of non-traditional learners who balance full-time careers, families, and social obligations with the requirements of their continuing education. The flexibility that an asynchronous and self-directed approach to learning provides is highly regarded, and these learners may not understand the value that increased learner-learner interactions can provide (Reisetter & Boris, 2004).

   Other factors that bear on the desire and efficacy of learner-learner interactions include the age, expertise, and motivation of the learner (Moore, 1989). Achievement outcomes in distance learning, compared to face-to-face learning, have been shown to vary depending upon the education level of the learner (Zhao et al, 2005). Learners may not feel confident to express their views and/or to challenge one another's ideas. Because writing is the medium of choice in conveying thoughts in an online environment, a learner with poor writing skills may also be reluctant to contribute to group discussions. Learners with less expertise may feel they have less to contribute than those with more expertise. Finally, research on cooperative learning has consistently demonstrated the need for learners to have clear understandings of the roles they play within the larger group, and what the expectations for fulfilling those roles are. Learners with experience in collaborative learning may be more ready to continue this type of interaction, whereas novice learners may require more support.

6. **Instructor engagement and feedback:** Arguably, the instructor's most direct role in facilitating learner-learner interaction comes from the quantity and quality of feedback they provide. In a recent meta-analysis examining factors that account for effective online course delivery, instructor involvement was the most significant moderator among all the identified factors (Zhao et al., 2005). Interactions between the teacher and students have been found to affect the quality of student experiences and learning outcomes in online education (Institute for Higher Education Policy, 2000).

While issues of timeliness, tone, and medium (e.g., response on discussion board, e-mails, announcements) are generally discussed and modeled as issues in faculty training, increasingly, there is an understanding that the quality of the feedback provided has significant impact on developing strong learning communities, in which learner-learner interactions are valued and encouraged. To achieve these desired learning outcomes, the instructor must assume a role that is both structured and systematic, so that the level of communication promotes a community of inquiry (Garrison & Cleveland-Innes, 2005). Instructors establish presence through their feedback in ways that support both the social and cognitive development of individual learners and the course as a whole. When instructors can provide timely, substantive, and individualized feedback, they help support the development of a community of inquiry (Garrison & Cleveland-Innes, 2005).

Solutions and Recommendations

Tier One: Expanding Initial Faculty Training to Emphasize Learner-Learner Interactions

The problem of increasing the instructor's ability to effectively foster learner-learner interactions in an online environment calls for a two-tier solution (see Figure 1). The first tier solution is to provide initial and ongoing faculty development that explains the model of interaction, articulates the theory of learning, the goals of the program/course, and general characteristics of the learners who participate that are unique to the IHE. Faculty development programs need to be more proactive in their inclusion of effective learning principles and strategies. An orientation to prevailing theories and practices of interaction, followed by explicit declaration and discussion on the IHE's particular focus, may help instructors refine their teaching practices to support the philosophy of the IHE and enhance learner outcomes. Levels of interaction in online courses would be an important construct to discuss, as well as explanations of how the instructor can assess their context and respond appropriately. The expanded model of types of interaction (Hillman et al, 1994; Moore, 1989) can provide an overarching framework for consideration. Moving beyond training in the technological aspect, and towards training that focuses on the nature and quality of feedback—perhaps through the use

Figure 1. Two-tiered solution to promote learner-learner interaction

Tier Two

Ecological
assessment provides
ongoing evaluation

Professional Development
builds the foundation for
considering learner-learner
interaction

Tier One

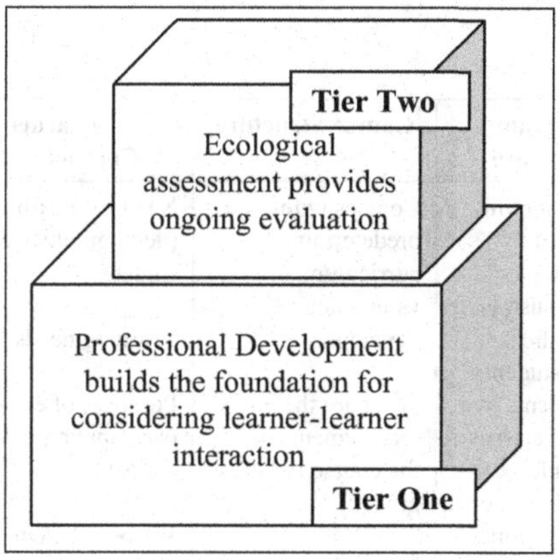

of case studies, model courses, and/or metacognitive strategies embedded within training models—may help instructors begin their approach to teaching online in ways that support the development of learner-learner interaction.

Tier Two: Ecological Assessment of the Online Environment

A second tier solution is geared towards instructors, and includes understanding the complex dynamics that comprise the online learning environment. The representation of the problem of increasing learner-learner interaction is presented in Table 1. Essentially, the model outlines the constraints under which an instructor operates and demonstrates the need for a complete representation of these constraints to develop effective solutions. Table 2 presents an ecological assessment tool that is based on this model. The ecological assessment provides instructors with a structured means of evaluating the specific constraints that either support or detract from opportunities for learner-learner interactions. As instructors use this tool to develop and evaluate their own courses, they should be guided by the question of priorities.

Our application of this tool is limited to a qualitative study to refine and consider how it might be applied to faculty development training opportunities and ongoing faculty/program evaluations. In this review, we found that the

Table 1. Problem demand: Increase learner-learner interaction in an on-line education environment

Constraints on Solution:

Technology	Program Structure	Course Structure	Learner Characteristics	Content
Does the course platform support/ include opportunities to engage in learner to learner interactions Group arrangements, discussion boards, chat rooms, document sharing areas	Is the Program structured by cohort, to support sustained relationships among students? Are students in a series of classes or a single, isolated course for professional development	Courses with predetermined curriculum vs instructor developed What are the requirements of the course (what is graded)	Need for flexibility (demographics of students) Learning needs Purposes of enrolling/ participating in the course Various student abilities	Nature of content may impact the opportunities for learner-learner interaction

Instructor feedback:
1. What avenues for providing feedback are available to the instructor?
2. Am I promoting social/cognitive/teaching presence through a variety of feedback styles?
3. Is the feedback timely? Substantive (addressing content, specific issues with an application, making connections to course and program content)? Individualized? (relevant and targeted to a specific learner)?

Solutions: *Depending upon the outcome of the analysis, different solutions may be warranted*

Consequences: *Is learner-learner interaction always the ultimate goal? To what end do we sacrifice other needs/elements?*

ecological assessment provided a more comprehensive review of the potential for increasing learner-learner interactions in an online setting, and specifically tailored the particular constraints under which each instructor operated (for a full report of that study, see Johnson, in press). For the purpose of this chapter, we briefly highlight some of the significant findings through the use of two specific examples that are relevant to the focus of the instructor's role in supporting learner-learner interactions.

We began our review of online courses by using the ecological assessment tool. This tool includes the six categories described above (see Table 2), along with guiding questions, a rating scale, and a comment section. In a more extensive application of this tool (see Johnson, in press), we examined courses provided by four institutes of higher education (IHE), including a large, online university

Table 2. Ecological assessment tool

Technology

Evaluation		Comments
1. The technology and course platform provide multiple opportunities for learners to interact	Y N U	
2. Group chat is possible	Y N U	
3. Document sharing features are enabled	Y N U	
4. Discussion boards are available and used	Y N U	
5. Assignments to smaller groups is possible	Y N U	
Overall Comments on technology:		

Program Structure

Evaluation		Comments
1. The program/degree is a cohort based approach	Y N U	
2. The course is within a program that includes a series of courses (not an isolated, one-time course)	Y N U	
3. The overall goals of the program encourage the development of collegial and collaborative relationships among students	Y N U	
Overall Comments on program structure:		

Course Structure

Evaluation		Comments
1. The course content and structure is pre-determined (not instructor developed)	Y N U	
2. Interactive discussion is a requirement of the course (e.g. requirement to discuss with classmates)	Y N U	
3. Group projects/work is a requirement of the course	Y N U	
Overall Comments on course structure:		

Table 2. continued

Learner Characteristics

Evaluation		Comments
1. The students are at a level of self-directed, independent learning	Y N U	
2. The students require flexibility in their learning environment (e.g. balancing family & work requirements)	Y N U	
3. The students have been taught the skills to interact effectively with one another to support L-L interaction	Y N U	
Overall Comments on student needs:		

Content

Evaluation		Comments
1. The course content easily lends itself to group assigned projects	Y N U	
2. Learners likely have professional experience relevant to this content area.	Y N U	
3. Content is challenging and requires a strong instructor presence	Y N U	
Overall Comments on content:		

Instructor Feedback

Evaluation		Comments
1. The instructor creates mediated presence on the course	Y N U	
2. The instructor provides clear rules of engagement and emphasizes the importance of L-L interaction	Y N U	
3. The instructor uses a combination of social, cognitive and teaching presence as required to support a community of inquiry	Y N U	
4. The instructor provides timely feedback	Y N U	
5. The instructor provides feedback that supports the needs of the students		
Overall Comments on instructor feedback:		

offering graduate-level degrees, a smaller college offering undergraduate and graduate degrees in online-only programs, a community college that offered a combination of live and online courses and serves typically underrepresented populations in higher education, and an online program designed to provide professional development opportunities for practicing teachers. Within these IHEs, we asked faculty development chairs to identify instructors who met two criteria: (1) they had more than one year of experience teaching online, and (2) they received positive student evaluations, particularly in the area of facilitating learner-learner interactions. We then asked these instructors for access to their courses, so that we could determine how our tool might be useful to analyze how instructors could improve the quality of learner-learner interactions. In this chapter, examples of reviews of two courses are included. We first present the reviews, followed by a summary that highlights how this assessment tool might be used to inform ways in which instructors can promote stronger learner-learner interaction.

Course Reviews

1. **Course A:**
   a. **Content:** This course is an introductory course for a master's program in public policy. This 12-week, 6-credit course introduces students to the university and the Master of Public Administration (MPA) program. The course also prepares students to use the learning platform as well as Internet tools, e-mail, Web browsers, and techniques of online communication. In addition, skills important for success in graduate education, including (a) self- management, (b) application of APA writing style, (c) use of the online library system, (d) scholarly writing, (e) ethical applications, and (f) critical thinking skills are introduced and applied.

   b. **Course structure:** This course took place over 12 weeks, and included weekly threaded discussion, individual assignments, and one group assignment with a group discussion area. The goal of the group assignment was to create, refine, and post a group response on a particular policy question. The discussion area was to be used for group discussion, consensus building and drafting, revising, and editing the group statement.

c.   **Program structure:** A sequential, cohort master's program requiring 52 credits of core courses with an option for specialization. Program completion is estimated at 24 months.

d.   **Technology:** The platform used can support asynchronous discussion boards, a document sharing section, and live chat sessions for the whole class or individual groups (no synchronous participation was required for successful completion).

e.   **Learner needs:** This program has an open enrollment policy (e.g., no GRE is required). For this particular program, learners must have a bachelor's degree from an accredited institution, and professional experience for admission. The majority of students are non-traditional, working professionals.

f.   **Instructor feedback:** Instructors can give feedback on the discussion board, in an announcement section, on individual applications, via e-mail, and through chat sessions. A specific look at the discussion board designed for group discussion found that the group discussion pages had no instructor input. There were several groups who posted one learner's initial discussion as their final work with no editing, revision, or discussion about the topic. Postings other than the one learner's response to the actual prompt included primarily procedural questions (e.g., "When is an assignment due?"). This finding was surprising, given that the instructor receives high ratings from students for providing feedback. Further scrutiny of the course showed that this instructor posted numerous announcements (averaging three per week), and posted numerous—but brief—replies to discussion boards in other places on the course.

2.   **Course B:**

a.   **Content:** The course is designed to help teachers plan and manage their literacy classroom as they implement the concepts and strategies they have learned throughout this degree program.

This course covers planning, organizing, and managing a balanced literacy program. It examines flexible grouping for differentiated instruction, incorporating literacy across the curriculum, integrating technology, working with parents and paraprofessionals, and pacing instruction.

b. **Course structure:** This is an eight-week course, with a weekly threaded discussion where learners are required to respond to the initial discussion question, and then to two of their classmates (on average, students had three responses each week;1-2 students of 15 posted an average of four responses). Weekly individual assignments are submitted via a dropbox. The instructor scheduled two voluntary opportunities for synchronous discussion during the eight-week course.

c. **Program structure:** A sequential, cohort master's program consisting of 10 courses.

d. **Technology:** The platform used can support asynchronous discussion boards, a document sharing section, and live chat sessions for the whole class or individual groups (no synchronous participation was required for successful completion of this course).

e. **Learner needs:** Learners in this course have a bachelor's degree, teacher certification, and have successfully completed nine previous courses in the program. The majority are current classroom teachers.

f. **Instructor feedback:** Instructors can give feedback on the discussion board, in an announcements section, on individual applications, via e-mail, and through chat sessions. In this course, the instructor created a voluntary process for peer editing applications, but no learners used this opportunity. A specific example of feedback provided on the regular discussion board to promote and encourage learner-learner interaction includes:

> "I often read helpful responses. N's to B is helpful, respectful, and instructional. As I read it, I knew that I was learning and that others would learn from N, too. Some day, I hope to hear that a lot of you are teacher-educators as well as teachers. Here is a model response that shows how to do this well. I have read others that are just as wonderful—N lucks out because I never thought to make this idea explicit before."

Here, the instructor pointed out that the learner's response was helpful, which may prompt more learners to read that particular posting more carefully. It may also promote more thoughtful responses to one another, as it highlights the fact that each learner has important insights to share. In terms of measurable outcomes however, no further postings from learners were made after this instructor feedback, and it is difficult to tell if postings made in other places reflected more thoughtful responses, since we could not determine which or how many students read this post. Possible explanations for the lack of response include that the course structure requires learners to only make three postings to meet requirements; the posting was made near the end of the course week, and learners may have already progressed to subsequent discussion boards; learners may not have responded to this specific posting, but it may have encouraged increased activity on subsequent discussion boards (though this hypothesis seems unlikely after review of the remaining discussion boards).

In another posting on the discussion board, the instructor made the following observation and comment:

Do you remember what we've learned about differentiated instruction? We need to be judicious about how we choose the agenda of a guided reading session. K is correct to say that decoding skills and fluency are important for struggling readers. But let's try to figure out where these readers learn the ideas and skills the more proficient readers' lessons are about. Are there good reasons that struggling readers can't discuss character traits or expand their vocabularies through learning multiple adjectives?

I would love it if there could be an expanded thread here that helps everyone see how the strugglers can also learn complicated ideas.

Here is the rub: processing difficulties do not preclude brilliant thinking. If we don't expose those who decode with more effort to the higher levels, ask for their opinions, ask for them to think of other episodes, they won't have the experience and then they will believe they can't.

What are ways around this problem? K has brought important issues to the surface. (An implied one is time: should the struggling readers have 2 sessions? A longer guided reading session?) Hmm...

In this response, we see that the instructor is making connections to prior course content which builds on their common experience and knowledge base. Additionally, she is inviting learners to expand on this posting, and finally, providing specific ways in which they might do so through the use of an example already provided by a learner. The observable results of this feedback included two additional postings made by learners. Each posting was made directly to the instructor, not to another learner. Again, although the instructor is providing feedback that attempts to engage learners with one another, the attempts do not appear to be as successful as might be expected.

Summary of Reviews

This review of courses highlights the need for a more comprehensive look at the online learning environment prior to making recommendations to instructors on how to improve and increase learner-learner interactions. For example, the instructor for Course A has many tools at his disposal, yet failed to intervene at a critical juncture in the course (e.g., group discussion boards). The instructor for Course B, however, provides feedback and support that exemplifies many of the best practice recommendations. However, the course structure is such that learners are not required to participate in peer editing, are only required to respond to two classmates each week (and that is all most do), and no synchronous or group work is required. Even when synchronous discussions were offered, learners did not participate.

One interpretation of these findings is that we measured learner-learner interaction only in observable and quantitative terms: through the number of responses on discussion boards, and participation in other discussion-like activities. Learners may benefit a good deal from one another by reading each other's postings on the discussion board, even if they choose not to respond further. Focus groups, questionnaires, or interviews with learners could provide important qualitative information on the impact that the instructors have on supporting the learners' interaction with one another. Another consideration that is unaccounted for in this model is learner preference for interaction. As noted in other research (Sharp & Huett, 2006), online learning may attract people who prefer to work independently—interacting with the content and/or with the instructor may be the preferred learning mode. All of these factors bear consideration as instructors evaluate approaches to improving the online education experience for a particular set of learners.

These reviews highlight important, possible applications of the ecological assessment tool that include:

- Instructors and faculty responsible for program/outcomes assessment may use this tool to conduct formative evaluations of their existing programs.

- By evaluating the context of the course and program, the instructor may find more effective ways to increase learner-learner interaction. For example, a request to a faculty chair to make synchronous chat, group work, and/or peer editing a *required* component of the course may lead to increased learner-learner interactions.

- A long-term application of this tool could be integration with learner evaluations to determine which elements are most effective depending upon degree, program, and/or course structure. One important element of online learning research is that although a variety of models exist, there is no delineation among practices that are effective for different kinds of learners and content areas.

- Program chairs responsible for developing curricula and revising courses may use the tool to determine ways in which the program and course structure may be varied to support increased learner-learner interaction.

- As suggested by Sharp & Huett (2006), learners come to the online education experience with many different needs. This tool may also be used to focus more on the specific needs of the learners, and the implications those needs carry for the instructor in supporting stronger interaction. For example, an instructor working with less-experienced and more diverse learners—especially those for whom English is not a first language, and those who have had a history of negative academic experiences—may use different methods to promote learner-learner interaction than an instructor working with learners in advanced degree programs who have experience of professional and collegial collaboration.

Although this assessment can provide a comprehensive evaluation of the learning environment, challenges to supporting learner-learner interaction remain. As mentioned previously, online learners may value the independent nature and flexibility of an online program, and be unwilling to coordinate schedules to collaborate and interact more with other learners. An increased focus on collaboration to promote learner-learner interaction may support strong learning outcomes, but may do so at the risk of detracting from some of the more practical advantages offered by online education.

Another challenge to supporting learner-learner interaction is that efforts to do so are difficult to measure. Learner-learner interaction is, to some extent, a latent variable, and measurements of the construct will always be subject to a level of interpretation. Typical measurements include analysis (primarily counts) of discussion board postings, correlations to student achievement, and student self-report of satisfaction with learner-learner interactions. The more elusive goal of determining the long-term effects of learner-learner interaction by measuring subsequent changes in behavior has yet to be realized. For example, when the number of discussion board replies to classmates increases from two to three, has achievement increased commensurately?

Implications and Future Trends

Research that helps to clarify the variables, behaviors, and processes in which instructors engage to support learning in an online environment is important. Translating that research into practice that completely addresses the constraints operating on the instructor in a complex context is critical. Though the work on this ecological assessment tool is limited to a qualitative review of its application, the principles, research, and theories on which it is based, will allow program developers, course designers, and instructors to more clearly target the variable of concern and devise appropriate solutions to the development of stronger learner-learner interactions.

Based on our reviews of both faculty training and course reviews, we offer the following recommendations to support online instructors in promoting stronger learner-learner interactions:

1. Provide initial and ongoing professional development opportunities that not only teach the instructor how to use the technology, but also examine pedagogical principles in the online environment.

2. Examine the specific context under which each course and program operates to determine the best means for increasing learner-learner interaction. Though resources that outline procedures for increasing learner-learner interaction are available and helpful, the recommendations are usually not context-specific. The ecological assessment tool provided in this chapter is one possible means with which to consider best-practices in

an applied, context-specific setting, allowing the instructor to choose methods most suitable to their particular learning environment.

3.   Instructors and program designers can use the assessment tool as an end of course evaluation to complement the feedback provided by learners.

In addition to these practical applications, continued research on the instructor's role in supporting learner-learner interaction is warranted. Further research should investigate the validity of the assessment tool by measuring pre/post levels of interaction and learner achievement after interventions are designed based on evaluation results, for example. Additionally, attempts to improve the ways in which we measure learner-learner interaction may significantly enhance efforts to promote it. Finally, though narrowly-focused research (e.g. examining the impact of an instructional change on a defined outcome) is beneficial in increasing our knowledge about effective online education, a parallel research agenda should continue to focus on "big picture" contexts to maintain thorough understandings, adequate problem representation, and relevant solution development.

Conclusion

Regardless of delivery method, the instructor's role in the education process is a critical determinant of overall effectiveness. In an online environment, one of the key challenges to effective course delivery is providing venues for and encouraging interaction among learners. Instructors need to consider the constraints under which they operate in order to effectively gauge where and in what manner they can support learner-learner interactions. Some of these constraints include the content, course structure, program structure, learner characteristics, and the technology. A comprehensive framework of the online learning environment allows instructors and IHEs to consider how best to support their learners. One way IHEs can develop reflective instructors is to include in faculty training discussion of learning theories and frameworks such as those discussed in this chapter to ensure that instructors not only use the technology available to them, but also engage in instructional practices that result in optimum learning.

References

Bandura, A. (1977). *Social learning theory*. New York: General Learning Press.

Boyer, E. (1991). The scholarship of teaching: From *Scholarship reconsidered: Priorities of the professoriate. College Teaching, 39,* 11-13.

Brown, A. L., & Palincsar, A. M. (1989). Guided, cooperative learning and individual knowledge acquisition. In L. B. Resnick (Ed.), *Knowing and learning: Essays in honor of Robert Glaser* (pp. 393-451). Hillsdale, NJ: Erlbaum.

Fulford, C. P., & Zhang, S. (1993). Perceptions of interaction: The critical predictor in distance education. *The American Journal of Research on Distance Education, 7,* 8-21.

Garrison, D. R., & Anderson, T. (2003). *E-learning in the 21st century: A framework for research and practice.* London: Routledge Falmer.

Garrison, D. R., & Cleveland-Innes, M. (2005). Facilitating cognitive presence in online learning: Interaction is not enough. *The American Journal of Research on Distance Education, 19*(3), 133-148.

Glaser, R. (1990). The reemergence of learning theory within instructional research. *American Psychologist, 45*(1) 29-39.

Hillman, D. C. A., Willis, D. J., & Gunawardena, C. N. (1994). Learner-interface interaction in distance education: An extension of contemporary models and strategies for practitioners. *The American Journal of Distance Education, 8,* 30-42.

Institute for Higher Education Policy. (2000). *Quality online: Benchmarks for success in internet based distance education.* Washington, DC: National Education Association.

Johnson, E. S. (in press). Promoting learner-learner interactions through ecological assessments of the online environment. *Journal of Online Learning and Teaching.*

Ko, S., & Rossen, S. (2004). *Teaching online: A practical guide.* Boston: Houghton Mifflin LaRose, R., & Whitten, P. (2000). Rethinking instructional immediacy for Web courses: A social cognitive exploration. *Communication Education, 49,* 320-338.

Levin, S. R., Levin, J. A., & Chandler, M. (2001, April). *Social and organizational factors in creating and maintaining effective online learning environments*. Paper presented at the annual meeting of the American Educational Research Association, Seattle, WA.

Loeding, B., & Wynn, M. (1999). Distance learning planning, preparation, and presentation: Instructors' perspectives. *International Journal of Instructional Media, 26*(2), 181-182.

McCauley, Jugovich, S., & Reeves, B. (2006). IT and educational technology: What's pedagogy got to do with it? *Educause Quarterly, 29*(4). Retrieved October 27, 2007, from http://www.educause.edu/apps/eq/eqm06/eqm0649.asp

Mezirow, J. (1998) On critical reflection. *Adult Education Quarterly, 48,* 185-198.

Moore, M. (1989). Three types of interaction. *The American Journal of Distance Education, 3*(2), 1-6.

Orvis, K. L., & Lassiter, A. L. R. (2006). Computer-supported collaborative learning: The role of the instructor. In S. P. Ferris & S. H. Godar (Eds.). *Teaching and learning with virtual teams* (pp. 158-179). Hershey, PA: Information Science Reference.

Reisetter, M., & Boris, G. (2004). What works: Student perceptions of effective elements in online learning. *Quarterly Review of Distance Education, 5,* 277-291.

Robinson, V. (1998). Methodology and the research-practice gap. *Educational Researcher, 27,* 17-26.

Roblyer, M. D., & Wiencke, W. R. (2003). Design and use of a rubric to assess and encourage interactive qualities in distance courses. *The American Journal of Distance Education, 17,* 77-98.

Russo, T. C., & Campbell, S. W. (2004). Perceptions of mediated presence in an asynchronous on-line course: Interplay of communication behaviors and medium. *Distance Education, 25,* 215-232.

Sharp, J. H., & Huett, J. B. (2006). Importance of learner-learner interaction in distance education. *Information Systems Education Journal, 4.* Retrieved October 27, 2007, from http://isedj.org/4/46

Slavin, R. E. (1991). Synthesis of research on cooperative learning. *Educational Leadership, 48,* 71-82.

U.S. Distance Learning Association. (2004). *Distance learning link program.* Retrieved October 27, 2007, from http://www.usdla.org/html/resources/dllp.htm

Zhao, J. J., Alexander, M. W., Perreault, H., & Waldman, L. (2003). Impact of information technologies on faculty and students in distance education. *Delta Pi Epsilon Journal, 45*(1), 17-33.

Zhao, Y., Lei, J., Yan, B., Lai, C., & Tan, H. S. (2005). What makes the difference? A practical analysis of research on the effectiveness of distance education. *Teachers College Record, 107*, 1836-1884.

Chapter VI

Collaborative Work in Online Learning Environments:
Critical Issues, Dynamics, and Challenges

Erman Yukselturk, Middle East Technical University, Turkey

Kursat Cagiltay, Middle East Technical University, Turkey

Abstract

The focus of this study is on issues that impact the success of collaborative working online learning groups. The issues of how such groups work collaboratively, how to facilitate them, and what makes work in such groups satisfactory and successful were explored. The data were colleted by semi-structured interviews from the participants in an online, project-based course. Hackman and Morris (1975)'s model was used as an analysis framework while interpreting the data. According to the results, it is found that group homogeneity plays a major role on successful group work. The second ma-

jor finding is the importance of face-to-face communication among online teams. The findings of this study are especially important for those people who are planning to organize activities which involve collaborative learning groups.

Introduction

Group work is an important part of the teaching and learning process in traditional face-to- face educational environments. Instructors can use it as an instructional strategy to create social interaction among group members. Learning is most effective when students work in groups, verbalize their thoughts, challenge the ideas of others, and collaborate to achieve group solutions to problems (Johnson, Johnson, & Holubec, 1994; Johnson, Johnson, & Stanne, 2000; Palloff & Pratt, 1999). Collaborative learning is a specific form of group work which is viewed as working together in small groups towards a common goal (Gokhale, 1995). Collaborative learning offers many benefits to learners and it is further defined as a technique that supports constructivist learning. Constructivists believe that knowledge is a result of social construction of meaning in a particular social context. Students interact not only with their instructor, but also with one another (Brandon & Hollingshead, 1999).

Given the increasingly widespread use of Information and Communications Technologies (ICT), individuals around the globe are beginning to participate collaboratively in organizations for learning and work (Riel, 1993; Travica, 1997). Specifically, a host of synchronous and asynchronous Internet and Web-based tools are being widely used to support and facilitate these purposes. As proposed by researchers and practitioners promoting social learning theories (Bonk & Cunningham, 1998) and distributed learning (see, for example, Thach & Murphy, 1994), a collaborative team approach may be the most effective means for learning and working in online or virtual environments.

The members of an online group generally do not have the advantage of face-to-face interaction and communication, but instead rely solely upon an assortment of computer-supported cooperative learning and work tools. The current state of technology is such that online team members can technically function well, despite being dispersed across the globe (Chinowsky & Rojas, 2003). With the help of ICT, more and more projects have been conducted by online teams. Even though group-based activities in organizations and educational institutions have significantly increased recently, research on group work has stayed behind (Guzzu & Salas, 1995). Graham (2002) stated that there is need for more educational research on computer-mediated teams.

In parallel to this need, this study explored issues in collaboratively working online learning groups in an online course. The analysis framework is based on Hackman and Morris (1975)'s model for analyzing the elements that impact group behavior and performance. They stated that groups are bounded by three phases of group patterns that include entry, process, and outcome elements. Entry elements consist of all contingency factors that affect group formation. Process elements are related to actual activities in which a group engages. Finally, outcomes are what the groups produce and achieve (Carabajal, LaPointe, & Gunawardena, 2003). In the scope of this study, the impact of these elements was analyzed in an online, project-based course. As a result, the researchers looked for answers for the following main research question:

•   How do group system variables (entry, process, outcomes) impact online group development in an online, project-based course?

While answering this main research question, the researchers tried to answer the following subquestion: What are the most important issues in creating and supporting groups that work collaboratively in an online environment? Some of the key issues that are addressed in this study are: group member characteristics, participation in group work among members, technology use (choice of communication medium) by group members, and the effect of other factors on the performance of such a group.

Method

Participants

The participants of this study were chosen from an online, project-based course which was offered in the Online Information Technologies Certificate Program. Table 1 summarizes the characteristics of the participants.

Table 1. The characteristics of participants

Participants	Gender	Age	Education	Occupation
Participant-1	Male	24	Undergraduate Student at Mechanical Engineering Department	Student
Participant-2	Male	35	Graduate of Civil Engineering Department	Civil Engineer
Participant-3	Male	32	Graduate of Economics Department	Inspector
Participant-4	Female	22	Undergraduate Student at Statistics Department	Student
Participant-5	Male	27	Graduate of Biology Department	Content Creator
Participant-6	Male	25	Graduate of Industrial Engineering	Industrial Engineer
Participant-7	Female	26	Undergraduate Student at Philosophy Department	Student
Participant-8	Female	25	Graduate of Electrical and Electronics Engineering Department	Electronic Engineer

Description of Online Certificate Program and Online Project Based Course

The Online Information Technologies Certificate Program (ITCP) is one of the first Internet-Based Education Projects of the Middle East Technical University in Ankara, Turkey. It is based on synchronous and asynchronous communication methods over the Internet, which is offered by the Computer Engineering Department. The online certificate program has been offered since May, 1998. It includes eight fundamental courses of the Computer Engineering Department, and comprises four semesters which last nine months. The courses in the program are given by the instructors of Computer Engineering Department. The main aim of the online ITCP is to train participants in the IT field. Furthermore, the online ITCP provides opportunities for people who would like to improve themselves in advanced IT area, and desire to make progress in their existing career (Isler, 1998; Isler, Vural, & Koc, 1998; Yukselturk, 2005). The program provides online lecture notes, learning activities, and visual aids. One instructor and two assistants are assigned for each course. Also, each course has an e-mail address, a discussion list, and chat sessions to provide interaction between instructors and participants. At the end of each term, there are face-to-face sessions for each course. During the face-to-face sessions, the instructors explain the course topics thoroughly, and students have a chance to meet with their classmates and instructors (Isler, 1997, 1998).

The Software Development Project is one of the courses of this online program. Students take it at the end of their program to apply their theoretical knowledge into practical problems. The main aim of this course is to develop a software project. This project can be developed alone or in groups of up to four members. Software development projects are divided into the following phases: project proposal, analysis, design, implementation, and test. Documents are prepared in each phase. These documents consist of requirements that groups will prepare during the course. For example, the document of project proposal consists of six parts: project's aim, definition, scope, methods and software tools that will be used, milestones, and plan. They are evaluated, and feedback is given to students by course instructors and two assistants. Each project phase is prepared by the students timely. The time table of project phases is given in the course Web site. At the end of the course, projects are presented to instructors and their fellows in a face-to-face session (Isler, 1997, 1998).

Procedure

This is a case study which is an in-depth study of a chosen event, activity, and process of a group using extensive data collection (Merriam, 1988). A case study approach is advantageous when "why" and "how" questions are being asked, and it is recommended when the investigator believed that the contextual conditions are highly relevant to the phenomenon under study (Yin, 1994). It means that case study method is useful to understand a particular situation, course, and program in depth, such as online, project-based course in this study. Qualitative methods (semistructured interviews and observations) were used to collect relevant data. Subjects were chosen among the students who attended the Software Development Project Course. 46 students attended the courses, and 28 students prepared their projects alone. In addition, 18 students decided to form eight different groups with two or three members to prepare their project. For this study, semistructured interviews were conducted with eight students to obtain information about the elements that impact their online group work processes. Students were chosen randomly from one member of each group. The interviews lasted about 30 minutes, and were conducted at the end of the semester. Interview questions were developed around the central themes related to the group system variables (entry, process, outcomes). For example: What are the group member characteristics? How do group members communicate with each other? What are the difficulties that group members are faced with? Moreover, each student was observed while presenting the course project in a face-to-face session.

In this study, the data process went through iterative cycles of examining the patterns and ideas that emerged from the collected data, exploring similarities and differences among the participants, and searching for confirming and disconfirming evidences that would be incorporated into the conclusions (Merriam, 1998; Miles & Huberman 1984).

In an initial data sort, the researchers first looked for similarities in the data from the participant interviews, the observations and the documents of each group. Second, the researchers looked for data that captured major differences among those groups. In order to clarify issues and to arrive at a list of critical issues of the process, categories and themes were created.

Findings

Data were analyzed according to Hackman and Morris' (1975) model: "entry," "process," and "outcome" elements or categories. For each category, critical issues and common characteristics were identified. These are described in the following sections.

Entry Elements of Online Groups

Under this item, three major categories emerged from the data: Issues about group member characteristics, group size, and task-related issues.

Group Member Characteristics

In this study, eight different groups with two or three members were formed while preparing their projects in the online, project-based course. The results demonstrated that there were several reasons stated by the participants to form a group in this online course. According to the participants, one of the main reasons of forming groups was that they supported and helped each other during their project. For example, one participant stated that one person might not see his or her mistakes, but members in the online groups could check other members' work, so they could better accomplish their projects. Another participant mentioned that they chose a comprehensive project, therefore it was hard to complete it alone. Moreover, all of the online groups—except one —chose group members who they already knew before the course or program. Also, four group members stated that they decided to form a group before determining a topic for the project. Only one participant found another group member by using the course discussion list.

The results of the study showed that group members had similar characteristics to those in the online groups. Members' gender and ages were nearly the same. In addition, many were students at the same departments, or graduated from the same departments. They knew each other before, and they could access and communicate with their group members easily in their daily life. Also, participants who already knew other group members expressed that they knew how members were going to behave in the project, and so they trusted each other. Moreover, all group members considered that they were literate about common computer technology at the beginning of their project. This software development project course is the last course of the certificate program. Before this course, participants completed six basic computer engineering courses, such as introduction to C programming, data structures and algorithms, database management systems, and operating systems. However, participants stated that they did not have much experience about preparing such a project. Also, they were interested in information technology, and they used some computer technology in their work settings. Only two members in different groups were good at some programming languages and database programming.

The results demonstrated that the members' personal characteristics and interests were divergent even though they had many similarities. For example, one participant stated that his/her group members had different characteristics, such as one of them is relaxed, the second one is stubborn, and the third one is harmonious. Also, members' professional occupations and interests were different in two groups, such as one of them is a teacher in a primary school, the second one is a content creator in a company, one of them works in a university, and one works in a company.

The member characteristics had several effects on the projects. Four participants mentioned that previous experience had not positively affected their projects, because the project topics were not related to their professional occupation. They expressed that limited knowledge about this kind of project development process led them to put forth more effort, especially when all members do not know about the topic. Members who were well-informed about project tasks guided the project and helped other group members when they needed it. In addition, members with different interests affected group works positively since members might see many things from different perspectives, but reaching agreement in the groups took more time. As a summary, participants mentioned about several advantages and disadvantages of homogenous and heterogeneous group characteristics.

Group Size

Participants mentioned that the size of online groups was determined by several factors in this type of online course. Four participants expressed that nature, scope, and aim of the project affected the group size. One participant mentioned that member properties might also affect the group size. He stated that member properties such as background knowledge and allocating time for the project might affect group size directly. In addition, most of the participants stated that two or three people are enough for this type of project. Only one participant thought that these types of project could be prepared alone. Moreover, participants mentioned advantages and disadvantages of group size with more or less members. For example, a more comprehensive project could be prepared, and work division among members was easier with more members in the groups. On the other hand, they thought that members might ignore their duties or might less wish to contribute their duties in the crowded groups, since they might think that one of the other members in the groups might complete the tasks. Also, one participant stated that it was difficult to reach agreements, or difficult to decide about project tasks with more members. Another participant mentioned communication problems in the groups with more members; for example, meeting or communicating with all group members at the same time or place might be a problem.

Task Related Issues

All participants mentioned that tasks in their projects were related to developing software project phases. Each group proposed different project topics in the course. For instance, one group prepared an online portal for inter-city travelers. Through this portal, one may find someone to travel together with and share the experiences. Another group prepared an online assessment system (e.g., quizzes, exams for instructors to use in their courses). The third group prepared a Web site for online shopping bookstores to receive an order. The other group prepared software for companies that sell products by installments to follow their customers' payments. Moreover, four group members stated that their friends and their relatives had mentioned their requirements. For instance, one member expressed that his father worked in a bookstore. He distributed books in a small town. His work was busy, especially in some months, and there was some disorganization in this bookstore, therefore he often mentioned his need to receive an order more easily, and more accessible by customers. In addition, there were many project ideas stated by members in a similar way at the beginning. They stated that they chose a feasible topic with common interests of all members. Although they had some ideas before the project, they investigated similar examples, and they adapted or got ideas from similar projects in real life. Also, participants mentioned that they learned or had to learn and use various programs, techniques, and methods while preparing their project phases. For example, they learned programming languages (e.g., Java, PHP, database, MS Access, My SQL), and used photo editors to draw shapes and objects. These were new for many members in the groups, therefore they were faced with several difficulties.

The online groups generally followed course requirements that were given in the time table at the beginning of the course. Course contents and examples helped them in preparing documentation. Participants stated that the course handout was crucial to complete the project components. Also, two participants mentioned that they made a plan according to the course time table. Actually, there were two ways groups followed for working during their project. In the first way, there was no work division among group members. These group members could meet often face-to-face in their daily life. They generally worked together with computers at the same place. If there were remaining works, one of the members finished them. In the second way, they made a plan before the project deadline of each phase of the project, and they met face-to-face, and discussed and worked at the same place. These group members could not meet face-to-face easily in their daily life. During the face-to-face meetings, they started with a simple idea, then improved it. They analyzed tasks, prepared drafts, and also they decided to divide tasks among members. Then, members completed their responsibilities alone with getting feedback from other members.

In both ways, participants stated that they worked irregularly—sometimes hard, sometimes little. For instance, they worked hard especially when a deadline became closer. Also, participants stated that work divisions among members were distributed according to the backgrounds or previous experiences of members, and also it depended on members' voluntary or convenient workload during that time.

Participants stated that during the face-to-face meetings, members discussed together, and listened to each other's views. They generally accepted ideas and reached agreement at the end of meetings. One participant stated that each member explained his or her ideas frankly during the group work. In addition, members who had more knowledge in the groups affected the decision, and members who dealt with the project more influenced the decision in the groups.

Process Elements of Online Groups

Under this item, we have found these major categories: issues about participation to group works, dynamics of group leadership, communication patterns, and finally, group history.

Participation in Group Works

In the online groups, the important issue was members' participation in the project. In this study, five group members stated that members worked equally in group work. They performed what they had planned. Also, they taught or assisted among members, and they sometimes controlled each other's works. However, three participants stated that group members did not work equally in their projects. Some members worked more to complete tasks in the project. Furthermore, two groups received help from their friends, such as computer specialists working in the same company when they needed. The reasons of seeking help from others and working unequally in the project were as follows: having less knowledge about project tasks, having not enough time due to members' other responsibilities (e.g., job, family), and having different expectations from their project. These findings are similar to the face-to-face project-oriented groups.

These online participants were different from traditional students, and they had various responsibilities (i.e., jobs, families) during their life in this study.

Therefore, they could not always spend enough time for their project tasks. Also, most of the participants had little knowledge about this type of project. Moreover, there were some differences in their motivations and aims to attend the online program, even though the major aim of almost all participants was the same at the beginning of the project. They prepared this project to improve themselves and learn new things from information technology field. In addition, some of them thought that they used it for special purposes (e.g., their family would use it in their job). Some participant thought they could get money by selling their project or this type of project. Other main aims were thinking it for social purposes, getting enough grades to pass the course, and using it in their job.

Leadership

In all groups, they did not select group leader at the beginning of the project. Especially, two members stated that there was no leader in the group, and one participant said that the leader appeared sometimes in the project. In addition, they thought that some members might take the leader role in the groups while preparing project tasks. For example, they guided other members when they needed. According to the participants, common characteristics of group leaders were as follows: more disciplined, more knowledgeable, more experienced, and proposers of the project idea. In addition, the participants who especially met less face-to-face stated that leaders worked more than other group members, and also they had more free time.

Communication Patterns

All groups used all communication methods and tools during their project. The results of the study showed that e-mail, online chat, phone calls, and face-to-face meetings were mainly used among members in the groups. Especially, all group members met face-to-face at least five times during the project before the project phase's deadline came. Also, some groups met face-to-face more, since members could often see each other in their daily life. During the face-to-face meetings participants discussed, worked, and decided something together, and then used communication tools to see and give feedback about each other's works. They used e-mail while writing short messages and sending their project files or related files. Members used phone for coordination and informing of their work, meeting plans, and so on. Most of the participants stated that they did not much use online chat during their project. Participants who met more face-to-face used computer-mediated communication tools rarely. In general, they used phone and e-mail. On the other hand, participants who met less face-to-face communicated much, especially when a deadline becomes closer, with the help of all communication methods (i.e., online chats, e-mail, phone, and face-to-face).

The results showed that members used all online communication tools; however, they preferred face-to-face meetings more. Two participants stated that in a short time they could talk about more things and work faster and spend more time on social activities. They thought that face-to-face meetings were more productive than online meetings. Also, one participant thought that they had to read the same documents and discuss them at the same time while preparing their project tasks, so they met face-to-face, and then implemented some part of the tasks together. In addition, they mentioned disadvantages of online communication tools. For example, one participant expressed that e-mail took much time to send or respond to, due to its asynchronous nature. Another participant stated that they talked to each other with ICQ and phone, but they were not enough. They needed face-to-face meetings to conclude their duties. Similarly, three participants mentioned that e-mail and phone calls were not enough, due to their limited knowledge about the project topic. They said that they also learned from each other during the face-to-face meetings.

Moreover, participants in the online groups mentioned that they did not much interact with course instructors. They generally contacted the course instructors when they were faced with problems in their project. They used generally the course discussion list to interact with the course instructors. Also, they used discussion lists to inform of their project progress, and to request clearance of their duties. They said that instructors replied to their messages in a short time. Furthermore, they used rarely the online chat session in the courses, due to the time inadequacy, being busy with their jobs, and having other responsibilities during chat session time in the online course.

Group History

After group work, members mentioned group history issues. Five participants stated that they knew each other more, they became closer, and now they communicate more in their daily lives. Furthermore, members in the online groups mentioned their other activities to each other while preparing their projects. For example, three members stated that they discussed project duties during lunch breaks. One participant shared friendly conversations often—that were related to daily life—among group members. Also, two university students stated that they met frequently face-to-face, due to being students at the same department; therefore, they attended the same activities, such as playing football. In addition, members who stayed in different cities met at the same place by traveling among cities while preparing their project tasks.

Outcome Elements of Online Groups

Under this item, issues about difficulties, conflicts, production, and satisfaction about group work are found as major categories.

Difficulties and Conflicts

Members in the online groups were faced with some difficulties while preparing their project phases. First, members mentioned that they were faced with finding an original project topic that would be prepared in a four-month online course. Second, most of them stated that they had anxiety at the beginning of the project, since they thought that their knowledge was inadequate, and they were incapable. Also, they stated that preparing project processes were too complex for them, and they did not know how to complete project phases, due to the limited knowledge. Therefore, they had to work hard and learn many things to prepare the project components in the given deadline. The third problem was living and working in different places. Participants mentioned that meeting at the same time with all group members was difficult, due to their busy schedules. They expressed that they might have different responsibilities when they decided to work together. It was difficult for some members in the online groups to allocate enough time for preparing their tasks, and find suitable time for face-to-face meeting and online chats.

Moreover, participants mentioned several negative events while preparing their projects. For example, three group members stated that some phases of the project were too difficult for them with having little experience. One of them mentioned that they worked all night to prepare some part of the project. Another participant explained that they did the same duties lots of times to prepare documents. Also, one participant mentioned problems in their computers, which were broken down. Furthermore, one participant talked about their remembrance. His leg was broken, and they worked with members with communicating MSN messenger tools. They started to work at 11 am, till 10 pm.

Participants stated that there was not much disagreement in the online group work. In general, when problems occurred, they discussed together how to solve it, and members guided each other for solving their problems. During the discussions, members did not insist on their ideas —they told opinions about all topics, and they sometimes accepted opposite ideas.

Production

All groups finished their projects at the end of the course. Six group members stated that they reached their basic aim of the project. They thought that they did the best that they could do while preparing their project, and they accepted that group members learned many things from each phase of the project. Only two participants thought that they did not reach the aim exactly, due to being busy and less knowledgeable about the project topic. They stated that their project still required more work. For example, one participant explained that they gave up some ideas and duties due to time inadequacy.

Satisfaction

The results showed that most participants were satisfied with group work in this online course. For instance, six participants stated that they were satisfied with group work, and they would regroup with the same group members. Two participants expressed that if they were not formed in the group, they would have been faced with more difficulties. They mentioned advantages of forming a group during the online course. For example, they stated that they shared success and failure among each other in the online group. They motivated and guided each other when they needed, and also they taught and learned from each other.

On the other hand, two participants criticized some points of group works in this online course, even though they were generally satisfied. In other words, they were dissatisfied with some points in the group work. According to them, one of the disadvantages was that it was difficult to reach a common decision point during the group work. Also, they stated that group work took more time than individual work.

Recommendations for Online Project-Based Courses

Some participants made recommendations for this online project-based course. For instance, not all students formed a group in this course, even though some of them were willing to form. Course instructors might help them in forming groups by finding appropriate members at the beginning of the course. Moreover, they thought that there should be at least one person who is knowledgeable about each project task in the group. He or she might guide other members when the problems arise. Therefore, they learned more things and worked more effectively in shorter time. Also, there was not much interaction among the groups in this course. Groups also should share their experiences and ideas with other groups during the course.

Discussion

This study analyzed the dynamics and factors that affected success and effectiveness of online groups. Eight online groups with two or three members were analyzed in an online project-based course. Participants preferred to form a group while developing their project, even though there was no enforcement in the online course. They expressed that they had gained significant benefits from group work. For example, participants stated that group members accomplished tasks that could not be done by individuals alone. They brought multiple perspectives to solve a single problem. Also, group work allowed individuals to observe perspectives of other group members, thus expanding each one's own perspective. It is a general consensus that information and communication tools offer one of the most exciting and effective ways to teach people how to collaborate by connecting groups, regardless of the location.

In this study, the dynamics that affect group learning are combined into entry, process, and outcome variables (Hackman & Morris, 1975). Entry variables in the group systems represented the design and compositional characteristics of a group, such as member personalities, knowledge, skills and abilities, group size, and task-related issues that influenced how groups performed.

Process variables in the group systems influenced group activities in which members engage, such as participation, leadership, communication pattern, and group history. Outcome variables in the group systems were related to what the groups produce and achieve during the course, such as difficulties, conflicts in the groups, and satisfaction and production of groups.

Group composition has a significant impact on group performance and effectiveness in any context in the literature. According to previous research (i.e., Hackman & Morris, 1975; Mennecke, Hoffer, & Wynne, 1992; Carabajal et al., 2003), while forming learning groups, the members' knowledge, skills, and abilities are significant factors. Carabajal et al. (2003) stated that each group member brings his or her knowledge, experience, belief, and abilities to the group. With regard to group member characteristics, one of the main issues raised in our study was group heterogeneity or homogeneity.

Several advantages and disadvantages of homogenous and heterogeneous groups are reported in the literature. For example, Cohen (1994) stated that heterogeneous groups provide more opportunities for learning, because a variety of new perspectives are exposed that enables production of creative, high-quality solutions for the students. This statement was supported by various studies in the literature (i.e., Guzzo & Dickson, 1996; Milliken & Martins, 1996; Volkema & Gorman, 1998). However, Schullery and Schullery (2006) stated that in heterogeneous groups, "communicative, cognitive, and cultural differences increase the potential for conflict, while decreasing desirable processes such as shared leadership, cohesiveness, information sharing, and satisfaction" (p. 543). Also, other researchers showed that homogenous groups bring higher levels of cohesiveness and satisfaction (i.e., Perrone & Sedlacek, 2000). As a summary, it might be possible to create real-life-like learning situations with heterogonous groups being dispersed across the globe, especially in computer-supported environments.

According to the results of the study, the group members generally preferred to form homogeneous groups in regard to entry variables. For example, members' gender and age levels were similar. They were students at or graduated from the same department. Their prior knowledge about computer technology and the online course project were limited. Also, members knew each other before, and they could access and communicate with their group members easily in daily life. So the homogeneity among group members affected fairly the selection of group members, activities in group processes, and group outcomes in this study.

In these homogenous groups, participants generally preferred to form groups with members who they already knew and they had previously worked with. In other words, they preferred to work with a group member who knew how to behave, and how to interact or communicate with each other. Trust is a critical issue in healthy group development. Handy (1995) and Lewis (1998) stated that trust is a key ingredient in successful virtual organizations, and in order to foster trust and start to work together effectively in virtual team, they need to meet in person.

Online or traditional groups are dependent on every member completing his/her assigned tasks in an efficient and effective manner. While completing tasks, equal participation is significant, since it leads to increased satisfaction for group members (Beebe & Masterson, 1997). Researchers found that conflict is more likely to occur in online groups when compared with face-to-face groups (Mortensen & Hinds, 2001). Also, conflict frequently occurs especially in the project group process, since group members have diverse skills, disciplines, knowledge, and experiences (Chen, 2006). On the contrary, the results of this study showed that there was not much of a problem with task distribution and task completion among members, due to the homogeneity in the groups. Members generally worked equally in group works, and they helped each other while preparing and completing their tasks. Task divisions were distributed based on members' experiences and convenient workload during that time. Furthermore, each participant agreed that they discussed their project components among members while making decisions, and they generally reached the agreement over time at the end of the meetings.

In addition to the benefits of forming homogenous groups, the results demonstrated that there were several difficulties in these groups. One of the major difficulties members were faced with was limited experiences about tasks in this type of project. Most members were faced with this kind of project for the first time. They did not know how to perform their tasks at the beginning. Furthermore, some members had time allocation problems in the groups. For example, some members had problems with spending enough time for their project duties, due to the other responsibilities (e.g., job, family). Therefore, members in the groups sometimes could not work at the same time together. Moreover, although members have a general goal for preparing their project (i.e., improving themselves and learning new things), each member in this study had a different implicit goal as well. These factors affected group effectiveness negatively during the group works. Vrasidas and McIsaac (1999) stated that group members' task orientations, strategy orientations, goal orientations, and motivation affect participation and interaction in the groups.

Also, researchers mentioned several factors that affect individual participation in online groups: members' responsibilities outside the online community (Kember, 1995), technical skills and equipment (Lea & Spears, 1992), and preferences and needs for interaction (Vrasidas & McIsaac, 1999).

It was found that one of the factors affecting group effectiveness was task-related issues, which included task types, division, coordination and interaction between members, and the ways they used them while performing their tasks. In this online course, participants had to complete their projects in four months. General tasks and types were defined clearly by the phases of software development project for participants. Also, a timeline and examples for completing project tasks were provided for each group at the beginning of the course. Course instructors evaluated groups' project progress and gave feedbacks regularly. Each document of groups was evaluated based on the requirements expected for each project phase. These feedbacks were given through course discussion lists and e-mail. If the groups needed more feedbacks, instructors helped them during online chat sessions. Groups generally completed the projects on time. This type of design helped groups to complete their projects. Groups started to work on the online course by proposing their project topics to the course instructors, and completed other requirements. Results showed that each group chose different project topics that related to meet the need in their real life requirements. Members reached the agreement of a common and feasible topic related to all member interests, after investigating similar ones in real life. As a summary, task types were extracted by the group members, based on their project proposals in the course. Task type is critical to the success and speed with which online groups make decisions in the literature (see Gallupe & McKeen, 1990; Daly, 1993). Also, research stated that group performance is highly dependent on developing clear plans, goals, and priorities. Groups' tasks were designed to require substantial task and goal interdependence (Porter & Lilly, 1996).

Group size, and their fit with the group's task, also played a very important role while creating learning groups. Actually, there is no common idea for an optimal group size for collaboration and cooperation learning in the literature. It is dependent on several variables, such as the type of task, the age and maturity of the group members, and the resources available to complete the task (Graham, 2002). Similarly, according to the participants in this study, group size was dependent on project properties, background knowledge of members, and allocating members' time for the project tasks. Furthermore, there is limited research related to size factors in online groups in the literature. Researchers suggested that small groups are more preferable for selecting group size (Johnson et al., 1994). In this study, preferable group size among participants was two or three people, which was enough for this type of project. Members stated that work division was easier in the groups with more members, but they thought that the more members in the group, the more they ignore their duties, and the less they wish to contribute to the duties. Also, they agreed that it was difficult to meet at the same with all group members, and to reach agreements about project subjects.

Group leadership is another process variable for a successful collaboration. Grenier and Metes (1995) stated that leadership in the virtual environment has a major influence on the outcome of the initiative. They mentioned that directions and boundaries are determined with the help of leadership in the projects. Although there is no clear leader among members in the online groups in this study, leaders who had more knowledge and guided other members appeared sometimes. Also, they had more time, worked hard, and generally stated a project idea.

Communication among group members is one of the most important process predictors of group effectiveness. Larson and LaFasto (1989) stated that groups must communicate effectively in order to establish clear and specific goals and objectives, so that they might function effectively as a group. The result of this study demonstrated that the face-to-face meetings were more productive than other communication types, even though participants used all types of communications, such as e-mail, online chat, phone calls, and face-to-face meetings during their project. For instance, they sometimes used e-mail to send short messages, send files, and make coordination, used phone calls to talk to each other in a short time, and used MSN messenger and ICQ tools to discuss their project's phases instantly. However, group members preferred face-to-face meetings more.

All groups whose members could meet often face-to-face in daily life, or could not meet face to face easily, made a plan according to the course re- quirements, and generally worked together face-to-face while preparing their projects. Especially, groups whose members could meet often face-to-face did not prefer to use computer-mediated communication tools. Actually, they did not need to use them. On the other hand, participants who met less face-to-face communicated with each other through all available communi- cation methods. They sent e-mails to each other, attended online chats, and met face-to face.

According to Warkentin, Sayeed, and Hightower (1999), people could use multiple modes of communication during the face-to-face conservations, such as voice tone, inflection, volume, eye movement, facial expressions, hand gestures, and other body language. However, the virtual environment brings some challenges to effective communication, including time delays in sending feedback, differences in salience and interpretation of written text, and assurance of participation from remote team members (Crampton, 2001). Furthermore, Salter and Gann (2002) found that, despite modern information and communication technologies, face-to-face interaction and the immediacy of sketching are still the most important elements for developing new ideas and solving problems. Similarly, the results showed that members preferred face-to-face meeting periodically, if it was proper for all group members. These face-to-face meetings were reported as a positive impact on group performance, and they helped the development of positive interpersonal relationships among group members. These findings were consistent with previous studies on the benefits of face-to-face meetings for virtual teams (e.g., Lewis, 1998; Saunders, 2000).

Online teams tend to have more of a task-focus and less of a social-focus than traditional teams, and virtual teams appear to lessen their task-focus over time (Walther & Burgoon, 1992). On the other hand, group members met regularly face-to-face physically, and also, they organized social activities with each other in the groups. For example, they met frequently face-to-face, and discussed their project duties during lunch breaks. These activities that strengthen the socio-emotional development of the group are other advantages of meeting face-to-face during group work projects.

Group performance and member satisfaction are two major outcome variables in group work studies (Powell, Piccoli, & Ives, 2004). In this study, almost all groups completed the major aims of their project, and they were satisfied with the online group work. According to Hackman (1989), these results are important, since member satisfaction influences their willingness to col-laborate and contribute to future group works. In addition, some participants mentioned difficulties that they were faced with during group work, and stated several recommendations for online, project-based courses. For instance, one of the difficulties for the participants was having little knowledge about project tasks. The second one was allocating enough time to work together for project tasks. Also, they stated that, sometimes, it was difficult to reach a common decision point during the group work.

One of the results of the study showed that interaction between members and instructors through communication tools was not enough. Group members generally contacted the course instructors through discussion lists when they were faced with problems in their project. Instructors could play a better role in stimulating interaction in CSCL environments. Burge (1994) found two types of instructor behaviors required in online collaborative learning: discussion management (e.g., providing structure, pacing and focusing the class discussions), and contribution (e.g., giving fast and relevant technical help, sending timely and individualized, content-related messages and feedback). Therefore, online instructors must make extra effort for distance learners to prepare more effective learning environments.

Implications for Practice

Learners in online groups may produce more than they ever could have working individually. This popular and new form of group learning comprises various dynamics that have very complex natures. Such a method can only be productive if we are well-prepared for potential problems, and ready to take necessary actions in advance. Based on the results of this study, the following recommendations can be offered for instructors or designers who will deal with similar computer-supported collaborative work:

- **Designing online course structure carefully:** The course content must be compatible with the students' entry behaviors. The projects must be related with real life experiences.

- **Helping form groups:** In the courses, students must be advised to form groups; they must be supported on this issue.

- **Keeping groups small:** Group size must be kept small.

- **Providing a leader member in groups:** Group member has to be picked among the most knowledgeable members. He/She must have available time for the project.

- **Suggesting face-to-face meeting to members, in addition to using CMC:** Online group members must be encouraged to have face-to-face meetings.

- **Interacting with group members:** Instructor must follow the groups' performance, and make all efforts to keep the interaction level high.

Conclusion

Distributed learning systems on the Internet are growing exponentially, and because of these systems, organizations reach greater numbers of students. Student mobility continues to increase across subject areas, geographic borders, and curriculum areas; therefore, increasing popularity of online group work is inevitable. Nevertheless, there are some cautions to consider while designing or using them in online collaborative environments. Therefore, there is need for more educational research that has focused specifically on online groups.

In this study, issues in collaboratively working online learning groups were explored in an online, project-based course. Analysis framework is based on Hackman and Morris (1975)'s model for analyzing the elements that impact online group behavior and performance. It was found that group homogeneity plays a major role in successful group work. The second major finding was the importance of face-to-face communication among online teams.

This study has some limitations. One of them was making group formation voluntary. For the next study, all members of the course must form a team. In this study, the participants had a chance to communicate face-to-face. So, geographically separated project members may act differently. This has to be explored. The nature of a project has also a significant role on the study. Similar studies need to be replaced on teams with different tasks.

References

Beebe, S., & Masterson, J.T. (1997). *Communicating in small groups*. New York: Longman.

Bonk, C. J., & Cunningham, D. J. (1998). Searching for learner-centered, constructivist, and sociocultural components of collaborative educational learning tools. In C. J. Bonk & K. S. King (Ed.), *Electronic collaborators: Learner-centered technologies for literacy, apprenticeship, and discourse* (pp. 25-50). Mahwah, NJ: Erlbaum.

Brandon, D.P., & Hollingshead, A.B. (1999). Collaborative learning and computer-supported groups. *Communication Education, 48*(2), 109-126.

Burge, E. J. (1994). Learning in computer conferenced contexts: The learner's perspective. *Journal of Distance Education, 9*(1), 19-43

Carabajal, K., LaPointe, D., & Gunawardena, C. N. (2003). Group development in online learning communities. In M. G. Moore & W. G. Anderson (Ed.), *Handbook of distance education* (pp. 217-234). Mahwah, NJ: Lawrence Erlbaum Associates.

Chen, M. (2006). Understanding the benefits and detriments of conflict on team creativity process. *Creativity and Innovation Management, 15*(1), 105-116.

Chinowsky, P., & Rojas, E. (2003). Virtual teams: Guide to successful implementation. *Journal of Management in Engineering, 19*(3), 98-106.

Cohen, E. (1994) *Designing groupwork: Strategies for the heterogeneous classroom.* New York: Teachers College Press.

Crampton, C. (2001). The mutual knowledge problem and its consequences for dispersed collaboration. *Organization Science, 12*(3), 346-371.

Daly, B. L. (1993). The influence of face-to-face versus computer-mediated communication channels on collective induction. *Accounting, Management, and Information Technologies, 3*(1), 1-22.

Gallupe, R.B., & McKeen, J. (1990). Enhancing computer-mediated communication: An experimental study into the use of a decision-support system for face-to-face versus remote meetings. *Information and Management, 18*(1), 1-13.

Gokhale, A. A. (1995) Collaborative learning enhances critical thinking. *Journal of Technology Education, 7*(1). Retrieved November 1, 2007, from http://scholar.lib.vt.edu/ejournals/JTE/v7n1/gokhale.jte-v7n1.html

Graham, C. R. (2002). *Understanding and facilitating computer-mediated teamwork: A study of how norms develop in online learning teams.* Unpublished dissertation, Indiana University, Bloomington.

Grenier, R., & Metes, G. (1995). *Going virtual: Moving your organization into the 21st century.* Upper Saddle River, NJ: Prentice Hall.

Guzzo, R., & Dickson, M. (1996). Teams in organizations: Recent research on performance and effectiveness. *Annual Review of Psychology, 47,* 307-38.

Guzzo, R.A., & Salas, E.S. (1995). *Team effectiveness and decision making in organizations.* San Francisco: Josey-Bass.

Hackman, J.R. (1989). *Groups that work (and those that don't)*. San Francisco: Jossey-Bass.

Hackman, J.R., & Morris, C.G. (1975). Group tasks, group interaction process, and group performance effectiveness: A review and proposed integration. In Berkowitz (Ed.), *Advances in experimental social psychology* (pp. 45-99). New York: Academic Press.

Handy, C. (1995). Trust and virtual organization: How do you manage people whom you do not see. *Harvard Business Review, 73*(3), 40-50.

Isler, V. (1997). *Sanal Ďaiversite*. Paper presented at Inet-tr '97: Türkiye Internet Konferansi, Ankara, Turkey.

Isler, V. (1998). *Distance education experiences of the middle east technical university*. Paper presented at the MEDISAT-EUREKA Joint Workshop: Internet as a Medium for Innovation and Technology Development in Eastern Mediterranean. Tubitak-Bilten & EU/INCO-DC.

Isler, V., Vural, H., & Koc, S. (1998). *ODTÛ sanal Kampüsü: Deneyimleri*. Paper presented at YA/EM '98: Yöneylem Arastirma Konferensi, Ankara, Turkey.

Johnson, D.W., Johnson, R.T., & Holubec, E.J. (1994). *Cooperative learning in the classroom*. Alexandria, VA: Association for Supervision and Curriculum Development.

Johnson, D. W., Johnson, R. T., & Stanne, M. B. (2000). *Cooperative learning methods: A meta analysis*. The Cooperative Learning Center at the University of Minnesota.

Kember, D. (1995). *Open learning courses for adults: A model of student progress*. Englewood Cliffs, NJ: Educational Technology Publications.

Larson, C., & LaFasto, F. M. (1989). *Teamwork: What must go right/what can go wrong*. Newbury Park, CA: Sage.

Lea, M., & Spears, R. (1992). Paralanguage and social perception in computer-mediated communication. *Journal of Organizational Computing, 2*(3-4), 321-341.

Lewis, R. (1998). Membership and management of a virtual team: The perspective of a research manager. *R&D Management, 28*(1), 5-12.

Mennecke, B., Hoffer, J. A., & Wynne, B. E. (1992). The implications of group development and history for group support system theory and practice. *Small Group Research, 24*(4), 524-572.

Merriam, S. B. (1998). *Qualitative research and case study applications in education.* San Francisco: Jossey-Bass Inc.

Miles, M. B., & Huberman, A. M. (1984). *Qualitative data analysis: A sourcebook of new methods.* Beverly Hills, CA: Sage Publications.

Milliken, F.J., & Martins, L. (1996). Searching for common threads: Understanding the multiple effects of diversity in organizational groups. *Academy of Management Review, 21*(2), 402-433.

Mortensen, M., & Hinds, P. (2001). Conflict and shared identity in geographically distributed teams. *International Journal of Conflict Management, 12*(3), 212-238.

Palloff, R., & Pratt, K. (1999). *Building learning communities in cyberspace: Effective strategies for the online classroom.* San Francisco: Jossey-Bass Publishers.

Perrone, K. M., & Sedlacek, W. E. (2000). A comparison of group cohesiveness and client satisfaction in homogeneous and heterogeneous groups. *Journal for Specialists in Group Work, 25*(3), 243-251.

Powell, A., Piccoli, G., & Ives, B. (2004). Virtual teams: A review of current literature and directions for future research. *Database for Advances in Information Systems, 35*(1), 6-36.

Porter, T. W., & Lilly, B. S. (1996). The effects of conflict, trust, and task commitment on project team performance. *International Journal of Conflict Management, 7*(4), 361-376.

Riel, M. (1993). *Learning circles: Virtual communities for elementary and secondary schools.* Retrieved November 1, 2007, from http://lrs.ed.uiuc.edu/Guidelines/Riel-93.html

Salter, A., & Gann, D. (2002). Sources of ideas for innovation in engineering design. *Research Policy, 32*, 1309-1324.

Saunders, C. S. (2000). Virtual teams: Piecing together the puzzle. In R. W. Zmud (Ed.), *Framing the domain of IT management: Projecting the future through the past* (pp. 29-50). Cincinnati, OH: PinnFlex Education Resources.

Schullery, N. M., & Schullery, S. E. (2006). Are heterogeneous or homogeneous groups more beneficial to students? *Journal of Management Education, 30*(4), 542-556.

Thach, L., & Murphy, K. L. (1994). Collaboration in distance education: For local to international perspectives. *The American Journal of Distance Education, 8*(3), 5-21.

Travica, B. (1997). *The design of the virtual organization: A research model.* Paper presented at the Association of Information Systems Americas Conference, Indianapolis, IN.

Volkema, R., & Gorman, R. (1998). The influence of cognitive-based group composition on decision-making process and outcome. *Journal of Management Studies, 35*(1), 105-121.

Vrasidas, C., & McIsaac. M. S. (1999). Factors influencing interaction in an online course. *The American Journal of Distance Education, 13*(3), 22-36.

Walther, J. B., & Burgoon, J. K. (1992). Relational communication in computer mediated interaction. *Human Communication Research, 19*(1), 50-88.

Warkentin, M., Sayeed, L., & Hightower, R. (1999). Virtual teams versus face-to-face teams. In K. E. Kendall (Ed.), *Emerging information technologies improving decisions, cooperation, and infrastructure* (pp. 241-262). Thousand Oaks, CA: Sage Publications.

Yin, R. (1994). *Case study research: Design and methods* (2nd ed.). Beverly Hills, CA: Sage Publishing.

Yukselturk, E. (2005). Online information technologies certificate program. *Turkish Online Journal of Distance Education-TOJDE, 6*(1). Retrieved November 1, 2007, from http://tojde.anadolu.edu.tr/tojde17/articles/erman.htm

Chapter VII

The Social Psychology of Online Collaborative Learning:
The Good, the Bad, and the Awkward

Donna Ashcraft, Clarion University of Pennsylvania, USA

Thomas Treadwell, West Chester University, USA

Abstract

Many social psychological phenomena that are found in face-to-face group work are also found in online group work (i.e., collaborative learning). In this chapter, we describe some of these more common phenomena, including social loafing, social categorization, and a variety of cognitive distortions. We also describe the stages that groups go through in order to become fully functioning teams. Because some of these experiences are unpleasant for both the instructor and the student, both faculty and students sometimes resist the use of collaborative learning. Furthermore, because of the anonymous nature of online group work, these negative experiences can be magnified.

We therefore make recommendations on how best to respond to and resolve them. We specifically draw on our experiences with Collaborative Online Research and Learning (CORAL) in order to demonstrate these phenomena and recommendations. CORAL is a teaching/learning method that integrates two course topics through assignments. Teams of students at two universities must complete together by utilizing video conferencing and other online tools.

Introduction

In this chapter, we examine problems instructors and students experience in collaborative learning by drawing on social psychological literature and our own experiences in implementing online collaborative learning. In particular, we draw on our experiences of teaching Collaborative Online Research and Learning (CORAL) (Treadwell & Ashcraft, 2005; Chamberlin, 2000) classes for more than seven years. CORAL is a constructivist pedagogy that allows students to form learning communities across sites. In CORAL, students at distant sites utilize a variety of electronic technology in order to jointly complete assignments of mutual interest. More specifically, students from two different universities, enrolled in two different courses, collaborate on semester-long projects designed to integrate course topics (e.g., developing research proposals related to both course topics). Students utilize video conferencing, discussion boards, file managers, online calendars, and chat rooms to communicate across, and within, sites to complete assignments. While completing their semester-long projects, students observe their own group's behaviors through a number of collaborative analyses, and are encouraged to modify any behaviors that are not collaborative. The collaborative analyses consist of a series of readings and exercises students complete and use to understand course material related to their own group's processes (for a more detailed description of the CORAL model, see Treadwell & Ashcraft, 2005).

We also make recommendations on how to minimize problems encountered during the life of collaborative teams. The majority of these recommendations are based on research findings in the social psychological literature demonstrating their success in other settings. Others are based on their anecdotal success in our CORAL course. Throughout the chapter, we use examples from CORAL to demonstrate how we apply these recommendations. In essence, we focus on the process that instructors need to utilize to ensure successful online collaboration among students. As Lee (2004) notes, there is little information that provides these types of practical guidelines for less-experienced, Web-based, instructional designers, although there is quite a bit of literature on assessing whether Web-based courses have been successful. We therefore take a process view of online collaboration, rather than a product view (Lee, 2004).

Collaborative and Cooperative Learning

In collaborative learning, students work together to achieve a shared learning goal (i.e., they form learning communities, reassuring the formation of collaborative ideas within a mutually-supportive environment encouraging scholarship). Although the terms collaborative and cooperative are used interchangeably within the literature, they should not be confused. In cooperative learning, students also work together to complete projects, but do so by dividing up the work among team members. In collaborative learning, students work on each aspect of a project by contributing and building on each other's ideas, along with sharing the workload. Thus, although cooperative learning (i.e., distributing work among team members) is part of collaborative learning, it is not the essential characteristic. Instead, the key characteristic of collaborative learning is the development of ideas through interactions with others. A benefit of collaborative learning over cooperative learning, among others, is students learning all the subject matter assimilated into a large project, rather than just the portion required by cooperative education. Beyond this, however, collaborative learning is more flexible and student-oriented. Cooperative learning is more directive, task-oriented, and teacher-oriented (Panitz, 1996).

While both types of learning are typically designed for—and usually take place in—the classroom, collaborative learning is especially conducive for online learning communities. Indeed, Furr, McFerrin, and Fuller (2004) state that "Distance education is collaborative education" (p. 211). By this, the authors imply that a clear advantage distributed collaborative learning has over face-to-face collaboration is the electronic technology. The technology creates a *disorienting dilemma*, allowing for an examination of—and subsequent change in—student work habits and attitudes, and thinking clarification (Palloff & Pratt, 1999). A disorienting dilemma is something that catches students' attention, a surprise that they further examine and reflect upon, thereby creating cognitive changes. In other words, students in collaborative online learning communities realize that the old work habits they are accustomed to in traditional face-to-face classes do not work well in a mutual learning environment. Students learn to modify their behaviors to be successful in their new learning environment, and these modifications create increases and improvements in learning.

Despite the fact that collaborative teaching methods have been found to be preferable to individualistic teaching methods (e.g., Johnson, Johnson, & Stanne, 2000), and despite the fact that collaborative learning contributes to social and cognitive development, many students and faculty demonstrate reluctance for collaborative and cooperative learning experiences, such as group work (e.g., National Institute for Science Education, [NISE] 1997; Rozaitis, 2005). Two key problems associated with group work include inequitable workloads, and disagreements among group members. This is true regardless of whether the group work is face-to-face or whether it is online and distance-based. In fact, many of the issues found in face-to-face group work are also found in online learning communities, but magnified because of the nature of the communication process in online work. Furthermore, students in distributed learning environments generally face additional challenges because of adjustments to the new learning environment (Kitsantas & Dabbagh, 2004). These issues, however, can be understood and minimized through employing the following social psychological principles.

Social Loafing

As mentioned, one of the more common complaints students have about collaborative work is the inequitable workload among team members (e.g., Felder & Brent, 1994; NISE, 1997; Rozaitis, 2005). Uneven distribution of workload is found in many settings. For example, "slacking" on the part of group members can be found even in such minimal effort tasks as clapping in a lab setting (Latane', Williams, & Harkins, 1979), and is commonly referred to as social loafing. Social loafing is a matter of expending less energy on a task than if one were working alone on that same task (Latane' et al., 1979). Thus, for example, students completing a paper in a group might expend less effort on its completion than if they were completing the assignment alone.

One of the primary explanations of this phenomenon is diffusion of responsibility (e.g., Harkins & Szymanski, 1989; Latane', 1981). Group members believe that someone else from the group or team will exert more energy, or do more work, and make up for their lack of effort. This is one reason that group work (collaborative learning) can be unsuccessful. Not only does the social loafer not learn the material because they are uninvolved in the project, but they force team members to redistribute assignment tasks, as well as handle the frustration involved with the inequity of this experience.

Another explanation includes the possibility that students are unsure of what to do when working with others, and believe that other team members are more informed about what behaviors are appropriate or required. They therefore relegate responsibility to those others who are viewed as better equipped to complete assignments.

In any case, online learning communities have an additional challenge: community members are not always physically present to encourage lagging team members to contribute, and, as Furr et al. (2004) note, in distributed courses, students may remain uninvolved and disengaged from team work, unless a strong effort is made to involve them. Fortunately, there are tactics that can be employed in order to reduce this problem for both face-to-face group work and multiple-site online learning communities.

Recommendations

Make individual team member contributions identifiable. One documented tactic involves organizing the efforts of each team member, such that the contribution of each one is obvious and identifiable (e.g., Williams, Harkins, & Latane', 1981). While making contributions identifiable might initially seem as though we are advocating cooperative—rather than collaborative—learning, it does not necessarily have to be cooperative. That is, it might seem as though we are suggesting that teams divide up tasks and then combine the products, rather than collaborate together on the entire project, but such an approach is not what we are proposing. Collaborative contributions can also be unique: For example, individual team members can edit their entire team paper using different colored fonts for each person. This "colored editing" approach allows all team members to check over the final product.

Minimize group size. Another consideration in minimizing social loafing is group size. In larger groups, individuals become anonymous, and so do their contributions, especially when those contributions are accomplished in the already anonymous realm of cyberspace. We therefore recommend minimizing group size for online communities, and find that groups of about six work best. In fact, NISE (1997) notes that students prefer teams of four to seven students in which to work. In CORAL, we integrate courses from two geographical locations, separating us physically by hundreds of miles. As a result, we refer to our teams as "online teams," with each team consisting of three team members from one site, and three team members from a second site. This number allows for adequate team interaction, ensuring that team members get to know each other's strengths and weaknesses, enabling stronger communication among team members in completing collaborative coursework assignments. In addition, with increased communication, team members learn to be aware of the various tasks other team members are performing, with the intention of decreasing confusion and increasing team productivity. While not all online teams consist of members from only two sites, minimizing group size is still recommended.

Encourage collaborative—rather than cooperative—work. A third consideration involves how the online teams divide up the various jobs necessary to complete the entire assignment. We find that teams often try to employ a cooperative—instead of collaborative—approach to complete assignments (i.e., students give each team member a different part of the assignment to complete, and then the team cuts and pastes the various parts of the assignment together). This is particularly true during the initial stages of team development (usually the first six weeks). While this does reduce some social loafing, due to the fact that team members' contributions are identifiable, there are problems with this approach. As noted earlier, one problem is that each student only learns his/her part of the assignment, and does not learn other necessary aspects of the material. We also find, however, that this cooperative approach results in poorly-written papers, because the teams often do not take time to integrate the various sections written by different team members. As NISE (1997) also notes, it is vital then, that teams be corrected when utilizing this approach, and encouraged to be more collaborative. To do this, we distinguish between cooperation and collaboration. Indeed, the first collaborative assignment CORAL students complete, in teams, is the writing of a short paper that describes, and compares, collaborative and cooperative learning. For each assignment, we encourage each team member to contribute to each section of each assignment. Thus, one student in an online learning community might be responsible for beginning her/his part of the assignment, but all other team members must read and comment on that section as well as other sections completed by individual team members. To illustrate, CORAL team members complete a collaborative task by utilizing a number of online technology tools: File managers are used to upload and download successive versions of papers, as well as various other team assignments. Chat rooms are utilized for team members to discuss individual reactions to assignment drafts, hash out differences of opinion, and clarify conflict. Web-based discussion boards are helpful for day-to-day interaction regarding the status of a team member's task, as well as keeping a daily communication log for the team as a whole. We also find that video conferencing is an especially valuable tool for encouraging cross-site collaboration. In fact, the teams who are most collaborative (and most functional) are those who discuss the various parts of the assignment before doing any writing (Treadwell & Ashcraft, 2005). This is time-efficient and collaborative, because the entire team agrees on what should be written, for example, to complete each section of a paper; the only thing left for team members to complete individually is the initial write-up. All the team members in their videoconference discussion have already completed the thinking and understanding portion of the assignment. The initial write-up is then followed by the entire team editing the paper, utilizing the color editing approach mentioned earlier.

It should also be noted, however, that the utilization of technological tools to complete cross-site collaborative work requires time management and organizational skills. In fact, Kitsantas and Dabbagh (2004) note that there is an even greater need for students in Web-assisted courses to engage in time management because of the challenge of adjusting to the use of the technology in the course.

Increase students' commitment. Another effective tactic shown to reduce social loafing in online learning communities is to increase team members' commitment to the successful completion of the assignment (e.g., Brickner, Harkins, & Ostrom, 1986). We rely on the teams themselves to utilize this tactic. Often, students want their instructors to fix problems they encounter working as a team. For example, students often approach their professors, complaining that a team member is not contributing enough. However, in order for teams to progress and become cohesive and functional, team members must solve their own problems. Therefore, if a team member is thought to be social loafing, the other team members must address this issue with that student, and professors must let teams know that this is their responsibility.

This is never a pleasant task, but it is necessary, for if the team does not address their interpersonal problem, it will continue throughout the semester, fester, and lead to even greater dissatisfaction and hostility. In fact, Scheer, Terry, Dolittle, and Hicks (2004) note 15 principles for supporting effective distance education, one of which is cultivating students' academic independence. It should be noted that interpersonal conflict is a natural part of an online collaborative course, as is learning how to cultivate social skills and reduce team conflict by implementing conflict negotiation.

Encourage extensive communication. In CORAL, because our teams consist of multiple students at two sites, we often find that team members from one site sees team members from the distant site as social loafers. Thus, team members across sites must communicate in great detail to each other, clarifying what aspect of the project they are working on. This can be done by posting messages on the teams' Web-based discussion boards, mentioning it during chat room conferences, or during video conference discussions. Often, students assume that everyone on the team knows what they are working on, because they have been discussing it at their own site, and make faulty assumptions, thinking all team members know what each person is completing. They assume that the other site also knows what they are doing, but because the distant site does not see them working, the distant site develops a simple cognitive distortion, assuming the worst (i.e., that their distant-site teammates are not contributing to the completion of the assignment). Everything considered, the more communication team members have with one another, the less likely they will experience confusion as to who is carrying out what task.

Increase team cohesion. An additional proven tactic to reduce social loafing is to strengthen group cohesiveness (Forsyth, 2006; Treadwell, Kumar, & Lavertue, 2001). A cohesive team cares about their team members and the successful completion of their tasks. In order to promote cohesiveness at the beginning of the semester, we encourage teams to determine a team identity, consisting of a team name, logo, and motto. Sherif (1958) similarly required his groups of boys to develop team names and flags in his classic study on intergroup conflict. While this may have a minimal effect on team cohesiveness, this task does serve an additional purpose: to get team members from distant sites to begin talking to each other. Additionally, we introduce superordinate goals in order to develop team cohesiveness across sites during the later part of the storming stage, or approximately the eighth week.

Introduce superordinate goals. Superordinate goals are goals that can only be achieved if all distant sites (i.e., the entire team) work together. Therefore, the potential for social loafing is reduced. Working toward a mutual goal also reduces animosity and social categorization, thereby helping students to overcome the us-versus-them bias (e.g., assuming that the distant site is composed of social loafers) that can develop in group work (Sherif, 1958). In Sherif's classic study, two groups of boys attended summer camp and were unknown to each other. In the first stage of the study, the boys formed group identities to represent their camp by choosing names and designing flags. They engaged in traditional summer camp activities, such as swimming, hiking, and canoeing. In the second stage of the study, the two groups became aware of each other when they were told that they would be engaging in competitions with the other camp. Prizes would be awarded to winners. This competition escalated to hostility between the two groups to such an extent that cabins were ransacked and flags were burned. In the third phase of the study, Sherif reduced the intergroup hostility by introducing a series of superordinate goals. Sherif defined superordinate goals as "goals that are compelling and highly appealing to members of two or more groups in conflict but which cannot be attained by the resources and energies of the groups separately…they are goals attained only when groups pull together" (pp. 349-350). The boys from both camps had to work together in order to fix their "broken" water supply, and to haul a truck up a hill. The introduction of the superordinate goals worked—hostilities dissipated.

Because an "us versus them" bias can develop so readily in multiple-site learning communities, it is critical then, that multiple-site teams be given superordinate goals. In CORAL, students are given the goal of collaborating on two major papers required for each team as their superordinate goal. It is collaboration that is the superordinate goal, not the completion of the papers. It is a goal that no one—and no one site—can achieve individually. Only by working together can the entire team achieve it. The assignments they are given are the means to achieve collaborative interaction among team members. Thus, in CORAL, students must learn to collaborate in order to earn good grades. If collaboration does not emerge, students' grades are significantly affected. Others also note the importance of this type of motivating factor (e.g., Felder & Brent, 1994). Students will only learn to collaborate if they are given incentives, but we have found that when students collaborate, all the other learning and completion of assignments fall into place. While this emphasis on collaboration as a superordinate goal may be appropriate for some course topics, it may not be as appropriate for other course topics.

However, it is possible for instructors to design other superordinate goals. In any case, if all team members are required to work together, social loafing cannot exist. The key to determining whether a goal is superordinate or not is in the answering of the question, "Can this goal be achieved only by the whole team?" If the answer is "no," then it is not a superordinate goal. For example, many of our CORAL students think that completing a paper together is a superordinate goal, but it is not. Theoretically, one student could complete the paper and put all team members' names on it. Therefore, it cannot be a superordinate goal.

One way that we encourage collaborative interaction among cross-site team members is by requiring students to complete different exercises at each site to understand their group processes. A whole picture of the team's processes is only gained by understanding the assignments of both sites. These exercises are combined (and related to each other) for the collaborative analyses to be completed and handed in. One site for example, examines team communication patterns; the other site examines bias and cognitive distortions. The topics are related, because communication patterns will be influenced by bias against certain team members, especially those at one site. Collaboration is necessary for the product to be successfully completed. If students use a cooperative approach, it is evident in a poorly-written, choppy paper, one that does not demonstrate the connection between site topics. Students are encouraged to be collaborative (i.e., the superordinate goal) because they want their papers to be evaluated positively. Other disciplines could use this approach as when, say, a physics class pairs collaboratively with a mathematics class. Math students could work with physics students to complete calculus-based physics problems.

Encourage distributed leadership. Often, online teams believe that they must designate one person as a leader, and this can become a coveted role, because it is perceived in a positive light. Initially, team members think that they have to have one person lead, and do not realize that all team members have to take on leadership responsibility. However, distributive leadership is preferential in online collaborative settings. In distributed leadership (Bennett, Wise, Woods, & Harvey, 2003), all team members share the leadership role, thereby reducing social loafing. Any team member can take it upon him/herself to take action that will help complete tasks successfully and help the team's development. Distributed leadership suggests that many more people are involved in the leadership activity than might traditionally be assumed. Thus, team leadership contributions that emerge should not be limited to a small number of people with formal senior roles. Distributed leadership, then, focuses on team achievement, rather than individual achievements. Student teams must be encouraged to adopt this collaborative leadership style, for it reduces tendencies toward social loafing.

Social Categorization: In-Groups and Out-Groups

As noted, team members in computer-supported collaborative learning environments have a tendency to automatically assume that distant-site team members are social loafers. They can also make many other unpleasant assumptions about their distant-site team members. Online collaborative teams seem to automatically divide themselves into "us versus them" (e.g., Harasty, 1997; Stephan, 1985) resulting in stereotyping and potential bias. Sometimes the "us versus them" bias involves one site pitted against another. In other cases, some team members bond, while others do not, and those that bond become the "us," whereas those who do not become the "them."

This tendency is explained in social psychological terms through the use of in-groups and out-groups. An in-group is a group to whom you, as a person, belong, and anyone else who is perceived as belonging to that group. In-group members have positive views of each other, and give each member preferential treatment. An out-group consists of anyone who does not belong to your group. Out-groups are viewed more negatively, and receive inferior treatment in comparison to that of in-group members. In-group members are perceived as being heterogeneous, and as having positive qualities, referred to as in-group differentiation (e.g., Lambert, 1995; Linville & Fischer, 1993). Out-group members are perceived as being "all the same," homogeneous, and as having more negative qualities. This is referred to as the homogeneity bias (e.g., Linville, Fischer, & Salovey, 1989). These concepts are used to explain hostility between social groups (e.g., Republicans versus Democrats, gays versus straights, whites versus blacks). Relatedly, this bias creates problems with teams becoming cohesive across distant sites, as a result of team members perceiving students from their site (or those they bonded with) as "our team," and automatically seeing students from the distant site (or those they have not bonded with) as not part of "our team." In CORAL, for example, one site is located in a rural area, and the other is located in a suburban east coast area. We often find that students from the rural area view the students at the east coast area as rude and pushy, whereas the east coast students view the rural area students as slackers because they are slower-moving. Again, however, there are methods to reduce this social categorization and associated hostilities (e.g., Gaertner, Mann, Murrell, & Dovidio, 1989).

Recommendations

Increase intergroup contact. One proven method for reducing social categorization is to increase intergroup contact, referred to as the contact hypothesis (e.g., Pettigrew, 1997). It is vital that all team members communicate extensively, in order to reduce cross-site conflict and stereotyping. Perkins and Giordano (2004), as well as many others (e.g., Birenbaum, 2004; Scheer et al., 2004), also note the importance of encouraging communication, especially in distance learning. Extensive communication permits team members to see similarities with others, fostering both synchronous and asynchronous communication with cross-site team members, hence reducing homogeneity bias. In CORAL, for example, we encourage teams to meet in chat rooms once or twice a week, in addition to meeting via video conference during class time, and utilizing discussion boards for asynchronous communication. It should be noted, however, that in order for increased intergroup contact to have the desired effect, the overall interactions must be neutral to positive. If the majority of cross-site interactions are unpleasant and negative, the hostility between groups will remain or increase.

Introduce superordinate goals. A second method for reducing social categorization is the introduction of superordinate goals (Sherif, 1958). As mentioned in the previous sections, the introduction of a task that can only be met through the efforts of all team members can significantly reduce the hostility between in-groups and out-groups, and increase team cohesion. By working together, team members begin to know each other as unique individuals, thereby eliminating some of the bias and hostility that is often found in multiple-site learning communities.

Recategorization. Another consideration for cross-site in-groups and out-groups is recategorization (e.g., Gaertner et al., 1989). Recategorization involves changing the boundaries of the in-group and out-group. While some teams cannot overcome the initial cross-site "us versus them" division, most teams can. But, when teams are able to overcome initial social categorization, other types of in-groups and out-groups can emerge. For example, at the beginning of the semester, we find cross-site social categorization to be very common, but as the semester progresses, team members are able to make connections with cross-site team members, who then become part of the in-group. Occasionally, the entire team becomes one in-group, a very favorable occurrence for collaborative learning. But, when only some team members bond across sites, the complexion of the team takes on a different look. In-groups emerge and consist of both same-site and cross-site team members, and the same for out-groups. We find that students who remain in the out-group tend to have work habits that are not conducive to team efforts and do not feel favorable to working as a team member. They are resistant to team work and try to give the impression that they are members of the team, but it is only an attempt to please authority figures (e.g., professors). They tend to be social loafers, or communicate less with the team, or are unpleasant to work with, regardless of which site they are located. Although teams can continue to work somewhat effectively with minimal contribution from these out-group members, it is obviously to the teams' benefit to be inclusive. Thus, we encourage groups of students to form whole teams that consist of all team members, but if they cannot—say, for personality conflict reasons—we instruct teams to continue to give those out-group members opportunities to work and become part of the in-group. However, teams are also coached to have a back-up plan if the work of the out-group member is not up to par with other team members, or not completed at all.

If recategorization does not occur naturally within the cross-site team, then we encourage it by asking students to work in pairs across two sites on individual sections of assignments. This allows cross-site team members to get to know each other as individuals, note their strengths, and see them complete work and convey this information to other team members at their site. In other cases where collaborative classes are purely Web-based and students bond over technology-assisted communication, asking in-group students to pair with out-group students should also have the desired effect.

Cognitive Distortions

We've mentioned that students often dislike group work because the learner had earlier negative group experiences where they felt responsible for completing all—or most—of the assignment adequately, and without the aid of group members. In some cases, team members believe that others will complete the assignment, and as a result, students fail to contribute. There-fore, other team members have to assume responsibility, and do complete the assignment alone. In other cases, students behave this way due to a lack of confidence in fellow classmates' ability to complete assignments to their standards. They believe that their academic skills are superior to those of their teammates, and that their teammates' quality of work will negatively affect their grade (e.g., Felder & Brent, 1994; NISE, 1997). In this case, other team members are willing to contribute to the completion of the assignment, but are not allowed to do so.

This is an example of a cognitive distortion called the self-serving bias, in other words, the tendency to attribute positive outcomes to internal causes, and negative outcomes to external causes (e.g., Brown & Rogers, 1991; Miller & Ross, 1975). Relatedly, the ultimate attribution error is a tendency to make more flattering attributions about members of one's own group than about members of another group (Hewstone, Bond, & Wan, 1983). These attributions are detrimental to the formation of a collaborative learning com-munity, and reflective of in-group/out-group biases. As a result, these types of individuals often think the team succeeded only because of their efforts, or their in-group's efforts, in completing a task. These individuals often attribute negative outcomes to out-group members. This perception, while occasionally true, is more often a cognitive distortion, an illusion manifested by these individuals, and calling attention to this concept may reduce some of the ill will that can develop in early stages of collaborative learning.

Relatedly, this type of cognitive distortion is especially common in certain high-achieving students. While some excellent students are quite adept at online collaboration, others are painfully unprepared for the experience. They often feel as though they are the only team members capable of completing adequate work, and are often dissatisfied with the work others produce. They therefore complete whole assignments alone, but then complain that they have completed all the work, and that no other team members are working. Other team members, in turn, can feel insulted by this lack of trust in their abilities, along with being referred to as social loafers by individuals who consider themselves better-quality students. In reality, this is not effective learning behavior for the individual, nor for their team. While this sense of responsibility and independence has been rewarded in other educational set-tings, it is contradictory to the purpose of online learning communities, and generally to collaborative learning.

Recommendations

Teach trust and mentoring. Because the reward structure in computer-supported collaborative learning environments is so different than that in traditional learning settings, these high-achieving students can feel frustrated and betrayed. What they are lacking is a sense of trust in working with others. Thus, taking time to help them trust their teammates is usually productive. For example, in CORAL, we often ask these types of students to take a chance, reduce their workload, and give other team members an opportunity to contribute. If they can force themselves to back off, they are often pleasantly surprised by the amount—and quality—of work their teammates can contribute. In addition, they need to be shown that it is their responsibility to help their teammates learn course material. Students such as these must be taught to be less independent and more concerned about the well-being of their team members instead of their own individual sense of well-being. Furthermore, they need to realize how their behavior is actually hindering team development and the learning of other team members.

Intellectualize. It is helpful, with this type of student, to intellectualize these experiences by labeling them as the self-serving bias or the ultimate attribution error, as a strategy to reduce feelings of discomfort that can be associated when challenging the appropriateness of their behavior. In effect, it is suggested that teams engage in metacognition (i.e., observe their own behaviors, apply labels to those behaviors, and determine whether they are appropriate for team development). If the behaviors are not helpful to team development, then their task is to develop solutions for those inappropriate behaviors. Not only do these metacognitive exercises help students to intellectualize and understand unpleasant online experiences, but they also contribute to developing a life-long learning process (Birenbaum, 2004; Kitsantas & Dabbagh, 2004).

Stages of Group Development

Students (and faculty) are sometimes reluctant to utilize collaborative learning, because they are uncomfortable with, and unprepared for, team conflict and conflict resolution (e.g., Felder & Brent, 1994). However, it is also useful to understand that long-term groups tend to pass through a number of stages, one of which is characterized by disagreement, ranging from mild to more extensive.

Tuckman and Jensen (1977) suggested that groups go through five stages of development, from their inception through their adjournment: forming, storming, norming, performing, and adjourning. Each has unique characteristics and implications for learning communities, but the characteristics of each stage are not set in stone, and it is sometimes difficult to determine when a team has moved from one stage to another. Occasionally, teams have characteristics from more than one stage. Thus, the stages are not as linear as Tuckman (1965) initially suggested.

Forming is the initial stage of group development. At this time, team members meet each other, and there is little interaction; the interaction that does occur is somewhat strained and superficial because, team members do not yet know each other. There is a lack of organization and confusion of team objectives. At this point, the team is just starting to forge an identity.

The second stage is storming, and can be stressful for team members, in that disagreements can occur. In storming, team members are often competitive over leadership positions, and there is disagreement about what team goals should be and how tasks should be accomplished. Sometimes these disagreements are mild and readily resolved. In other cases, the disagreements are much more major, resulting in repetitive—and sometimes inappropriately-handled—arguments. Many students are unprepared for dealing with conflict, and see this stage as something to be avoided. However, disagreements and arguments, while unpleasant, are a normal part of teamwork, and are necessary for the growth of the team. It can be contentious, unpleasant, and even distasteful to members of the team who are averse to conflict. In fact, disagreements can occur more frequently in online groups as a result of the lack of non-verbal cues when communicating with tools such as chat rooms and Web-based discussion boards. Video conferencing does allow for face-to-face contact, but students, during the initial stages of computer-supported collaborative learning communities, are fearful of bringing attention to problems they see regarding other team members during this type of interaction. They are often concerned about hurting another team member's feelings, or negatively affecting team development and cohesiveness, but their reluctance to address problems early often fosters team conflict later. The storming stage is when students start complaining about other team members (e.g., they are slacking, they are pushy) or that other team members do not listen to their ideas.

The storming stage is one of the primary reasons students (and instructors) avoid collaborative learning.

The third stage of Tuckman's model is norming. In norming, teammates have accepted their differences, and are beginning to find ways of coping with those differences. Team members often work through this stage by agreeing on rules, values, professional behavior, shared methods, working tools, and even taboos. During this phase, team members begin to trust each other. Motivation increases as the team gets more acquainted with team assignments. They capitalize on each other's strengths, and find ways to compensate for each other's weaknesses. For example, the team may accept one teammate as being disorganized, and ask that teammate to complete particular tasks they are good at by giving them specific instructions and deadlines. As another example, team members may accept one teammate as overly talkative during videoconference exchanges, thereby dominating the conversation. The dominating team member may be allowed to express their opinions, yet other team members may insist on moving forward, covering other important agenda items. Acceptance of individual differences and respect for each other are key characteristics of this stage.

In the performing stage, learning communities are fully functioning. They understand the tasks they need to complete, and how to complete them collaboratively. They also have rules in place for managing conflict and disagreements adequately and appropriately. At this point, the learning community is relatively self-sufficient, and the teams engage in their own self-assessment. The instructor has very little need to intervene. Finally, the adjournment stage is entered, and the learning community disbands.

Recommendations

Start with simple collaborative tasks. To help teams move from the forming to storming stage, it is useful for instructors to assign uncomplicated collaborative tasks at the inception of the online learning community. These can be designed to help students form a group identity, get to know each other on a more personal level, and learn how to use the technological tools. Perkins and Giordano (2004) also note the importance of an ice-breaker at the beginning of a Web-based course. The initial collaborative assignment demonstrates the difficulty students can expect working as a team. It serves as an example of the types of problems students may run into during the semester, and gives instructors the chance to show teams how to identify the problems they might encounter, and methods they can use to correct them.

Encourage constructive discussion of team concerns. If students avoid conflict, issues never get resolved, similar problems surface over and over again, and the team does not progress in development. Instead, they remain at the uncomfortable storming stage. Thus, instructors facilitating online learning communities must be prepared for this stage, and help students deal with it appropriately. In order to progress through storming and move on to norming, students must be encouraged to diplomatically address and resolve concerns about their team or individual teammates, and an atmosphere of acceptance of differing opinions must be nurtured. Sometimes disagreements develop into verbally-violent and personal exchanges as a result of individual differences regarding ideas about how to deal with conflict, or because concerns not discussed earlier in team development begin to fester. This is an obvious sign that conflict is getting out of control. When—or if—this happens, it is useful to encourage students to focus on team goals rather than personality conflicts, along with keeping team members centered on completing assignments. For example, if teams are avoiding confrontation in CORAL courses, the professors ask them to diplomatically address their concerns over video conference. Video conferencing is better than chat rooms or discussion boards for this type of confrontation, because both verbal and nonverbal cues are used, and there is less likelihood of misunderstandings. Tone of voice (which is not available in chats or discussion boards) can be instrumental in reducing the possibility of conflict escalating.

Intellectualize. We also find it useful to help students intellectualize the situation, using it as a learning experience, thereby reducing some of the emotional component of the disagreement. For example, depending on the circumstance, it might be useful to draw attention to possible in-group and out-group biases that contributed to the conflict during the storming stage of development. These concepts are intertwined with the content of the CORAL courses we teach, and might be useful in other courses as well.

Encourage understanding of team norms. Norms form throughout the various stages of group development. Norms, unspoken rules for behavior, can be both positive and negative. For example, as noted earlier, sometimes learning communities form a negative norm that does not allow disagreement to occur or to be addressed. Students agree with each other for the sake of preserving the peace. In other cases, norms of social loafing, or not working hard enough, develop. In still other cases, teams motivate each other to develop positive norms, such as checking Web-based discussion boards daily, completing assignments before deadlines, and developing agendas for video conferences and online chat sessions.

Understanding team norms is critical for teams to examine their own growth. Group development emerges in stages, and team members have to understand what stage of growth they are in, in order to better address stage-determined issues and move on. Recognizing and identifying positive and negative norms are useful, so those that are not conducive to team development can be addressed and changed. Becoming aware of team norms and understanding them is foremost for students, and facilitates completing collaborative assignments designed to learn course material. In some cases, students object to this internal team examination because, for some disciplines, it is not related to course topic. However, this belief that courses or disciplines are unrelated is an illusion, and students need to understand that their major courses do not operate in a vacuum. Indeed, Johnson, Johnson, and Smith (1991) maintain that regular self-assessment of team processes is a vital feature of successful collaborative learning experiences.

Accept fluctuation between the storming and norming stages. In the norming stage, we also sometimes find that teams become complacent with their success in overcoming the problems of the storming stage. They feel that, because they no longer argue, that they have reached the pinnacle of team performance. In actuality, this is not true, and teams can still fine-tune their collaborative efforts. It should also be noted that teams sometimes fluctuate between the storming and norming stages. It is therefore not uncommon for teams to regress to storming and even the forming stage. Perhaps this is most confusing to team members–understanding regression. Students' interpretation of this is normally negative, yet it simply indicates that there are internal team processes that need further examination. With this as one explanation for regression, students begin to reframe their experience into a more positive structure, and at times, it is necessary for instructors to point out this explanation. It must be kept in mind that students are usually not aware of stage regression and fluctuation, and it is essential that professors emphasize the normalcy of stage and team vacillation.

Encourage teams to develop rules. To help teams move from initial forming and storming stages to more comfortable and collaborative norming and performing stages, it is helpful to encourage teams to develop positive rules of team behavior. This could include rules about how frequently team members talk on discussion boards or chat rooms, as well as rules about how to deal with disagreement and conflict. It could also include rules about how the team completes assignments. All of these issues are not firm in the forming and storming stages, and need to be discussed in order for the team to function.

Summary

In summary, students and faculty, in both face-to-face and distant-site classes, often resist the use of collaborative learning because of common, troublesome, behavioral events. These include unequal distribution of work among team members and friction among team members. Problems such as these can be magnified with online collaborative teams as a result of the less-personal electronic communication technology that does not always allow for non-verbal communication cues. We have made a variety of recommendations on how best to cope with these side effects of group work, and these suggestions are consistent with Johnson et al.'s (1991) criteria for successful collaborative learning, which includes positive interdependence, individual accountability, face-to-face interaction, appropriate use of interpersonal skills, and regular self-assessment of group functioning. However, because online (as opposed to face-to-face) team problems can be exaggerated, additional requirements are necessary for successful computer-supported collaborative learning. Thus, we see five recommendations as especially important:

1. *The introduction of superordinate goals* is beneficial in fostering distributed team cohesion and commitment, and reducing cross-site hostilities. Superordinate goals encourage students to collaborate and reduce social loafing, since students learn that they can only succeed if the whole team succeeds and works together.

2. *The intellectualization of unpleasant team processes* is helpful in reducing emotionally aversive group experiences, and learning from them. Labeling unpleasant, yet common, events with technical terms removes some of the emotional distress associated with group or individual conflict, and discussing methods for resolving these issues generally is practical, and less threatening, than personalizing them.

3. *Distributed leadership* encourages collaboration (rather than coopera-
    tion), and reduces social loafing. Many students have a preconceived
    idea that there can be only one leader in a team. Changing this assump-
    tion, and encouraging distributed leadership whereby all team members
    take on leadership roles as necessary, encourages all team members to
    contribute significantly to completing assignments, and increases team
    commitment and cohesion.

4. *Distinguishing collaborative versus cooperative approaches* to complet-
    ing group work for students is helpful in aligning student and instructor
    expectations, especially considering that students enrolled in Web-based,
    or Web-assisted, courses are unsure as to what work habits will best
    contribute to success in a collaborative learning environment.

5. *Teaching trust and mentoring* assists independent students in their struggle
    to share workload with their teammates. Considering that Web-based
    courses can create an atmosphere of anonymity (and independence),
    taking time to instruct students on how to connect, and relate, with
    other students online is useful in creating a sense of community and
    teamwork.

Because there are a variety of online learning communities, there will be
a variety of team experiences. Some online teams might experience all the
phenomena noted here; others might only experience a few. Nevertheless,
awareness of these issues, and methods useful in minimizing them, assist
both faculty and students in reducing unpleasant behavioral events that result
in reluctance to utilize a collaborative learning pedagogy.

The success of collaborative online courses depends on the appropriate use
of pedagogy and related technologies, not just on the introduction of technologies themselves.

For collaborative learning to be effective, professors must view teaching
as a process of developing and enhancing students' ability to learn. The
collaborative educator's role is not to transmit information, but to serve as
a facilitator for learning. This involves creating and managing meaningful
learning experiences, and stimulating students' thinking through real world
problems.

References

Bennett, N., Wise, C., Woods, C., & Harvey, J. (2003). *Distributed leadership*. National College for School Leadership. Retrieved November 4, 2007, from http://www.ncsl.org.ui/literaturereviews

Birenbaum, M. (2004). A hypermedia learning environment that supports knowledge construction and affords opportunities for self-regulated learning. *Journal on Excellence in College Teaching, 15*(1/2), 143-166.

Brickner, M., Harkins, S., & Ostrom, T. (1986). Personal involvement: Thought provoking implications for social loafing. *Journal of Personality and Social Psychology, 51*, 763-769.

Brown, J. D., & Rogers, R. J. (1991). Self-serving attributions: The role of physiological arousal. *Personality and Social Psychology Bulletin, 17*, 501-506.

Chamberlin, J. (2000, April). *One psychology project, three states.* Monitor on Psychology, pp. 58-59.

Felder, R. M., & Brent, R. (1994). *Cooperative learning in technical courses: Procedures, pitfalls, and payoff (ERIC Document Reproduction Services NO. ED377038).* Retrieved November 4, 2007, from http://www.ncsu.edu/felder-public/Papers/Coopreport.html

Forsyth, D. R. (2006). *Group dynamics* (4th ed.). New York: Brooks/Cole.

Furr, P., McFerrin, K., & Fuller, F. (2004). Constructive and disruptive ad hoc communities in higher distance education: An analysis of synchronous and asynchronous settings. *Journal on Excellence in College Teaching, 15*(1/2), 211-229.

Gaertner, S. L., Mann, J., Murrell, A., & Dovidio, J. F. (1989). Reducing intergroup bias: The benefits of recategorization. *Journal of Personality and Social Psychology, 57*, 239-249.

Harasty, A. S. (1997). The interpersonal nature of social stereotypes: Differential discussion patterns of in-groups and out-groups. *Personality and Social Psychology Bulletin, 23*, 270-284.

Harkins, S., & Szymanski, K. (1989). Social loafing and group evaluation. *Journal of Personality and Social Psychology, 56*, 934-941.

Hewstone, M., Bond, M. H., & Wan, K. C. (1983). Social factors and social attributions: The explanation of intergroup differences in Hong Kong. *Social Cognition, 2*, 142-157.

Johnson, D. W., Johnson, R. T., & Smith, K. A. (1991). *Cooperative learning: Increasing college faculty instructional productivity (ASHE-ERIC Higher Education Report No. 4)*. Washington, DC: The George Washington University, School of Education and Human Development.

Johnson, D. W., Johnson, R. T., & Stanne, M. B. (2000). *Cooperative learning: A meta-analysis*. Retrieved November 4, 2007, from http://www.co-operation.org/pages/cl-methods.html

Kitsantas, A., & Dabbagh, N. (2004). Supporting self-regulation in distributed learning environments with Web-based pedagogical tools: An exploratory study. *Journal on Excellence in College Teaching, 15*(1/2), 119-142.

Lambert, A. J. (1995). Stereotypes and social judgment: The consequences of group variability. *Journal of Personality and Social Psychology, 68*, 388-403.

Latane', B. (1981). The psychology of social impacts. *American Psychologist, 36*, 343-356.

Latane', B., Williams, K., & Harkins, S. (1979). Many hands make light the work: The causes and consequences of social loafing. *Journal of Personality and Social Psychology, 37*, 822-832.

Lee, J. Y. (2004). Guidelines for designing Web-based instruction in higher education. *Journal on Excellence in College Teaching, 15*(1/2), 31-58.

Linville, P. W., & Fischer, G. W. (1993). Exemplar and abstraction models of perceived group variability and stereotypicality. *Social Cognition, 11*, 92-125.

Linville, P. W., Fischer, G. W., & Salovey, P. (1989). Perceived distributions of the characteristics of in-group and out-group members: Empirical evidence and a computer simulation. *Journal of Personality and Social Psychology, 57*, 165-188.

Miller, D. T., & Ross, M. (1975). Self-serving biases in the attribution of causality: Fact or fiction? *Psychological Bulletin, 82*(2), 213-225.

National Institute for Science Education. (1997). *Collaborative Learning: Small group learning page*. Retrieved November 4, 2007, from http://www.wcer.wisc.edu/archive/cl1/CL/default.asp

Palloff, R. M., & Pratt, K. (1999). *Building learning communities in cyberspace: Effective strategies for the online classroom*. San Francisco: Jossey-Bass Publishers.

Panitz, T. (1996). *A definition of collaborative versus cooperative learning.* Retrieved November 4, 2007, from http://www.city.londonmet.ac.uk/deliberations/collab.learning//panitz2.html

Perkins, S. S., & Giordano, V. A. (2004). Distance learning interactions: Implications for design. *Journal on Excellence in College Teaching, 15*(1/2), 105-117.

Pettigrew, T. F. (1997). Generalized intergroup contact effects on prejudice. *Personality and Social Psychology Bulletin, 23*, 173-185.

Rozaitis, B. (2005). *Scenes from a classroom: Making active learning work.* Center for Teaching and Learning Services, University of Minnesota. Retrieved November 4, 2007, from http://www1.umn.edu/ohr/teachlearn/workshops/activelearning/resistance.html

Scheer, S. B., Terry, K. P., Dolittle, P. E., & Hicks, D. (2004). Online pedagogy: Principles for supporting effective distance education. *Journal on Excellence in College Teaching, 15*(1/2), 7-30.

Sherif, M. (1958). Superordinate goals in the reduction of intergroup conflict. *American Journal of Sociology, 63*, 249-356.

Stephan, W. G. (1985). Intergroup relations. In G. Lindzey & E. Aronson (Eds.), *Handbook of social psychology* (Vol. 3, pp. 599-658). New York: Addison-Wesley.

Treadwell, T., & Ashcraft, D. (2005). A pedagogy for collaborative online research and learning: The CORAL model. *National Society for Experiential Education Quarterly, 30*(1), 10-17.

Treadwell, T., Kumar, V. K., & Lavertue, N. (2001). The group cohesion scale-revised: Reliability and validity. *International Journal of Action Methods, 54*(1), 3-12.

Tuckman, B.W. (1965). Developmental sequences in small groups. *Psychological Bulletin, 6396*, 384-399.

Tuckman, B. W., & Jensen, M. A. C. (1977). Stages of small-group development revisited. *Group and Organizational Studies, 2*, 419-427.

Williams, K. D., Harkins, S., & Latane', B. (1981). Identifiability as a deterrent to social loafing: Two cheering experiments. *Journal of Personality and Social Psychology, 40*, 303-311.

Section III

Professional Development
Case Studies

Chapter VIII

Collaborative Learning Among Faculty:
Using Course Management Systems to Support Faculty Development

Ellen L. Nuffer, Keene State College, USA

Abstract

In higher education today, faculty members are faced with ever-increasing expectations for their teaching, scholarship, and service. Faculty in the 21st century college and university must teach with technology, incorporate student research opportunities into the curriculum, employ active learning strategies while accommodating learners with disabilities, engage in scholarship at the edges of the traditional disciplines, demonstrate multiple forms of scholarship in a professional portfolio, implement classroom and departmental assessment strategies, and provide service to the discipline and community in addition to the college. These complex roles frequently require faculty to collaborate with staff, administrators, students, and peers for the most effective engagement in these new modes of scholarship, service, and teaching. Faculty development professionals are faced with the challenges of supporting faculty in this new environment, and in particular with finding ways to facilitate the sharing, interacting, discussing, questioning, and brainstorming necessary for success in a highly-demanding work environment. Given the time constraints that are endemic in today's academy, creative solutions that will facilitate collaboration are necessary.

Introduction

This chapter will examine principles of adult learning and cognition, as well as theories and perspectives on collaboration that inform best practices in supporting faculty as they find creative ways to work together. These best practices are examined in their applications to faculty collaboration using course management system software (e.g., BlackBoard). Four projects that exemplify the new and challenging roles of faculty as teachers, scholars, and contributors in the new academy are described and analyzed. Recommendations for the future are then discussed.

The Principles of Adult Learning

The design of supports for faculty development and faculty collaboration should rest on the principles that promote effective learning and change. In the same way that excellence in curriculum and pedagogy in any classroom should be informed by the practices that have been shown to be developmentally appropriate to the population in question, so too should faculty development practices follow what is known about adult learning. The following paragraphs review some of the adult learning literature, and examine the principles of adult learning that are most clearly relevant to the special case of learning in those adults who happen to be faculty members.

Malcolm Knowles is known by many as the "father of andragogy"—the science of teaching adults (Bash, 2003). Knowles's work was initially written to help guide how one teaches the adult returning to, or perhaps first starting, higher education. He contended that teaching adults is most successful when the needs and motivations of the learner are primary, rather than the wants and desires of the instructor (Knowles, 1970). Later work by Knowles and his colleagues recognized that adult learners can vary considerably in their reasons for engaging in further learning, and that not all adults are the self-motivated and self-directed learners that early scholarship in adult learning implied. Knowles went on to describe the information about adult learners that must be considered by instructors: the motivation, prior experiences, readiness to learn, orientation to learning, and the problem solving capabilities of the learners (Swanson, Holton, & Knowles, 1998). When compared to the typical college-aged student, the adult learner has a much greater diversity of background and experiences, as well as breadth of reasons for engaging in further learning. Instructors must take this range of experience and mo-tivation into account in order to engage the adult student in learning, and encourage that student to strive even further. Faculty developers frequently find themselves in similar situations—faced with groups of faculty members with wide ranges of experiences, perspectives, and motivations for attending faculty development events. Faculty developers who recognize that their instructional choices should honor this diversity and capitalize upon it will find greater success in meeting their instructional goals.

Honigsfeld and Dunn (2006) have also examined the characteristics and learning styles of the adult student, but particularly focused on the issue of choice. They found that adult learners perform better when they can select from different types of resources and assignments, choose with whom they work, and have some control over the ways in which they can complete their assignments and present their final work. They also emphasized the importance of adults knowing their own learning preferences in making these choices. Those individuals who work with faculty and extrapolate from this work will find that their workshop and study group participants will experience more satisfaction when they can choose with whom they collaborate or consult, and can select the materials and resources they will use. Providing faculty members with experiences that enable them to understand their own learning preferences and styles will increase their abilities to make wise choices and therefore will increase satisfaction as well.

Bash (2003) also considered characteristics of adult learners, and found there to be five important dimensions that distinguish the adult learner from the more traditional-aged college student. Adult learners are (1) predominantly autonomous and self-directed, needing a sense of control over the learning environment in which they engage. Adult learners have (2) had significant life and work experiences that they need to connect to new information that is presented. They are (3) oriented to goals, their own and those of the instructor, and appreciate understanding the relevance of information, activities, and assignments. Adult learners are (4) practical, wanting to know how information will be useful to them, and finally, (5) have a high need for respect for the knowledge and experience that they bring with them. Faculty developers should heed these findings to ensure the success of their faculty development programs. Faculty members will probably learn more and have higher levels of satisfaction if they can have some control over the content and form of the development activity, if they have multiple opportunities to discuss and connect their own experiences with the information presented (if it is done in an atmosphere of respect), and if they are "invited in" to the presentation, allowing them to understand the reasoning and practicality behind particular approaches.

Other researchers have applied the work of Knowles and others in the area of adult cognitive development to specific populations of adult learners, such as professionals engaged in continuing professional development. Nuffer and Linder-Crow (2000) have suggested that psychologists engaged in continuing professional education (CPE) must be prepared to take responsibility for assessing their own cognitive characteristics and motivations for learning, in order to select the appropriate match with a CPE experience (i.e., a course, workshop, or seminar). Additionally, instructors or designers of these CPE experiences for psychologists must clearly communicate their methodologies to the potential consumer. These methodologies may include commercially- (conferences or workshops) or independently- (study groups or book circles) designed programs combined with other- (presenters and instructors) or self-directed approaches. With full knowledge of the CPE approach, the learner can match his/her own expectations and personal characteristics with that methodology, working towards a "match" that will lead to the most successful learning experience. Most critical to ensuring success is self knowledge of the learner and disclosure of the instructional approach to ensure a good methodological- characteristics-expectations match. Applying this to faculty development means that faculty members must have opportunities to choose among possible faculty development offerings, should understand the approaches that will be used in each, and be able to recognize their own preferences and styles.

The literature about adult learners—whether focused on adults returning to college after a gap of several years, those starting further education for the first time as non-traditionally-aged students, or practicing professionals seeking additional skills—indicates that there are several practices that promote effective learning and change. Reviewing these adult learning principles, one can conclude that faculty development (which is at its core a learning experience) will be most successful when:

1. Experiences are designed that recognize the rich experiences of the participants.
2. Participants are given the opportunities to make choices based on self-knowledge about their own needs and characteristics.
3. The information presented is relevant and practical.
4. Opportunities are afforded for each participant to be acknowledged as worthy of respect.
5. Methodologies are clearly communicated to participants so that they may exercise choice, autonomy, and self direction.

The Social Aspects of Learning

Many contemporary learning theorists and cognitive psychologists have drawn upon the classic works of Albert Bandura, Lev Vygotsky, Jean Piaget, and others to describe the importance of the social environment in learning. Theories about how one's understanding is meaningfully constructed through interactions with others have revolutionized our thinking about the teaching and learning process. These researchers have helped us to recognize that teaching is not merely the conveying of information, and that learning is not solely dependent on a two-way interaction between one teacher and one student. Rather, successful teaching and learning depend on the development and maintenance of strong social relations and an environment of trust within the classroom. Once established, this then gives rise to an atmosphere in which ideas can be presented and appraised, leading to thoughtful dialogue and discussion. The presence of other active participants in the learning environment is critical, because it encourages those present to examine their personal understanding of an issue. This leads to what has been called the "meaning making" of information for every one individual (Merriam & Caffarella, 1999). When individual learners can make personal meaning of information, they are better able to apply that learning to diverse situations and to remember it.

Orvis and Lassiter (2006) looked more specifically at the importance of such social aspects of the learning environment as the ability to interact with one another, share information, and coordinate actions, regardless of the age of the learners. Deatz and Campbell (2001) noted that specific tasks such as discussing, summarizing, and clarifying, when used in a group setting, allow students to learn material more deeply and make stronger connections with other content. In both studies, students were able to better understand information, and to make greater personal connections with the material, when provided with opportunities to share, discuss, and clarify.

Moller, Huett, Holder, Young, Harvey, and Godshalk (2005) specifically examined the social aspects of the online learning environment. "Online collaboration, in the form of peer work groups and learning communities, increases engagement in the learning process" (Moller et al., 2005, p. 138). According to these researchers, the level of engagement reflects the amount of effort and motivation. They go on to say that strong interpersonal commitments of the other members of the learning community provide support for motivation and engagement in the learning. Additionally, confidence leads to greater engagement in learning, and is also influenced by other members of the learning community providing encouragement and support.

Rovai (2002) has also found that a learning community can be successfully developed in the "virtual classroom." His research focuses on the particular importance of developing the community aspect of the learning community, and recommends sensitivity regarding the adverse impact of too much structure on dialogue, development of expectations for level and timeliness of contributions, use of an appropriate level of instructor social presence, development of norms around minimizing use of the authoritative tone, attention to achievement of the task as well as maintenance of the group process, and application of teaching styles that match learner needs while encouraging learners to grow. Additionally, Rovai recommends that virtual learning communities consist of no fewer than 10 and no more than 25 learners.

Reviewing the social aspects of learning, one can conclude that faculty will learn best when:

1. Strong personal commitments to the group and to each other's learning exist.

2. They are encouraged to discuss, share, give each other feedback, and clarify each other's work.

3. Dialogue is not overly structured, but occurs in an atmosphere of shared expectations and norms.

4. attention is paid to the maintenance of the group process, as well as accomplishment of the task.

A Theory of Collaboration

Wood and Gray (1991) describe the literature about collaboration as utilizing a myriad of definitions for collaboration. In their meta-analysis of nine different definitions, they isolated the critical common elements, and used that to craft a metadefinition: "collaboration occurs when a group of autonomous stakeholders of a problem domain engage in an interactive process, using shared rules, norms, and structures, to act or decide on issues related to that domain" (p. 146). Wood and Gray build on that definition to describe the essential elements of collaboration, which include the importance of mutual recognition of a problem, agreement on a legitimate convener, acceptance of the role of stakeholder, and agreement on a set of shared norms.

If one were to specifically apply that definition to the domain of faculty learning, collaboration would be most successful when a group of faculty:

1. Mutually recognize that there exists a problem in teaching, scholarship, or service which they want to address.

2. Agree on a convener or facilitator of their work on the problem who has legitimacy.

3. See themselves as stakeholders regarding the problem.

4. Can agree on a set of shared norms and structures used to make decisions about that problem.

Best Practices in Faculty Development Using Collaboration

This chapter began with a description of the current challenges that face faculty today as teaching, scholarship, and service become more complex. This complexity requires faculty to collaborate with others as they learn how to engage in these new roles. Faculty development that takes principles of adult learning—including attention to the importance of the social aspects of learning—into account will be required. Several characteristics of best practices in this area have been identified:

- Faculty will engage in collaboration when they recognize that a problem can only be solved by working with other faculty.
- This recognition can be enhanced when faculty have opportunities for self- reflection and development of self-knowledge.
- When engaged in collaboration, faculty will find their learning to be more successful and satisfying.
- Successful collaborations give opportunities for choice in the ways in which faculty share, discuss, and give feedback while assuring that each faculty member contributes at a level that fits within the group norms for participation.
- These collaborations need to be facilitated or convened by someone who has legitimacy and who pays attention to the group process in addition to the accomplishment of the task.
- Faculty development experiences have the greatest chance for continued success if faculty feel respected for their knowledge, experiences, and contributions.
- A hybrid approach of face-to-face meetings and use of asynchronous learning environments allows for groups of 10-25 to learn, share, and interact in ways that support successful collaborations and learning.

The Collaborative Projects

The Faculty Resource Center (FRC) at Keene State College, a small public liberal arts college in New Hampshire with 190 full-time faculty members and approximately 200 part-time adjunct faculty, organizes new faculty orientation, and supports projects that have faculty development as a component. The FRC has supported a number of faculty groups implementing new pedagogies, investigating general education models, administering internal grant funding programs, and engaging in curricular changes. In each of these cases, faculty members have recognized that their work would be enhanced by greater collaboration with peers. The groups each discovered that essential components of their work involved learning and sharing information with each other, but found there to be many obstacles to real collaborative learning.

These obstacles included difficulties in scheduling meetings, lack of trust in unfamiliar colleagues, and disciplinary differences in vocabulary and comfort with particular pedagogies. Collaboration was needed and wanted, but the process by which it would be supported was initially unclear.

The FRC chose to utilize a series of interactive Web pages, using the course management system Black Board, designed to support the collaboration that would enhance the success of each project. These Web pages supported the faculty members' mutual development of learning goals, encouraged sharing of information and resources, helped develop an atmosphere of respect for each others' contributions, and aided participants in the gathering of beneficial feedback through the interactive capabilities of the Web pages. Four projects in particular will be highlighted. Each project posed unique sets of circumstances (because of the faculty role to which each project was linked), and resulted in different approaches to the design of the course management system Web pages. Each project will be described, and the faculty role that the project represents will be noted (engagement in new forms of scholarship, use of more interactive pedagogies, fulfillment of service obligations, and design of curricula that will attract and retain students). The challenges of fulfilling that particular faculty role will be discussed, and the ways in which application of the principles of best practice in collaboration maximized the success of the project will be described. Each project engaged in "hybrid collaboration"—using the Web pages to share, chat, review, and revise, as well as utilizing regular face-to-face meetings. In the case of each project, faculty members found that the use of the Web pages enhanced their abilities to collaborate, which in turn enhanced the success of the projects.

General Education (Integrative Studies Program) Committee

In this project, a group of faculty and academic staff were charged with reviewing an old proposal for general education revision that had never been approved, gathering current information about national models, and proposing a new general education program. This is an example of the new kinds of scholarship in which faculty are expected to be engaged—the scholarship of integration (seeing patterns across disciplines and applying these unique approaches to solve problems) and the scholarship of application/engagement (applying theory to solve pressing problems). Both of these types of scholarly endeavor are enhanced by working collaboratively with faculty members from other disciplines towards finding a solution to a real issue facing the academy. When faculty members from multiple disciplines regularly work together on a project about which they care deeply, they are more likely to propose unique solutions, not based in any one discipline, to that project. In order to do this, faculty members must be able to easily share resources (in this case, through Web-based postings of articles and Internet links) and review and discuss draft materials (in this project, by using chat and e-mail). The public nature of interactive Web pages enhanced civility among group members, and brought a form of peer review to the activities.

In this General Education Committee project, many of the original group members had never worked together before. Some individuals came to the task with very specific agendas that they wanted to be implemented immediately. Several group members did not perceive themselves as true stakeholders in the task, because they did not see the change as having much impact on them, placing the probability of collaboration at risk. The initial Committee charge was imposed on the group, and therefore the group members had difficulty agreeing upon learning goals for the group. Because of these circumstances, and given what we know about collaboration, the group could be seen as needing help in understanding the impact of any changes in general education requirements and agreeing on the background information to be gathered in order to successfully meet the Committee charge.

In order to support the group's attainment of these objectives, Black Board pages were developed that encouraged members to share and discuss information from other colleges and disciplinary societies in "Course Documents" and "External Links." Eventually, subcommittees formed and "Group Pages" were used to develop, share, and critique first and second drafts of the proposal sections chosen by each small group. "Discussion Forums" were used for the entire group of 25 to comment on subcommittee work. The group members were able to choose their own level of commenting and feedback, and subcommittees developed norms for the level of expectations. According to collaboration theory, respect and acceptance among group members is critical. Because there were multiple ways in which faculty members could share, discuss, give feedback, or contribute information and resources, they reported a high degree of acceptance, and a true collaborative learning situation was established.

Universal Design for Instruction Learning Community

In this project, one faculty member (Dr. Stephen Bigaj) was principal investigator for a grant-supported project in which principles of universal design were applied to pedagogy in higher education. This project built on the principles for universal access to both public and home amenities, regardless of disability, that have become accepted practice in the architecture and design community. The project began with the claim that an accommodation originally designed for an individual with a disability (low drinking fountains, curb cuts, wide bathroom stalls, etc.) may be appreciated by a wide variety of individuals (small children, people using wheeled backpacks, those carrying multiple parcels). Applying this to the design of learning experiences, an accommodation that may meet the needs of a student with a disability (tape recording lectures, developing "self checks" for understanding difficult material and completing complex tasks) may also be found useful to students who do not share those same challenges. The Universal Design project explored this idea by investigating nine principles of universal design for access to instruction. The principles of universal design include (#2) flexibility in use–design materials and strategies to accommodate a wide range of abilities by offering choice in methods or approaches, and (#5) tolerance for error–design materials and approaches in such a way that anticipates that students may have a range of background skill and pace of learning. Examples of other principles are equitable use (ensure that all students can access all materials), perceptible information (all materials are presented in a way that minimizes the impact of sensory challenges), and instructional climate (atmosphere encourages inclusivity and espouses high expectations).

In this project, twenty faculty members gathered once per month to discuss the principles and the applications to their own classrooms. Faculty members shared some of the challenges they experienced with the individual principles. This project fulfilled the faculty role of teaching using new, learner-centered approaches. Many of the faculty members involved were not tenured faculty, and felt uncomfortable sharing their pedagogical challenges too freely. However, some very senior faculty members with well-established teaching credentials were engaged in the project as well. Their willingness to share their own difficulties with application of each of the principles (How do I incorporate "tolerance for error" in my laboratory when I have concerns about safety?) ensured that a collaborative atmosphere was established. BlackBoard pages were developed to share challenges, ideas, and triumphs and provide feedback in a mutually-supportive atmosphere. Pairs of faculty volunteered to be the primary presenters for each session. Faculty had autonomy in choosing when and with whom they paired. "Folders" in the "Course Documents" were used to post descriptions of pedagogical applications. "Discussion Forums" were used to provide feedback and pose questions for clarification. Group norms were discussed, and time was set aside to ensure that faculty members felt as though their concerns were heard and understood, and that their contributions were valued. Attention to process and respect enhanced the nature of the collaborative atmosphere, and tremendous learning was accomplished.

Undergraduate Research Committee

In this project, a committee of faculty from across the campus reviewed applications from students for internally-funded research awards. The committee members changed yearly, came from different disciplines, and reviewed applications from students in majors all over the college. This led to challenges with consistency in how applications are read and scored. This type of committee is seen as primarily fulfilling the service to the college role; however, in the new academy, faculty are expected to work across the disciplines and teach each other about research methods, ethical implications, and disciplinary-specific approaches, in order for committee members to read and react fairly to the wide variety of applications. Black Board was used to set up "Folders" in the "Course Documents" to post the applications and all supporting materials. "Discussion Forums" were used to pose questions for clarification, particularly when a proposal referenced technical information in the purview of some, but not all, Committee members. "Folders" were also created that were made "Not Available" by the FRC Director to archive material from previous years of applications. These were used on occasion to provide examples for new Committee members of past decision-making processes.

This group, as did others, met the definition of a "hybrid" collaboration group—one in which some of the collaborations took place in a computer-supported environment, and others took place face-to-face. This approach met with great success, because it was time-efficient, and faculty had the autonomy (a requirement for true collaboration) to choose whether to admit ignorance about an issue and ask colleagues for enlightenment or to learn about it in another way by themselves. This approach also established an atmosphere that respected the knowledge that others offered, lending itself to another successful collaboration for learning.

Thinking and Writing

In this project, a group of faculty and support staff were directed to develop and implement a pilot freshman seminar course (Thinking and Writing). This project included full-time senior level faculty, brand new faculty, part-time adjunct faculty who would be implementing the pilot, and academic affairs support staff who would not be teaching the course at all. Norms for collaboration were non-existent in this group that mixed administrative staff with faculty at different levels of seniority and status. Additionally, because this was a new course (and, as such, was seen primarily as fulfilling the teaching role for faculty) there were no models for collaboration on which to draw; therefore, there were no mutually agreed-upon leaders or learning goals, one of the requirements for collaboration. However, the group had great enthusiasm about collaboration.

The Black Board pages for this project were designed so that they facilitated the sharing of challenges and ideas, and provided feedback in a climate of support. "External Links" were utilized to share Web-based citation guides and academic honesty tutorials. "Folders" in the "Course Documents" were used to share new course descriptions and writing assignments. "Discussion Forums" were developed for feedback on assignments and policies. There was less collaboration utilizing the Black Board pages on this project that the other projects described. More collaboration, more sharing, discussing, and questioning occurred in the face-to-face meetings. It is hypothesized that because the course was being pilot-taught at the same time that faculty were trying to learn from each other, there seemed to be less time to go to the Web site and read, discuss, share and give respectful feedback. Because this is an on-going group, the nature and success of the collaborative learning will continue to be assessed.

Recommendations for the Future

It is clear that faculty need to engage in collaborative learning with their peers to fulfill roles required in the new academy, such as engaging in new forms of scholarship and service, and designing and utilizing more interactive pedagogies that will attract and retain more students. Faculty developers can help to support that collaboration through the design of work groups and learning communities for faculty using adult learning principles, including those that embrace social learning theory. The literature suggests that individual faculty will be more likely to engage in collaboration after self-reflection enabling them to recognize that problems can be solved only by working with other faculty members. When faculty members collaborate, they find greater job satisfaction, particularly when choices are afforded to them in the ways they will share, discuss, and give feedback. Faculty members are more likely to experience success in work groups and learning communities when those groups are facilitated by an individual skilled in group process, who can build an atmosphere of trust and respect for group norms. Additionally, the literature suggests that hybrid collaboration groups, those that meet, share, and discuss in computer-supported environments as well as meet face to face, can meet with success in achieving work-related and learning goals.

The projects described in this chapter utilized interactive Web pages, using the course management system Black Board, and designed to enhance the success of each project through supporting faculty collaboration. These projects represent the complexity of faculty roles in the new academy, including the engagement in new forms of scholarship and service, and designing new approaches to curriculum and implementing new forms of pedagogy. In each case, the success of the projects was enhanced by the encouragement of collaboration through carefully-designed interactive Web pages which allowed faculty members to share ideas, review draft documents, post questions and links to resources, give feedback, and request support. Additionally, faculty members gathered in face-to-face meetings on a regular basis.

These computer-supported collaborations allowed faculty members to control their choices regarding approaches to group work, establish mutually agreed-upon group norms for engagement, and foster sharing, discussion, and feedback in an atmosphere in which each faculty member can share life experiences and feel respected—all necessary conditions to true collaboration. Faculty developers should consider supporting hybrid collaborations to enable faculty members to engage successfully in the new roles demanded by the new academy.

References

Bash, L. (2003). *Adult learners in the academy*. Bolton: Anker Publishing.

Chickering, A.W., & Gamson, Z.F. (1991). Applying the seven principles for good practice in undergraduate education. *New Directions for Teaching and Learning, 47*. San Francisco: Jossey-Bass Inc.

Deatz, R.C., & Campbell, C.H. (2001). *Application of cognitive principles in distributed computer based training* (Research product 2001-03). Alexandria, VA: U.S. Army Research Institute for the Social and Behavioral Sciences.

Honigsfeld, A., & Dunn, R. (2006, Winter). Learning style characteristics of adult learners. *Delta Kappa Gamma Bulletin*, pp. 14-17.

Knowles, M. (1970). *The modern practice of adult education*. Chicago: Association Press.

Merriam, S., & Caffarella, R. (1999) *Learning in adulthood: A comprehensive guide* (2nd ed.). San Francisco: Wiley.

Moller, L., Huett, J., Holder, D., Young, J., Harvey, D., & Godshalk, V. (2005). Examining the impact of learning communities on motivation. *The Quarterly Review of Distance Education, 6*(26), 137-143.

Nuffer, E.L., & Linder-Crow, J. (2000, August). *Adult ways of knowing: Making continuing education work for professionals*. Presentation at the American Psychological Association Annual Convention, Washington, DC.

Orvis, K.L., & Lassiter, A.R.L. (2005). Computer-supported collaborative learning: The role of the instructor. In S.P. Ferris & S.H. Godar (Eds.), *Teaching and learning with virtual teams* (pp. 158-179). Hershey, PA: Idea Group.

Swanson, R.A., Holton, E., & Knowles, M. (1998). *The adult learner: The definitive classic in adult education and human resource development*. Houston: Gulf Professional Publishing.

Wood, D. J., & Gray, B. (1991). Toward a comprehensive theory of collaboration. *Journal of Applied Behavioral Science, 27*, 139-162.

Chapter IX

Development of Online Distributed Training:
Practical Considerations and Lesson Learned

Eileen B. Entin, Aptima Inc., USA

Jason Sidman, Aptima, Inc., USA

Lisa Neal, eLearn Magazine, USA

Abstract

This chapter discusses considerations and tradeoffs in designing and developing an online teamwork skills training program for geographically distributed instructors and students. The training program is grounded in principles of scenario-based learning, in which operationally realistic scenarios are used to engage students in actively forming links between classroom and real-world applications of key concepts. The chapter focuses on supporting active engagement of learners, and meaningful and thought-

ful learner-learner interactions appropriate to the subject matter (Neal & Miller, 2006). We describe lessons learned in the development of a distributed training program that interleaves asynchronous and synchronous training modules (Neal & Miller, 2005) to leverage the advantages of both self-paced and group learning, provide opportunities to practice the teamwork concepts being trained, create social presence, and promote interaction and reflection among the course members.

Introduction

The value of peer learning is well known, especially for domains in which people will apply what they learn in collaborative settings, but it is challenging to design courses that effectively incorporate and support peer learning. When learners are copresent in the classroom, it is easier to devise exercises that facilitate peer learning. Currently, most training outside of the classroom is self-paced, eliminating peer and instructor contact, due to the perceived cost reduction and the greater ease of implementation. It is a challenge to develop online training that incorporates these rich human interactions while respecting the time constraints under which learners operate, yet it can lead to deeper learning that is more memorable and more easily applicable (Neal & Miller, 2005; Notess & Neal, 2006).

This chapter discusses considerations and tradeoffs in designing, developing, and evaluating an online training program for an instructor and students who are geographically distributed. The discussion will take readers through the development process, starting with analysis of audience and goals, to the challenges in acquiring and adapting course material to the online format, and finally the implementation and evaluation. We focus on considerations involved in supporting active engagement of learners, and meaningful and thoughtful learner-learner interactions appropriate to the subject matter (Neal & Miller, 2006).

Training is successful only when there is a demonstrable performance improvement; for that to occur requires opportunities for demonstration, practice, and feedback, as well as for declarative learning (Cannon-Bowers, Tannenbaum, Salas, & Volpe, 1995). Furthermore, training that involves teams, rather than individuals, requires that the practice and feedback is conducted in a team environment. Whereas in the past training has been traditionally delivered in a face-to-face, classroom-like environment (Neal & Miller, 2006), our goal was to develop a *distributed* training program that includes elements of didactic instruction and demonstration, as well as the opportunity for practice and feedback in a team-based environment. The training program we developed was designed to train civilian and military emergency medical team members in teamwork skills and in methods for enhancing teamwork; the approaches used are applicable to any training where learners will not be practicing in isolation.

This chapter is written through the lens of our experiences in developing the teamwork training program. The program was developed for medical professionals, and in that sense is different from the academic environment where students are still in a learning mode, and have not yet had experience in their chosen profession. Nonetheless, we suggest that many of the points discussed in this chapter are relevant for academic instructors teaching courses that involve the students in practice and application, as well as for instructors in a professional training program.

In discussing the issues involved in developing this online training course, we organize the discussion around two major phases of development: research leading to the development of substantive materials and factors considered during the development of the course materials and process. Although the two phases are not totally independent of one another, for the purposes of exposition, they can be usefully separated.

We note that while our approach is based on both sound theory and substantial experience, as well as feedback we received during formative testing of the program, at this writing, the specific techniques we implemented in our training program have not been validated by a thorough training evaluation. Therefore, while this chapter can make training developers aware of some of the key considerations that led to our implementation approaches, it cannot offer empirical proof of their effectiveness. Additional research is required for that.

Teamwork Skills Training

Teamwork skills (Sims, Salas, & Burke, 2004) are valuable in many settings, but in emergency medical settings, they are crucial to the safety and well-being of patients. Many medical teams are ad hoc, and they, in particular, need to rapidly increase team proficiency when brought together by implementing effective leadership, backup behavior, and the other components of teamwork. Teamwork training and assessment in a remote and networked environment (T-TRANE) is a teamwork skills training program for emergency medical teams that is delivered using Web-enabled collaborative technologies (see Entin, Lai, Sidman, Mizrahi, Stewart, Neal, Mackenzie, & Xiao, 2007 for a more complete description of the program). The program assumes students are skilled in clinical techniques, but have minimal formal knowledge of teamwork.

The goals of T-TRANE are to train emergency medical teams, be they ad hoc or enduring teams, to understand and use teamwork skills. Due to the difficulties of arranging lengthy training for such learners, the focus of the course is not on a theoretical understanding of teamwork skills, but on the components of teamwork as applied to emergency medicine. The course is specifically designed to do this through the use of real video footage and authentic textual scenarios culled from emergency medical personnel. Furthermore, the course objective is the immediate application of skills in the workplace, and this is accomplished through questions about and reflection on daily practice.

In order to achieve the course goals, T-TRANE is comprised of information about and examples of teamwork skills and scenario-based training exercises that provide practice in strategies to promote teamwork such as conducting pre-planning and debriefing sessions. The program includes four modules, with both live (synchronous) interactive sessions and self-paced (asynchronous) sessions that students complete within scheduled intervals. The first module provides definitions and examples of five critical teamwork skills: communication, monitoring, back-up, leadership, and team orientation (Sims, Salas, & Burke, 2004). It discusses internal and external threats that may disrupt effective teamwork, and the use of planning and debriefing as strategies for promoting effective teamwork. Modules 2 through 4 reinforce and apply the concepts and strategies discussed in Module 1, and provide opportunities for the students to apply these concepts in their current work. Scenario-based exercises ask the students to identify the teamwork skills that were displayed in a video-based or verbally-described situation and the threats that emerged to disrupt effective teamwork, and show how these threats could be addressed in a debriefing.

The training is led by an instructor who is experienced in the emergency medical domain, but who is not necessarily an expert in teamwork training.

An extensive Instructor's Manual supports the instructor in planning and delivering the course. The approach used in this program can be adapted to any domain in which ad hoc teams are formed or when teams need to perform well together.

Pre-Development Considerations

Planning any online program requires consideration of many factors, most importantly the target learners and the topic, the constraints that arise due to these factors, and the course objectives that will satisfy stakeholders (Neal & Miller, 2005). In this section, we discuss some of the issues that we grappled with in the program-planning stage, when certain decisions that would frame the subsequent development needed to be made.

Identifying the Target Learner Population and Other Stakeholders

Many of the decisions about training system development occur before any curriculum is drafted or any courseware is designed. While content and functionality are obviously critical components to any training system, they can only be optimally designed when the training consumer is considered (Neal & Miller, 2005). Consumers of training are not only the trainees themselves, but instructors, administrators, and potentially other people who may purchase, assign, deliver, or study training content. These stakeholders may vary widely with respect to their level of expertise in the training domain, level of familiarity with the training technology, and so on. Therefore, determining who the consumers of the training are, and what unique relevant characteristics they possess, is a critical first step in training development.

For our training program, we identified three categories of stakeholders: administrators, instructors, and students. All three groups were medical professionals in emergency medical units: department heads (administrators), attendings (instructors), and residents (students). As emergency medical providers, their defining common characteristics were their education level and their extremely busy schedules; and these factors demanded three requirements of our training system. First, we needed to find a way to allow time- and location-independent access to the training. If their schedules suddenly permitted some time for training, then we wanted learners to be able to access the course and use their time productively. Second, the course needed to be efficiently designed, and instructors well-prepared, so that everyone's valuable and limited time was optimally used during training sessions. Finally, and most importantly, course materials needed to be appropriate, relevant, and immediately applicable, capitalizing on existing knowledge and experience.

Identifying Course Objectives

As any course is being developed, it is important to be clear about the course objectives. For the teamwork training course we developed, we had several key objectives, including: enabling distributed (rather than colocated) training, providing opportunities to practice the teamwork concepts being trained, promoting interaction and reflection among the course members, and circumventing the need for a teamwork trainer to deliver the course. All aspects of the program were developed in light of these objectives.

Identifying how Training is Delivered

Before development of a distributed training program starts, the development team must ascertain what options are available in terms of "where" in space the team will meet–in particular, whether it is desirable to use an asynchronous or synchronous method only, or whether both technology options are blended into a solution that is in harmony with user requirements and constraints (Shneiderman, 2002). Once that is decided, the challenge is to use each mode to its best pedagogical advantage (Neal & Miller, 2006). Relevant considerations here, due to the nature of the topic, were the need to present realistic scenarios, to provide opportunities to practice together, and to promote and reinforce training through independent reflection and group discussion (Notess & Neal, 2006).

Synchronous sessions allow for dynamic interchange of ideas and promote social networking, since learners have better opportunities to get to know each other (Neal & Miller, 2005). This is especially important for teaching teamwork, where there are limited opportunities for practice through role-play or sharing of insights without real-time interaction. Even with the value of synchronous sessions, they can be challenging to incorporate into training, since they require all participants to be available at the same time. Participants may be distributed across multiple time zones, further complicating the task of identifying suitable times to meet. In our case, this was further constrained by busy schedules that were often out of the participants control since they could be paged at any time. Furthermore, synchronous technology is more complex to introduce.

Asynchronous learning is the most common way of delivering e-learning (Neal & Miller, 2005). It circumvents the scheduling difficulties, because learners can choose a time that is convenient and can work at their own pace. On the other hand, the only interaction is through discussion forums, which are less dynamic, and there is less of a sense of belonging to a class, since the class never "meets" (Neal & Ingram, 2001). In addition, because the time commitments are not rigid and harder to reinforce, it is easier for students to lag behind, which creates problems when students are out of sync.

In order to leverage the advantages of both self-paced and group learning, we decided upon a blended solution that would interleave asynchronous and synchronous training modules (Neal & Miller, 2005). For a few hours over the course of the entire training program, the students would be required to participate in synchronous modules. They could complete asynchronous training modules at their convenience within a specified period of time. Defining a time window in which each asynchronous module had to be completed was necessary, because the modules had to be completed in a specified order, and the students' responses to exercises in the modules needed to be integrated and distributed to the class members by specified times. Given the busy schedules of our training consumers, we believed that this was an effective compromise between demands on time and the desire for dynamic interchange among students.

Technology Usage

The delivery of the synchronous sessions proved to be a considerable challenge, both logistically and practically. Logistically, coordinating synchronous sessions requires finding a common meeting time, a challenge with varied schedules and time zones, ensuring that all computers have the necessary hardware (speakers, microphones) and software, providing login names and passwords to access the Web site, and so on. While advances in technology, as evidenced by the growing popularity of remote meetings and e-learning and the sophistication of supporting technology, provide solutions to all of these logistical challenges, whether learners know how to use the latest technology is another matter.

We identified several Web-conferencing platforms capable of running synchronous sessions with distributed users. While most people in our target population know how to access the Internet and interact with a Web site, fewer are knowledgeable about and comfortable using Web-conferencing tools, such as voice-over-Internet protocol (VoIP), as a method of communication. Consequently, our pilot test of one Web-conferencing platform barely got past introductions. Our untrained group demonstrated a dismal display of what military personnel refer to as "comms discipline." People were unaware of when other people were talking, and therefore interrupted communications, of whether what they were saying was being heard by others, and so on. Indeed the technology itself was functioning fine; the people, however, did not know how to use it appropriately and were not being adequately facilitated.

In order to allow consumers to avoid the frustrating and unproductive pilot test experience, we decided to integrate within the training program a structured introductory synchronous session in which people could (a) test that they could connect to the Web-conferencing platform, (b) ensure that their computers contained the necessary hardware and software to view training content and to communicate with others, and (c) be taught protocols for online communication. Although this required an additional synchronous session (and the time commitment and logistical preparation that goes along with that), the benefit of knowing how to use the technology outweighed the cost of not being able to conduct the sessions at all, or to conduct ones that would not accomplish our pedagogical objectives.

Instructor Preparation and Support

One of the goals we established for the training program was that the instructor did not have to be a subject matter expert in teamwork, since that would have required bringing in an outside person to deliver the training, for which hospitals may not have the resources. Rather, we felt it was more important that the instructor was experienced in the application domain–in this case emergency medicine–and could therefore apply the training concepts to a range of teamwork situations he or she experienced. Having identified ways to allow anytime, anywhere access to training (and being trained on the tools necessary to conduct the training), we then faced our second dilemma with respect to our training: preparing nonexpert instructors to deliver our train- ing content. The defining feature of this training was the focus on teamwork in emergency medicine, not on the delivery of the medicine itself. While emergency medical units are populated with qualified medical instructors, these medical experts are not experts in teamwork. Our challenge, therefore, was to implement measures to allow nonexpert instructors to be sufficiently prepared to facilitate discussions of teamwork.

We created several methods to prepare instructors to facilitate the course. First, from a logistical perspective, we needed enough preparation time for instructors to become familiar with the course prior to delivering it. We therefore hard-coded triggers within the training system that would alert instructors to upcoming deadlines well in advance. For example, when an administrator assigns an instructor to a course, an e-mail is automatically sent to the instructor weeks in advance of the class.

While instructors had plenty of advance notice prior to leading sessions, they still required the requisite domain knowledge to truly facilitate ses- sions. One of the key resources we included within the training system was an Instructor's Manual that included background information on teamwork skills such as communication, monitoring, and back-up. The Instructor's Manual also contained a guide to each of the training modules, highlighting key teaching points along the way.

Additional aids were implemented within the synchronous sessions to provide instructors with timely notices of what to talk about and when. When using the synchronous platform, the instructor could see notes within the training content that the trainees could not see. The notes within the Instructor View might point out a key instance of teamwork from a video clip, or suggest a critical question to ask to get trainees to think about teamwork instead of taskwork. Again, this feature of the training allowed nonexpert instructors to confidently and competently facilitate discussion on teamwork.

Despite our best efforts to reduce the workload on an instructor, there were still significant preparation and facilitation responsibilities for the designated instructor. All of these responsibilities, of course, do not include actually providing any feedback to students on their self-paced exercises. This task, as any school teacher or college professor knows quite well, is time-consuming and labor-intensive. Given our priority to minimize the time commitment of all of our consumers, we decided to diffuse the responsibility of reviewing student work across the trainees themselves. We included an administrative functionality within the training system by which Instructors could designate trainees to be Peer Leaders for a given training module. Peer Leaders would be responsible for reviewing completed assignments and identifying key themes within them that would promote discussion in subsequent synchronous sessions.

Lessons Learned

In sum, many decisions were made about training development prior to developing any training content. The following lessons learned may be useful for future instructional designers developing distributed training:

- **Tailor your training to your consumers:** Consumers may be more than the trainees themselves. There may be administrators and instructors as well who will purchase, facilitate, or interact with your training system. These populations need to be identified from the start and their needs considered for training to be successful.

- **Blended learning is not just an effective pedagogical approach**. It is a practical compromise between achieving learning objectives and acknowledging real-world time constraints.

- **Instructors do not have to be experts:** However, the burden is on the training developers to implement measures to allow nonexperts to effectively deliver training.

- **Students can be more than just students:** Diffusing some of the instructor's responsibility to Peer Leaders can alleviate some of the burden on the instructor. Providing students with additional responsibilities may increase their level of commitment to the course and enhance their educational experience since they think more deeply about the training materials.

- **Just because technologies exist that enable distributed learning does not mean that people know how to use them:** The capabilities of some technology may exceed people's ability to use it. Be sure to allow adequate preparation time to ensure that consumers of all ages, education levels, and technical expertise can be comfortable with and fully exploit the training technology, so that it does not get in the way of the learning it is supposed to deliver.

Substantive Development Considerations

How course material is designed and delivered is dependent on the learners and topic, as well as on the course objectives. While a decision to offer a blended course, incorporating synchronous and asynchronous interaction, fosters many pedagogical approaches beyond the self-paced "electronic page-turner" model, many decisions and some creativity needs to be applied to design a course that meets learners' needs and meets course objectives.

In this section, we explain some of the considerations and issues that arose as we developed the training program content. As noted previously, the program we developed used a blended approach, but we focus here primarily on the challenges in development of asynchronous training modules, where engagement and student interaction are more difficult to achieve than in synchronous modules.

Materials for Exercises

The training program we developed is grounded in the principles of scenario-based learning in which operationally realistic scenarios are used to engage students in actively forming links between classroom and real-world applications of key concepts. Scenarios place students in a particular context and encourage them to think about cause and effect (Neal, Miller, & Perez, 2004). Therefore, our first challenge when developing training materials was to create engaging scenarios upon which the training content would be based.

Our preference was to use real experiences within emergency medicine as the source for examples and training exercises. This was possible because our medical subject matter experts had independently developed a library of video recordings of cases treated at a major medical trauma center. Our plan was to use the video clips both to provide illustrations of teamwork skills and give the students practice in applying teamwork skills by giving them the opportunity to recognize, assess, analyze, and perhaps even role-play aspects of teamwork from multiple points of view.

The challenge was in how to select and use the video clips effectively. However, the key dilemma was that the video recordings we drew from were made for different purposes than the training program we were developing. As a result, we found that they were not indexed according to teamwork concepts captured in the videos, so the development team had to spend many hours going through videos to find ones that were relevant for the purposes of the examples and exercises. A further problem we encountered was in finding clips in which both the video and audio portions were of sufficiently high quality that they could be understood both visually and aurally. While for their original purpose there was not a need for clear audio, for teamwork training, where verbal communication is a central skill, the audio portions were critical. As a result, we had to work through the videos that we selected multiple times to insure that we understood what was being said and captured it in a transcript that could be played along with the video. Where that was not possible, we needed to find other alternatives.

An alternative in scenario-based training is for the developers to generate their own exercise materials. The advantage of creating original scenarios from scratch is that training developers can tailor them to the specific training objectives. Although it was not possible to create videos of our original scenarios, we found that a scenario could be described effectively in text format. We therefore worked with both civilian and military emergency medical practitioners to develop and integrate several authentic textual scenarios along with the video clips.

Creating Social Presence

Social presence is a variable that may affect learner-instructor interactions in distance education courses and is an important aspect for effective online learning (Volery, 2001). Because of the lack of physical, face-to-face contact in Web-based courses, students may not feel the instructor's presence in the course, and they are less likely to be aware of the presence of other students. The absence of the visual cues that normally exist in the traditional classroom may lead to feelings of isolation or lack of connection with students and instructors in the Web-based environment (Atack & Rankin, 2002; Billings, Connors, & Skiba, 2001). Getting to know the instructor is more difficult in a Web-based environment because of the absence of the face-to-face interaction and the lack of visual cues. Furthermore, students' perceptions of social presence are significant predictors in students' perception of overall learning (Richardson & Swan, 2001).

As a way of creating social presence at the outset of the course, we provided the ability for both the instructor and the students to enter profiles in which they provided information about themselves related to the course and their professional background. In addition to the text-based information, the instructor and students can upload a picture, which could increment the sense of knowing one's fellow students. Participants are urged to upload their profiles before the course begins, so that everyone has an understanding of who the other course members are. This is important because sharing personal information at the beginning of team formation boosts member satisfaction and communication (Kahai & Cooper, 1999) and increases feelings of social cohesion (Zaccaro & McCoy, 1998).

Engaging Learners

The active engagement of learners in forming connections between existing and newly-presented material is known to be an important aspect of facilitating learning, retention, and comprehension, and is supported by a large body of literature (e.g., Mayer, 1997; Soraci, Carlin, Chechile, Franks, Wills, & Watanade, 1999; Slamecka & Graf, 1978; Wittrock, 1989). Active involvement of students in the learning process can be ensured by cuing important concepts with open-ended questions, providing multiple examples in different formats, and perhaps most importantly, providing opportunities for discussion, which helps in actively forming links between classroom and real-world experiences.

The first module in the training program, we developed was asynchronous in format and primarily didactic in nature. Especially because it was the first one and set the tone for the rest of the course, we felt is was important to ensure that it was engaging as well as informative. We provided audio clips from high-profile and experienced medical personnel testifying to the importance of effective teamwork. We used pictures and video clips to provide examples of the teamwork skills we were training. While most of the examples were taken from the emergency medical domain, we also included examples from other domains–including, for example, aviation and sports–to illustrate the importance of teamwork skills in a wide range of domains.

But still we were concerned that the module did not require the learner to become actively engaged. We explored a number of available online courses and found that, for the most part, they provided useful lessons in what *not* to do. The courses we reviewed tended to foster what might be called a "read and click" mindset, in which the learner passively reads the information that is presented and clicks to move on, without any deep processing of the material. We were concerned that the first module in the training program, which is primarily didactic in nature, could foster this kind of behavior. Yet we wanted to establish at the outset that the training program required active participation.

To clearly establish the interactive nature of the program, we inserted reflection questions early in the first module. These questions required the students to think about the material being presented in terms of their own experiences, and to periodically reformulate their ideas as new concepts were introduced. To ensure that students actively engaged with the material, they were required to submit their responses to the instructor and, in addition, to provide a relevant work experience in an online student forum. The requirement to submit their responses to the instructor established accountability; it was made clear that the instructor would be reading the students' responses and would discuss them with the group in the next module, which was conducted synchronously. The requirement to enter their experiences in the forum, and then to read the other students' entries, reinforced the reflective nature of the training; in addition, it set the expectations for learner-to-learner interaction.

Promoting Learner-Learner Interaction

In *learner-learner* interaction, students help themselves to learn, by sharing ideas and discussing problems, often in a real or virtual group setting (Moore & Kearsley, 1996). LeBaron and Miller (2004) describe the successful infusion of various instructional techniques, including the use of discussion forums and role plays, implemented within an online graduate-level course, to provide for the social construction of peer knowledge, and facilitate an overall sense of course community. Further, when an online course facilitates the structured discussions that enrich and provide context to learning, learning is more enjoyable and more social (Neal, 2002). Orvis and Lassiter (2006) recommend that instructors focus on learner-learner interactions as early as possible in a course.

In the synchronous sessions the instructor can facilitate learner-learner interactions. Our challenge was how, in a distributed, asynchronous environment, to create interactions among the students in a timely and effective manner. One solution was to use a process whereby each student's responses to the exercise questions were submitted to one of the students in the training program who was assigned by the instructor to be the *peer leader* for a particular module. The peer leader was responsible for reviewing all the students' responses, summarizing them, and providing comments to all the trainees. This mechanism served several purposes. It motivated the students to provide thoughtful responses, it engaged the peer leader in the training, and it provided an efficient way that the students could share the other students' perspectives. In addition, the use of the peer leader shifted a task away from the instructor.

A second mechanism for encouraging learner-learner interaction was a "forum" where students could post ideas and comments and respond to other students' postings (Neal & Miller, 2005). At the end of each asynchronous module, the student was asked to think about a situation in his or her experience where issues relevant to the concepts and techniques trained in that module had arisen, and to describe that situation in a posting to the discussion forum. The students were then encouraged to read the other students' postings and respond to them. These ideas were available to all the students, who could then comment upon them in a "chat" dialogue about a particular topic. Although the text-based forum does not have the spontaneity of a live online session, research suggests that online asynchronous discussions possess the ability to invite a higher level of learner-learner interaction than occurs in face-to-face settings (Chih, 2004).

In addition to its use in discussing the exercises, the discussion forum was available for student discussion on any topic. This opportunity is particularly useful for student teams that will be working in field settings, where it is useful, and even sometimes necessary, to know about team members skills, interests, and concerns that fall outside the medical domain. For example, in a field setting, it may be important to know who is able to drive an ambulance or who has had experience with specialized field equipment.

Together these mechanisms allowed students to respond to questions, reflect on what they were learning, and exchange relevant experiences and ideas with peers. The fact that the postings were public served as a motivator to engage in the conversation. That students were describing real experiences generated "deep" responses from their peers, based on how the description resonated with their own experiences (Notess & Neal, 2006).

Lessons Learned

In sum, many decisions were made to achieve training that engages learners and promotes learner-learner interaction. The following lessons learned may be useful for instructional designers developing distributed training:

- **Involving subject matter experts as a resource eliminates some of the burden of developing training materials:** The developers' role becomes tailoring the materials to meet the specific training objectives.

- **Engage the student immediately:** Set the precedent that active learning will take place early in the first training module.

- **Learner-learner interaction can be synchronous or asynchronous:** Do not be of the mindset that interaction has to be synchronous. Asynchronous interaction can be achieved through the use of email and discussion forums, and can set the stage for future synchronous interactions.

Conclusion

In this chapter, we have discussed some of the considerations and challenges that arose as we planned and developed a teamwork training course, how we resolved them, and our lessons learned. Any course has unique requirements for which a unique solution must be crafted to provide an optimal solution to training on a given topic for a group of learners. As we have described, in our case, decisions about delivery methods and approach were based not only on existing theory, but also on the abilities and constraints of the targeted learner population and the other stakeholders, and the requirements imposed by the topic. Furthermore, we needed to be realistic about the opportunities provided and limitations imposed by the technology in order to ensure that the selected technology served to facilitate learning rather than impede it. Given these considerations, we tried to be creative in developing a training program that met our course objectives, engaged learners, and led students to immediately apply what they learned in their professional practice. While our recommendations are based on research, theory, and experience, future research is necessary to empirically validate our approach.

References

Atack, L., & Rankin, J. (2002). A descriptive study of registered nurses' experiences with Web-based learning. *Journal of Advanced Nursing, 40*, 457-465.

Billings, D. M., Connors, H. R., & Skiba, D. J. (2001). Benchmarking best practices in Web-based nursing courses. *Advances in Nursing Science, 23*, 41-52.

Cannon-Bowers, J.A., Tannenbaum, S. I., Salas, E., & Volpe, C.E. (1995). Defining team competencies and establishing team training requirements. In R. Guzzo & E. Salas (Eds.), *Team effectiveness and decision making in organizations* (pp. 330-380). San Francisco: Jossey-Bass.

Chih (2004, April). *Research in interaction and durations of online asynchronous discussions.* Presentation at American Educational Research Association Meeting.

Entin, E. B., Lai, F., Sidman, J., Mizrahi, G., Stewart, B., Neal, L., Mackenzie, C., & Xiao, Y. (2007). A Web-based teamwork skills training program for emergency medical teams. In J. Westwood et al. (Eds.), *Medicine meets virtual reality 15.* Amsterdam: IOS Press.

Kahai, S., & Cooper, R. L. (1999). The effect of computer mediated communication on agreement and acceptance. *Journal of Management Information Systems, 16*, 165-188.

LeBaron, J., & Miller, D. (2004). The teacher as agent provocateur: Strategies to promote community in online course settings. In T. Latomaa, J. Pohjonen, J. Pulkkinen, & M. Ruotsalainen (Eds.), *eReflections: Ten years of educational technology studies at the University of Oulu* (pp. 109-125). Retrieved November 6, 2007, from http://herkules.oulu.fi/isbn9514276329/

Mayer, R. E. (1997). Multimedia learning: Are we asking the right questions? *Educational Psychologist, 32*, 1-19.

Moore, M. G., & Kearsley, G. (1996). *Distance education: A systems view.* Belmont: Wadsworth Publishing Company.

Neal, L. (2002). Talk to me: Discussion is the key to engaging online courses. *eLearn Magazine.* Retrieved November 6, 2007, from http://www.elearnmag.org/subpage/sub_page.cfm?article_pk=6142&page_number_nb=1&title=COLUMN

Neal, L., & Ingram, D. (2001). Asynchronous distance learning for corporate education. In K. Mantyla & J. Woods (Eds.), *2001/2002 ASTD distance learning yearbook.* McGraw-Hill.

Neal, L., & Miller, D. (2005). Distance education. In R. Proctor & K. Vu (Eds.), *The handbook of human factors in Web design* (pp. 454-470). Lawrence Erlbaum Associates.

Neal, L., & Miller, D. (2006). The use of technology in education. In H. F. O'Neil & R. Perez, (Eds.), *Web-based learning: Theory, research, and practice*. Lawrence Erlbaum Associates.

Neal, L., Miller, D., & Perez, R. (2004). Online learning and fun. *eLearn Magazine*. Retrieved November 6, 2007 from http://www.elearnmag. org/subpage/sub_page.cfm?article_pk=12265&page_number_nb=1&title=FEATURE%20STORY

Notess, M., & Neal, L. (2006). Deep thoughts: Do mandatory online learning activities help students leave surface learning behind? *eLearn Magazine*. Retrieved November 6, 2007, from http://www.elearnmag.org/subpage. cfm?section=opinion&article=75-1

Orvis, K. L., & Lassiter, A. L. R. (2006). Computer supported collaborative learning: The role of the instructor. In S. P. Ferris & S.H. Godar (Eds.), *Teaching and learning with virtual teams*. Hersey, PA: Idea Group.

Richardson, J. C., & Swan, K. (2001). The role of social presence in online courses: How does it relate to students' perceived learning and satisfaction? *World Conference on Educational Multimedia, Hypermedia and Telecommunications, 1*, 1545-1546.

Shneiderman, B. (2002). *Leonardo's laptop: Human needs and the new computing technologies*. Boston: MIT Press.

Sims, D. E., Salas, E., & Burke, C. S. (2004). *Is there a big five in teamwork?* Paper presented at the 19th Annual Conference of the Society for Industrial and Organizational Psychology, Chicago, IL.

Slamecka, N. J., & Graf, P. (1978). The generation effect: Delineation of a phenomenon. *Journal of Experimental Psychology: Human Learning & Memory, 4*, 592-604.

Soraci, S. A., Carlin, M. T., Chechile, R. A., Franks, J. J., Wills, T., & Watanabe, T. (1999). Encoding variability and cuing in generative processing. *Journal of Memory & Language, 41*, 541-559.

Volery, T. (2001). Online education: An exploratory study into success factors. *Journal of Educational Computing Research, 24*, 77-92.

Wittrock, M. C. (1989). Generative processes of comprehension. *Educational Psychologist, 24*, 345-376.

Zaccaro, S. J., & McCoy, M. C. (1998). The effects of task and interpersonal cohesiveness on performance of a disjunctive group task. *Journal of Applied Social Psychology, 18*, 837-851.

Section IV

Diversity in
CSCL Environments

Chapter X

Gender and Diversity in Collaborative Virtual Teams

Anna Michailidou, University of Macedonia, Greece

Anastasios Economides, University of Macedonia, Greece

Abstract

Computer supported collaborative learning environments (CSCLEs) is one of the innovative technologies that support online education. Successful design and implementation of such environments demand thorough analysis of many parameters. This chapter studies the impact of diversity in learner-learner interactions in collaborative virtual teams through a social and cultural perspective. Social differences include gender, race, class, or age. Cultural differences refer to matters like how an individual's cognition, values, beliefs, and study behaviors are influenced by culture. Instructors must take into consideration the factors that influence individuals' diversity, and invent new ways to implement successful collaboration. This is crucial, especially regarding teams scattered on different countries or even continents. Social and cultural differences influence an individual's performance in a learning environment. Such differences must be adequately studied by both the educational organization and the instructors in such a way that the learning procedure will become a positive experience for all the members involved.

Introduction

It is beyond any doubt that adequate education is one of the key factors for successful embedment of the synchronous man to a world that becomes increasingly digitalized. The increased use of information and communication technologies (ICTs) generated a major modification in both the pedagogical and educational methodologies (Andrews & Schwarz, 2002). This refers to the teacher-learner relationship and embraces matters like personalized learning, collaboration, interaction, and evaluation.

The approach of participative learning offers the possibility of developing novel learning environments that support collaboration, rapid interaction and feedback, real time communication, information seeking, and problem solving. The learner has the opportunity to construct knowledge through a process of discussion and interaction with both other learners and teachers (Michailidou & Economides, 2003).

Diversity in computer supported collaborative learning environments (CSCLEs) is a complex concept. It is one thing to create diversity by recruiting learners—of different nationality, cultural background, race, gender, sexual orientation, religion, discipline, and another thing to develop a supportive educational environment in which individuals of diverse backgrounds can perform at their highest levels and contribute fully to the learning procedure (Chen, Czerwinski, & Macredie, 2000). Even more challenging is the task of fully integrating the varied knowledge experiences, perspectives, and values that learners of diverse backgrounds bring into the educational environment.

This chapter begins with a discussion concerning the issue of collaboration in virtual teams. Afterwards, diversity in collaborative virtual teams is being studied, along with its impact in learner-learner interactions. Some suggestions to the instructors for facilitating effective learning in a collaborative computer-supported environment are also included. Finally, the conclusions are presented along with future trends.

Collaboration in Virtual Teams

A virtual team is a group of people who work interdependently across space, time, cultures, and organizational boundaries on temporary, nonoccurring projects with a shared purpose, while using technology (Lipnack & Stamps, 2000). Virtual teams are utilized in multiple settings, including education (teams formed among students of distance learning classes), professional development, as well as corporate and community organizations.

The use of virtual teams is growing in popularity, especially in work-related and educational organizations. There are many advantages for using virtual teams in an educational setting. These include the creation of learning communities and the opportunity to work collaboratively to generate new knowledge. Working in virtual teams presents unexplored opportunities for peer interaction as teams create new knowledge to resolve the problem assigned. Additionally, it asserts that the best conditions for intellectual accomplishment are environments that are motivated by discovery, the reciprocal feedback between mutually-respected individuals, and the free exchange of ideas. Conclusively, virtual teams have become a vehicle for distance education, through which group work is accomplished in demanding learning environments (Anderson & Garrison, 1998).

The current chapter analyzes the gender and diversity impact in collaborative computer-mediated environments formed basically for educational purposes. Therefore, if the instructors study the diversity issue in a potential learning virtual team, then some solutions might occur, concerning the embodiment of diversity parameters and their impact in the success factors of a collaborative task.

Diversity intensively influences the performance of a virtual team in an educational setting. Many significant factors constitute diversity like those related to differences in social and cultural characteristics, gender, ethics, knowledge, educational experiences, and future expectations. For most virtual teams to be effective, some degree of diversity is both desirable and necessary. If all the team members have the same perspectives, histories, work experience, and academic training, then, theoretically, the creativity and problem solving potential of the team is limited. When facilitated properly, a team will be more effective than a single person will. For example, virtual teams that develop new ideas and problem solving are often composed deliberately of people of various ages, interests, religious backgrounds, or academic disciplines. Therefore, diversity on learning virtual teams has been shown to be positively associated with performance if process challenges are addressed (Chen et al., 2000; Paulus, Legett, Dzindolet, Coskun, & Putman, 2002).

Although diversity is connected to positive outcomes, it also has been linked to negative ones, like difficulties in managing cooperation. While a diverse team can generate a wider array of ideas, solutions, and perspectives, it may also require special management to both release and harness that diverse energy. The collection of differences in a diverse virtual team may bring more conflict within the team if these differences are not managed with insight to the idiosyncrasies of the team membership.

Gender is among the characteristics associated with diversity and is known to influence team behaviours (Barrett & Lally, 1999). Many surveys were designed to explore whether men and women feel differently about being part of a learning team. More specifically, some questions arose: Are there differences in the degree to which men and women are satisfied with team performance? Are there differences between what men and women see as the primary difficulties faced by a team? And if gender differences exist, how do they influence team performance? The assessment of gender and diversity influence in learner-learner interactions in a CSCLE is a crucial issue concerning the determination of the educational value of such an environment (Gunn & McSporran, 2003). In order for educators to balance the benefits of diversity with its possible costs, they must be aware of the factors that constitute diversity and their influence on team performance.

The Impact of Gender and Diversity in Learner-Learner Interactions

In the current section, the discussion focuses on the social and cultural differences of individuals that shape diversity in a collaborative virtual team.

Social Differences

Social differences focus on race, gender, class, age, or sexual orientation. The individual's identity in these social categories is derived both from the knowledge of what it is like to be part of a particular group (e.g., women) and from the way others view the value of being a member of that group (Abnett, Stanton, Neale, & O'Malley, 2001).

Gender-based differences in performance and communication style in computer supported learning environments were deemed as an important element for research (Blum, 1999; Gunn & McSporran, 2003; McLean & Morrison, 2000).

Fewer girls and women study or have jobs in engineering or computer science; in schools and homes, boys often dominate computer use, while females are typically less confident about using technology and have less experience with it (Blum, 1999; Brosnan & Davison, 1994; Ford & Miller, 1996; Hatton, 1995). There have been identified common differences in the behavior of male and female students in technology-based instructions. These differences include self-reported levels of confidence in ability to work successfully with technology, and patterns of interaction. It was found that women talked less, contributed less frequently, did not receive positive feedback to their contributions, and did not appeal to the same sources of support (Ausburn, 2004; Barrett & Lally, 1999).

Similarly, Gunn and McSporran's (2003) study found gender differences in motivation, confidence level, flexibility, and access. Men stated that they were very confident and enjoyed using the online materials, whereas women stated they were apprehensive about using the materials and about their overall ability for the technical aspects of the course. In addition, women reported that they had more problems with access, such as having to share the computer with other family members or friends. Richardson and Turner (2000) also stated that females responded significantly more negatively toward CSCLEs than males. This outcome may arise from the fact that female students are not as computer-literate as male students, and therefore less confident. Another explanation may be that some elements of working in such an environment may not be compatible with the needs of female students.

There are also several research studies that found gender differences in the learning outcomes. Studies of gender-related patterns in epistemological knowledge demonstrated that female students tend to view learning from a connected and relational path, rather than an individualistic perspective (Baxter-Magolda, 1992). It was also found that females performed better than males in mixed-gender online courses, and generally, female groups demonstrate a more positive attitude towards teamwork and collaboration tasks, as compared to males (McSporran & Young, 2001; Young, Dewstow, & McSporran, 1999). However, these studies show mixed results. Some found that women are more successful in Web-based learning, while others found that men performed as well too (McSporran & Young, 2001; Mehlenbacher, Miller, Covington, & Larsen, 2000). This is partly due to culture's role as a moderating factor affecting gender differences (Mortenson, 2002). In individualistic cultures, people tend to be opinion-oriented and straight-forward, whereas in collectivistic cultures, task dominates over personal relationships (Chang & Lim, 2002). Countries such as Canada and USA are typically associated with individualistic cultures, while most Asian countries, such as Singapore and Taiwan, are inclined towards collectivism (Hofstede, 1991). Mortenson (2002) found that the typical gendered behavior was only supported in Euro-American subjects. Males were as likely as females in using supportive modes of communication in Asian subjects. In addition, Watkins, Adair, Akande, Cheng, Fleming, Gerong, Ismail, McInerney, Lefner, Mpofu, Regmi, Singh-Sengupta, Watson, Wondimu, and Yu (1998) discovered that the gender stereotypes, with females valuing social relationships more, apply only to individualistic western countries.

The existing literature concerning gender differences in a computer conferencing environment has evidently addressed variations in terms of communication styles and participation rates between males and females (McLean & Morrison, 2000). Females tend to display a more socio-emotional behavior, nonaggressive strategies, and a stronger compliance concerning others' differentiations. In contrast, males are typically associated with aggressive and active strategies. Generally, they support their opinion in a stronger manner and express independence (Ausburn, 2004; Barrett & Lally, 1999). Furthermore, research suggests that women are more comfortable than men with team-based evaluations and rewards. This may be partly due to findings by gender theorists that men's relationships tend to be defined by role and status, while women tend to value relationships based on communication and understanding (Bostock & Lizhi, 2005; Gunn & McSporran, 2003; Herring, 2000).

Analysis of written dialogue in computer mediated communication systems reveals gender variations in message style. In particular, females tend to be more punctual and use frequently apologies, questions, personal orientation, and support. Males' language includes strong assertions, self-promotion, challenges, and sarcasm (Herring, 2000). Bostock and Lizhi, (2005) studied the gender differentiations that occurred in student asynchronous online discussions. The research findings indicated that female groups had significantly more messages per student than male groups. Mixed groups were more variable than single-gender groups, while the messages contributed by males in mixed groups were especially changeable. More females were less confident of using computer applications and less positive regarding new technology challenges. They also demonstrated higher average final report marks, although they had expressed fears about finding the course difficult.

Clearly, gender is one of the many factors associated with team performance and cohesion in CSCLEs. Concerning the role of the instructor in managing gender differences in virtual teams with the purpose of promoting collaboration and influencing learner-learner interactions, the following list is presented (Barrett & Lally, 1999; Johnson & Aragon, 2003; Knight, Pearce, Smith, Olian, Sims, Smith, & Flood, 1999; Potter & Bathazard, 2002):

- Gender differences and needs may be addressed by tailoring distance programs or by creating peer groups with similar learning backgrounds and interests. The instructor would organize discussions about gender similarities and differences.

- Strategies for promoting inclusion regarding gender issues suggest equally profiling men and women in curriculum illustration in both traditional and nontraditional roles. Care should be taken to be sensitive to diversity in sexual orientation. The instructor would create mixed teams and ask them to play a game or to develop a project.

- An instructor should keep in mind that male participants will tend to be most comfortable when team's objectives are clarified to the greatest possible extent, and the individual roles of team members are defined. Whilst female participants appear to be most comfortable when communication and other group maintenance activities are clearly valued, along with task activities.

- Instructors might choose to discuss common gender differences with their team members to raise awareness and understanding. For this purpose, they can use teambuilding exercises with discussions of differences in personality types, levels of participation, technology issues, and so on.

Ethnic-racial, economic-class differences and barriers occur in most learning groups, since it is common for individuals initiated from different races or social classes to participate in the same computer-mediated learning environment. Wegerif (1998) showed, through a study of a multicultural computer-mediated course, that social factors, like ethnicity, have an impact upon the learning procedure. In particular, he stated that when ethnicity differentiations corresponding to language or race differences are not taken under account, lead to decreased participation rates, and willingness in collaboration. Similar studies had also been conducted by other researchers (Kember, 2000; Kennedy, 2002; Vogel, Lou, van Eekhout, van Genuchten, Verveen, & Adams, 2000). In cases where the learning environment allows racist hints concerning racial or economic-class backgrounds, individuals hurt demonstrate negativism, unwillingness in participation, and abstention to any collaborative task. As a result, the team coherence is damaged, and the whole learning procedure fails.

One of the key issues facing all educational environments, both traditional and computer mediated (and indeed lifelong learning), is how to create tolerance for minorities in an environment characterized by diversity (Obidah, 2000; Volet, 1999). Intolerance is conceptualized basically as a matter of attitudes, and is said to be constituted by prejudice.

The instructor should confront ethnic or racial differences within the members of a virtual team by using information summarized below (Chow, Shields, & Wu, 1999; Chen et al., 2000; Bonner, Marbley, & Agnello, 2004):

- The context supporting the courses in such an environment should be adequate and neutral in terms of ideas and learning outcomes. This develops a sense of equal confrontation among the participants, resulting in an increase of involvement in the learning procedure, and in satisfactory collaboration terms.
- If racism is an issue in a learning environment, then participants must become acquainted with other cultures and find the courage to challenge stereotypes and appreciate others. The instructor would:
    ° Enable learners to share personal photos (e.g., family, friends, and place of origin), videos, ethnic-traditional music, tourist information about their countries, and so on.
    ° Provide information about learners' ethnicities and races.
    ° Organize discussions about learners' ethnic-racial similarities and differences.
    ° Create a common basis of views accepted by all.
    ° Unify and integrate opposing views and ideas.

- Illustrations in distance learning delivery can include culturally appropriate personal names and culturally accepted phrases. This illustration embraces the students' background and serves as an engaging point to keep their interest.

- Matters that relate to prejudice and attitudes must be confronted through teaching about "other cultures." That requires a dismantling of institutionalized practices of racism—whether in employment or education or in social welfare. It also entails a direct confrontation with racist ideologies—for example, in curricula. The instructor would:

  ° Find common ground among conflicting opinions (e.g., two learners from different nations describe a battle between their nations from a single compromised point of view).

  ° Create mixed teams and ask them to complete a project.

  ° Ask learners to collaboratively develop concept maps on controversial issues.

Concerning economic class differences, an instructor would (Howard & Levine, 2004; Paulsen & St. John, 2002; Walpole, 2004):

- Enable the participation of the lowest economic class learners by either encouraging scholarships or tailoring the required economic resources of a project to these learners.

- Provide the appropriate background information to students lacking it, due to their economic situation.

- Create mixed teams and ask them to complete a project.

- Encourage learners to share their living experiences.

- Foster mutual understanding and respect.

Age differences and barriers correspond mainly to different life experience, educational background, professional status, and maturity (Gaskell, 2000). Age should be taken under consideration in group formation, especially when it influences team effectiveness due to differences that might occur in prior educational background and technology adequacy. For example, it is evident that all participants should be familiarized with technology demands and frustrations, especially in a virtual learning environment.

Turner (2000) conducted a research with the purpose of investigating individual difference factors with respect to computer use generally, as a means of informing e-learning instructional design. The learning team included 170 undergraduate students (103 Chinese and 67 UK) who completed tasks, and also a questionnaire on their knowledge of the Internet and how effectively they used it. The results indicated a difference in the affective and cognitive components of attitudes between different age groups, such that the younger age group (17-19 years) reported more positive attitudes than the older age group (21-32 years). It is possible that this may relate to differences in education and exposure to the Internet.

In some cases (Chioncel, Van Der Veen, Nildemeersch, & Jarvis, 2003; Mehrotra, 2003), both younger and older learners with the same educational background reported that participating in an age-diverse group was a positive experience. Older learners felt that the younger group respected their opinions, and the age mix in the virtual classroom finally provides a multitude of ideas. Instructors noted that older learners fear failure, more than younger learners (Chioncel et al., 2003). There has also been expressed the opinion that older learners have difficulty with multitasking, and as a result, require more understanding from other learners regarding their capabilities. Furthermore, older adult learners are less confident in using information and communication technologies and need more time to remember the necessary information for understanding the material. Consequently, if they feel confident and relaxed, being a part of the educational environment, they will learn more.

Older adult learners most commonly have their own views and opinions on certain subjects, and therefore, they will challenge teachers on the information that they give. The teacher has to invent ways in order to get older adults to challenge their ways of thinking and open their minds to new ways of perceiving knowledge (Mehrotra, 2003). Older adults also have a lot of maturity regarding their studies and will give help and advice to younger students. They have better attendance, are more mannerly, and in most cases are more grateful for the opportunity to learn.

The instructor would confront age differences within the members of a virtual team by using information summarized below (Liang & McQueen, 1999; Merriam & Simpson, 2000):

- Age differences and barriers may be addressed by tailoring distance programs or by creating peer groups with similar learning backgrounds and interest.

- Delivery systems for different age groups relate most prominently to the amount of—and degree of—interactivity. Therefore, instructors must facilitate interactivity procedures between the participants of different age groups, introducing both synchronous (e.g., chat) and asynchronous (e.g. e-mail) ways of communication.

- Instructors must also analyze all the evidence concerning the individual characteristics of any participant related to age, like prior educational background, professional skills, and expectations, and suggest realistic solutions that confront any potential learning issue on an equal basis for each and every learner. In order for this to happen, instructors should receive feedback information (with interviews, interactive exercises, etc.) throughout the learning procedure.

- Since older adult learners are more sensitive to failure, they need more individual or one-to-one attention.

The above discussion concerning the social differences among learners in a CSCL educational environment is being summarized in Table 1. The first column contains the Differential Factor corresponding to Social Differences and the second column the Behavioral Attitude affecting Learner- Learner Interactions that might occur in a CSCLE.

Cultural Differences

Cultural differences focus on how individuals' values, beliefs, norms, communication styles, and study behaviours are influenced by the culture in which they grew up or live. Cultural differences may help the instructors to understand how students can best adapt to new educational environments (Hughes, Wickersham, Ryan-Jones, & Smith, 2002). Cultural differences are harder to "see," but may be much more important causes of misunderstanding among learners participating in multicultural educational organizations. Taking under consideration relevant cultural differences and preconceptions is a crucial step into creating effective international learning teams (Myers & Tan, 2002).

Hofstede (1991) defined a cultural model in which cultures vary along five dimensions: Power distance, collectivism/ individualism, femininity/mascu-

Table 1. Social differences and behavioral attitude affecting learner-learner interactions

Social Differences		Behavioral Attitude affecting Learner-Learner Interactions
Differential Factor		
Gender Differences	Females	• They display more socio-emotional behavior, non-aggressive strategies and a stronger compliance concerning others' differentiations. • They usually perform better than males in mixed-gender online courses. • They demonstrate a more positive attitude towards teamwork and collaboration tasks. • In dialogues, they tend to be more punctual and use frequently apologies, questions, personal orientation and support. • Analysis of written dialogue in computer mediated communication systems revealed that female groups write more massages per student than male groups. • They have lower confidence with IT applications.
	Males	• They are associated with aggressive and active strategies. • In dialogues, they use language with strong assertions, self-promotion, challenges and sarcasm. • According to some studies males were as likely as females in using supportive modes of communication in collectivistic countries. • They are more confident about using technology.
Ethnic-Racial, Economic-Class Discrimination	Present	• Individuals are being hurt and demonstrate negativism, unwillingness in participation and abstention to any collaborative task. • The team coherence is damaged and the whole learning procedure fails.
	Not present	• There is a sense of equal confrontation among the participants resulting in an increase of involvement in the learning procedure and in satisfactory collaboration terms. • The learners become acquainted with other cultures and find the courage to challenge stereotypes and appreciate others. • The learners form a harmonious, democratic educational environment that supports cultural pluralism.
Age Differences (when prior educational background and technology adequacy are not at the same level among individuals)	Taken under consideration	• Team members will correspond better in learning tasks. • Team members may feel more comfortable with each other.
	Not taken under consideration	• Team coherence will be jeopardized. • Many difficulties will occur concerning the achievement of a learning task.
Age Differences (when prior educational background and technology adequacy are at the same level among individuals)		• Both younger and older learners with the same educational background, find that participating in an age diverse group is a positive experience. • Older learners fear failure, more than younger learners. • Older learners are less confident in using information and communication technologies. • It is common for older learners to challenge teachers on the information that they give. • Older learners and in particular adults have a lot of maturity regarding their studies.

linity, uncertainty avoidance, and long term/ short term orientation. Taken together, these dimensions provide a means of characterizing and comparing different cultures, as well as providing a meaning for the use or nonuse of computer-mediated software. For example, cultures reflecting more "collectivist" tendencies, such as Chinese and those in the Middle East may actually use collaborative software more effectively than individualistic cultures like those of the U.S. or Australia (Chung & Adams, 1997).

Cultures can be learned and reflect the patterns of thinking, feeling, and acting (Harris, 1987). The underlying theme is that culture is an abstraction from concrete behaviour, but not behaviour itself. Culture is transmitted mainly by symbols, constituting distinctive achievement of human groups, including the embodiments in artifacts (Chow et al., 1999). It is in this sense that culture characterizes the whole way of life of a group. It is a pattern of traditions that can be transmitted over time and space. Three qualities underlie its centrality: it is learned, much of it exists at a non- or unconscious level, and it helps structure thought perception and identity (Mayers & Tan, 2002).

Cultural sensitivity must be included in the initial design stages of a collaborative virtual learning environment (Rovai, 2002). A level of cultural sensitivity could be incorporated into the design of the system, such that users' individual identities can be expressed, while simultaneously supporting community development. For example, cultural sensitivity is paramount in designing interaction systems (Mudur, 2001; Raybourn, 2001). In answer to this call, data collected from ethnography, questionnaires, and persona development provide the basis for designing cultural and organizational cues into the community-based system, in order to engender identification among the members of the community of practice.

Lessons learned both from face-to-face and computer-mediated communication tell us that the quality of successful collaborations depends largely on sharing cultural information like this concerning the values, beliefs, and norms of individuals. That minimizes uncertainty in interpersonal relationships and enhances interaction and collaboration among the participants (Chow et al., 1999). In much the same way, collaborating organizations, individuals, or communities of practice share cultural information to reduce uncertainty and strengthen notions of common ground (Wenger, 1998). Cultural information often shared across and within members of organizations includes values, goals, and histories that are shared, negotiated, and cocreated by the members. The future success of collaborative work in community-based virtual environments requires not only understanding the sociocultural dynamics that manifest in online communication and communities of practice, but also considering how the design of these environments can support intercultural communication with cultural of organizational contextual cues (Leevers, 2001).

A significant factor relative to the development of a collaborative community is the mutual engagement of participants. Mutual engagement refers to participants' cocreation and negotiation of actions or meanings, and relates to communication styles that each participant has developed. Consequently, mutual engagement is facilitated by communication, whether occurring in the face-to-face context, or virtually (Fai Wong & Trinidad, 2004). Observations of heterogeneous groups, whose members are of different (national) cultural backgrounds, revealed a wider variety of skills, information and experiences that could potentially improve the quality of collaborative learning (Rich, 1997). An improvement such as this could be obtained in a CSCLE, since the number of concurrent conversations that a medium can support, along with the reprocessing of messages during communication, can help learners of different cultures to gain a more accurate understanding of each other, thus improving performance (Yu, 2001). Additionally, it has been demonstrated that designing subtle cultural and contextual cues into a text-based collaborative virtual environment such as a multi-user dimension, object-oriented (MOO) is an effective way to encourage collaboration and awareness of intercultural communication, including the negotiation of power and exploration of identity (Raybourn, 2001). This aspect is particularly important for non-native speakers. Nevertheless, a direct consequence of cultural diversity is communication distortion, because basic modes of communication differ among people from different cultural backgrounds (Easley, Devaraj, & Crant, 2003).

Learners have different strategies, approaches, and capabilities for learning that are a function of prior experience and heredity. Individuals are born with and develop their own capabilities and talents. In addition, through learning and social acculturation, they have acquired their own preferences for how they like to learn, and the pace at which they learn (Ford, 2000).

Therefore, a learner's study behavior, especially when he is a part of a heterogeneous group, becomes more positive in the case of his participation in the cultural cocreation process. The cultural cocreation process includes the formation of a "new culture," which arises from the interactions in the educational setting between all the participating cultures. In effect, together, users co-create a "new culture" that is neither one nor the other, but a combination of the two, or three, and so on (Lim & Zhong, 2005). The successful future design of intelligent community-based systems requires considering how the design of these environments support intercultural communication and a greater awareness of cultural orientations in both the organizational and educational context.

Several studies indicate that individual success or failure on a learning task depends upon the level to which learners are able to cross a threshold from feeling like an outsider to feeling like an insider (Muirhead, 2000; Wegerif, 1998). In collaborative learning, students learn by recognizing flawed reasoning of others during a discussion. Prior studies have highlighted the importance of the discussion session in collaborative learning activities (Lave & Wenger, 1991). However, text-based computer mediated communication facilitates important features with respect to communication that are radically different from the face-to-face setting (Dennis & Valacich, 1999). The parallelism afforded by collaborative learning systems is expected to help learners of different cultures to gain a more accurate understanding of each other, thus improving performance. This aspect is particularly salient for nonnative speakers, since the spoken language disappears altogether after the utterance (Herring, 1999).

Conclusively, a significant factor that increases the feeling of alienation between the participants in a learning procedure is the different native **language**. This means that there must be defined a common communication language for the course, something that corresponds to a different level of adequate language knowledge for the participants. Although this may always be a problem, it is possible that with a sufficiently strong sense of community, learners with less experience on the language being used would be able to overcome their fears (Myers & Tan, 2002).

Table 2 summarizes some of the outcomes corresponding to cultural differences and their impact on learner-learner interactions. The first column contains the Differential Factor related to Cultural Differences, and the second column, the Impact on Learner- Learner Interactions that might occur in a CSCLE.

From the above discussion, it has become clear that cultural diversity plays an important role in implementing successful collaboration in virtual environments. Therefore, the instructor could follow some of the recommendations listed below:

- The instructor needs to foster critical engagement, to help people to connect with, and own, those aspects which accord with their sense

Table 2. Cultural differences and their impact on learner-learner interactions

Cultural Differences		Impact on Learner-Learner Interactions
Differential Factor		
Values, beliefs, norms (when shared among the participants)		• Minimize uncertainty in interpersonal relationships. • Enhance collaboration tasks. • Better implementation of interaction techniques and feedback among the participants in a virtual learning environment.
Communication styles	**When they are developed in a way that enhance communication among the participants.**	• Support information sharing. • Support real time spontaneous communication. • Enhance mutual engagement between the participants (mutual engagement refers to participants' co-creation and negotiation of actions or meanings). • Heterogeneous groups, whose members are of different (national) cultural backgrounds, reveal a wider variety of skills, information and experiences that could potentially improve the quality of collaborative learning. • Multiple concurrent conversations that a medium can support are expected to help learners of different cultures to gain a more accurate understanding of each other, thus improving performance.
	When they are not taken under consideration.	• Communication distortion may appear because basic modes of communication differ among people from different cultural backgrounds.
Study behaviors (when taken under consideration)		• A learner's study behavior especially when he/she is a part of a heterogeneous group becomes more positive in the case of his/hers participation in the cultural co-creation process. • The cultural co-creation process includes the formation of a 'new culture' which arises from the interactions in the educational setting between all the participating cultures. This new culture is accepted by all members and helps in the development of any study behavior that affects positively the learning procedure.
Language		• Different level of adequate language knowledge for the participants results to limited participation. • With a sufficiently strong sense of community, learners with less experience on the language being used would be able to overcome their fears.

of themselves, and of what is good and right. At the same time, it is to reject certain things, to encourage the desire and ability to change values, behaviors, ideas that are unjust or that inhibit well being (Swigger, Alpaslan, Brazile, & Monticino, 2004).

- Many people do not explicitly share information about their cultural background or educational organization for a variety of reasons, including diverse orientations toward privacy and public versus private information (Raybourn, 2001). Therefore, the instructor must invent ways to motivate users to identify more strongly with their community of practice, and take the first steps towards opening a chat with others whom they may share common interests with, but do not know well enough to feel comfortable communicating with in a virtual environment. In order for this to happen:

  ○ The instructor could organize a discussion forum supporting themes of common interest among the participants.

  ○ A set of educational tasks (e.g., exercises) given by the instructor would motivate the participants to increase e-mail or chat communication. This would reduce nervousness among the participants, and encourage them to support and share their own cultural background.

- Most users who inhabit virtual worlds like to leave their mark on the shared space, whether it is through building artifacts (objects) or becoming influential members of the community (Selim, 2003). Allowing each person to contribute to development or design of the space creates more community, which could help individuals to surpass cultural differences that hinder collaboration, like language barriers. A graffiti board, or bulletin board, arouses curiosity and participation among the community by arousing interest among teammates—whether it is curiosity about other members of the community, or the shared space itself. The instructor could participate in creating more motivating environments by designing for user fun, curiosity, and fantasy exploration.

- Both designers and instructors could consider giving the right to participating members to express themselves anonymously in a virtual setting—for example, only for a few sessions at the beginning of a learning procedure. Certain anonymity can create more equitable communication (especially for newcomers) reducing the appearance of hierarchy and power in a collaborative environment, and fostering more peer-based communication events (Volet, 1999). A virtual tour of the learning space, and perhaps a FAQ on the formal and informal cultural norms, will help a participant to feel more like part of the team, and thus identify more strongly with the community. A team gallery of interests might be an informal mechanism for obtaining meta-level information on the team culture and individual identities.

- Avatar movement may be based on common cultural attributes, or common social interests, in addition to movement throughout the space based on keywords and common work products. Educational agents could connect users of common social and cultural interests, and provide reasons for the movement in the space. Cultural information about the team (hobbies, families, etc.) may be made available in the learning space via interactive objects (Myers & Tan, 2002). The instructor should encourage learners to interact in real time where there are mutual concerns or interests, and evaluate certain cultural characteristics, incorporating them into an adaptive community-based virtual environment in order to offer enhanced support for intercultural communication among remote learners.

- Different national cultures emphasize distinct values and are associated with diverse languages. It is apparent that the presence of different languages, and the inability to speak and comprehend these different languages, creates barriers to efficient knowledge sharing throughout the organization. In the case of multinational learning groups, a lot of knowledge might be lost in translation, or due to the inability to articulate the knowledge in the project's working language (Myers & Tan 2002). A good way to diminish the negative consequences of language barriers is to emphasize active listening skills, patience, and understanding. Despite language differences, it is important to enable all members an equal opportunity to be heard. The difficulty of studying and communicating in a second language exacerbates the problem of equal participation, especially in the case of a CSCLE. Until students have built up sufficient fluency in the lower-level language skills (Raybourn, Kings, & Davies, 2003) to be able to express their understanding in their own words in the language of instruction, they may find it difficult to display their newly acquired knowledge. Therefore, the instructor must encourage learners with less language experience, and help them to overcome their difficulties in expressing their opinion, and actively participate in the learning procedure.

- Learners have different strategies, approaches, and capabilities for learning that are a function of prior experience and heredity. Individuals are born with and develop their own capabilities and talents (Ford, 2000). Instructors need to help students examine their learning preferences and expand or modify them, if necessary. They also need to attend to learner perceptions, as long as these differences are adapted to by varying instructional methods and materials.

Conclusion and Future Research

As several studies have observed (Adler, 1997; Watson, Kumar, & Michaelsen, 1993), diversity within teams is a reality for educators and organizations. It is also an important social value for synchronous society. For these reasons, it is important that research clearly and accurately elucidate the true impact of diversity in learning-teams. This requires moving beyond studies of simple demographic effects and broad generalizations about the effects of diversity on teams, to understanding how these differences arise and are experienced in specific contexts. Only then, both learners and instructors will be able to manage differences effectively and understand in detail how diversity really affects individuals in different types of educational organizations.

In the current chapter, diversity issues that arise from both social and cultural differences are analyzed. Social differences focus mainly on race, gender, class and age. While cultural differences focus on how individuals' cognition, values, beliefs, communication styles, and study behaviors are influenced by their culture. The impact of these factors on the learner-learner interactions are being summarized in Tables 1-2.

Online learning and virtual learning environments demand that the role of the instructor will be the one of the facilitator in the learning process, rather than that a of knowledge dispenser. Conclusively, in order for the instructor to attain successful collaboration, diversity and all its factors that affect learners' interactions must be adequately analyzed and studied. A number of constructive suggestions to be used by the instructor in both the design and the implementation of learning activities are presented in the bulleted paragraphs throughout the "The Impact of Gender and Diversity in Learner-Learner Interactions" section.

A teaching and learning environment located within a technological context can be used to support instructor-learner and learner-learner communication, and to aid collaborative learning across different cultures. An individual's learning process, combined with synchronous or even asynchronous inter-activity with other learners, can be enhanced with the proliferation of communication technologies. Such technologies can strengthen and increase additional communication cues during group activities (Aviv, 2000). Due to their unique features, CSCLEs provide strong support for the collaborative learning process. They help in teaming up groups of people who are unable to meet face-to-face and facilitate group interactions.

By using CSCLEs, learners from an individualistic cultural context might emphasize more on group achievement or relationship than before, and learners from a collectivistic context might become more independent and insistent on their own opinion during the reasoning process. Future research should work toward greater understanding of this aspect. In addition, problems of cross-cultural learning might be due to differences in language, cultural values, and the types of learning strategies preferred.

Recent technological developments have opened new perspectives for the cooperation between human learners, virtual humans, and anthropomorphic robots, especially in an augmented virtual reality environment. This kind of learning environments can be defined as DigiMech learning environments (DMLE) (La Russa & Faggiano, 2004; Nijholt, 2005). The richness and variety of users' possible interactions in such environments go far beyond the simple sensorial use of the virtual realities. The existing research, literature, experiences, practices and academic know-how support that DMLEs have extensive educative and cognitive potentials, especially in distant education context, and need further explorations. In addition, the associated social awareness mechanisms and diversity factors need to be explored further, including the issue of how robots and virtual humans perceive and interpret the social situations in the community they are a part of.

References

Abnett, C., Stanton, D., Neale, H., & O'Malley. (2001, March 22-24). The effect of multiple input devices on collaboration and gender issues. In *Proceedings of European Perspectives on Computer-Supported Col-*

laborative Learning (EuroCSCL) 2001, Maastricht, The Netherlands (pp. 29-36).

Adler, N. J. (1997). *International dimensions of organizational behavior.* Cincinnati, OH: South-Western College Publishing.

Anderson, T. D., & Garrison, D. R. (1998). Learning in a networked world: New roles and responsibilities. In C. C. Gibson (Ed.), *Distance learners in higher education* (pp. 97-112). Madison, WI: Atwood.

Andrews, T., & Schwarz, G. (2002). Preparing students for the virtual organization: An evaluation of learning with virtual learning technologies. *Educational Technology & Society, 5*(3).

Ausburn, L. (2004). Gender and learning strategy differences in non-traditional adult students' design preferences in hybrid distance courses. *The Journal of Interactive Online Learning, 3*(2), 1-17.

Aviv, R. (2000). Educational performance of ALN via content analysis. *Journal of Asynchronous Learning Networks, 4*(2).

Barrett, E., & Lally, V. (1999). Gender differences in an online learning environment. *Journal of Computer Assisted Learning, 15*, 48-60.

Baxter-Magolda, M. B. (1992). *Knowing and reasoning in college: Gender-related patterns in student's intellectual development.* San Francisco: Jossey-Bass Publishers.

Blum, K. D. (1999). Gender differences in asynchronous learning in higher education: Learning styles, participation barriers and communication patterns. *Journal of Asynchronous Learning Networks, 3*(1), 46-66.

Bonner, F., Marbley, A., & Agnello, M. F. (2004). The diverse learner in the college classroom. *E-Journal of Teaching and Learning in Diverse Settings, 1*(2), 246-255.

Bostock, S. J., & Lizhi, W. (2005). Gender in student online discussions. *Innovations in Education and Teaching International, 42*(1), 73-85.

Brosnan, M. J., & Davison, M. J. (1994, February). Computerphobia: Is it a particularly female phenomenon? *The Psychologist*, pp. 74-78.

Chang, T., & Lim, J. (2002). Cross-cultural communication and social presence in asynchronous learning processes. *e-Service Journal, 1*(3).

Chen, C., Czerwinski, M., & Macredie, R. (2000). Individual differences in virtual environments. Introduction and overview. *Journal of the American Society for Information Science, 51*(6), 499-507.

Chioncel, N. E., Van Der Veen, R. G. W., Nildemeersch, P., & Jarvis, P. (2003). The validity and reliability of focus groups as a research method in adult education. *International Journal of Lifelong Education, 22*(5), 495-517.

Chow, W. C., Shields, M. D., & Wu, A. (1999). The importance of national culture in the design of and preference for management controls for multi-national operations. *Accounting Organizations and Society, 24*, 441-461.

Chung, K., & Adams, C. (1997). A study on the characteristics of group decision-making behaviour: Cultural difference perspective of Korea vs. US. *Journal of Global Information Management, 5*(3), 18-29.

Dennis, A. R., & Valacich, J. S. (1999). Rethinking media richness: Towards a theory of media synchronicity. In *Proceedings of the 32nd Hawaii International Conference on System Sciences*, Hawaii.

Easley, R. F., Devaraj, S., & Crant, J. M. (2003). Collaborative technology use to teamwork performance: An empirical analysis. *Journal of Information Systems, 19*(4), 247-268.

Fai Wong, L., & Trinidad, S. G. (2004). Using Web-based distance learning to reduce cultural distance. *The Journal of Interactive Online Learning, 3*(1).

Ford, N. (2000). Cognitive styles and virtual environments. *Journal of American Society for Information Science, 51*(6), 543-557

Ford, N., & Miller, D. (1996). Gender differences in Internet perceptions and use. In *Proceedings of the Elvira Conference* (pp.87-100). London: ASLIB. Retrieved November 9, 2007, from http://www.shef.ac.uk/~is/home_old/gender.htm

Gaskell, T. (2000). The process of empirical research: A learning experience? *Research in Post-Compulsory Education, 5*(3), 349-360.

Gunn, C., & McSporran, M. (2003). Dominant or different? Gender issues in computer supported learning. *Journal of Asynchronous Learning Networks, 7*(1), 14-30.

Harris, M. (1987). *Cultural anthropology* (2nd ed.). Harper and Ross.

Hatton, D. (1995, November 18-21). Women and the "L": A study of the relationship between communication apprehension, gender and bulletin boards. In *Proceedings of the 81st Annual Meeting of the Speech Communication Association*, San Antonio, TX.

Herring, S. C. (1999). Interactional coherence in CMC. In *Proceedings of the 32nd Hawaii International Conference on System Sciences (HICSS)*.

Herring, S. C. (2000). Gender differences in CMC: Findings and implications. *The CPSR Newsletter, 18*(1). Retrieved November 9, 2007, from http://www.cpsr.org/publications/newsletters/issues/2000/Winter2000/herring.htm

Hofstede, G. (1991). *Cultures and organizations: Software of the mind.* McGraw-Hill.

Howard A., & Levine, A. (2004). Where are the poor students? A conversation about social class and college attendance. *About Campus, 9*(4), 1924.

Hughes, S. C., Wickersham, L., Ryan-Jones, D. L., & Smith, A. (2002). Overcoming social and psychological barriers to effective on-line collaboration. *Educational Technology & Society, 5*(1).

Johnson, S. D., & Aragon, S. A. (2003). An instructional strategy framework for online learning environments. In S. A. Aragon (Ed.), *Facilitating learning in online environments, new directions for adult and continuing education* (pp. 10, 31-44). San Francisco: Jossey-Bass.

Kember, D. (2000). Misconceptions about the learning approaches, motivation and study practices of Asian students. *Higher Education, 40*, 99-121.

Kennedy, P. (2002). Learning cultures and learning styles: Myth-understandings about adult (Hong Kong) Chinese learners. *International Journal of Lifelong Education, 21*(5), 430-445.

Knight, D., Pearce, C. L., Smith, K. G., Olian, J. D., Sims, H. P., Smith, K. A., & Flood, P. (1999). Top management team diversity, group process, and strategic consensus. *Strategic Management Journal, 20*, 445-465.

La Russa, G., & Faggiano, E. (2004). Robo-eLC: Enhancing learning hypermedia with robotics. In *Proceedings of ICALT, Joensuu, Finland* (pp. 465-469).

Lave, J., & Wenger, E. (1991). *Situated learning: Legitimate peripheral participation.* Cambridge, UK: Cambridge University.

Leevers, D. (2001). Collaboration and shared virtual environments—from metaphor to reality. In R. Earnshaw, R. Guedj, A. van Dam, & J. Vince (Eds.), *Frontiers of human-centered computing, online communities and virtual environments* (pp. 278–298). Springer.

Liang, A., & McQueen, R. J. (1999). Computer assisted adult interactive learning in a multi-cultural environment. *Adult Learning, 11*(1), 26-29.

Lim, J., & Zhong, Y. (2005). Cultural diversity, leadership, group size and collaborative learning systems: An experimental study. In *Proceedings of the 38ᵗʰ Hawaii International Conference on System Sciences.*

Lipnack, J., & Stamps, J. (2000). *Virtual teams people working across boundaries with technology* (2ⁿᵈ ed.). New York: John Wiley & Sons.

Mayers, M., & Tan, F. (2002). Beyond models of national culture in information systems research. *Journal of Global Information Management, 10*(1), 24-32.

McLean, S., & Morrison, D. (2000). Sociodemographic characteristic of learners and participation in computer conferencing. *Journal of Distance Education, 15*(2).

McSporran, M., & Young, S. (2001). Does gender matter in online learning? *Association for Learning Technology Journal (Alt-J), 9*(2), 3-15.

Mehlenbacher, B., Miller, C. R., Covington, D., & Larsen, J. S. (2000). Active and interactive learning online: A comparison of Web-based and conventional writing classes. *IEEE Transactions on Professional Communication, 43*(2), 166-184.

Mehrotra, C. M. (2003). In defense of educational programs for older adults. *Educational Gerontology, 29*, 645-655.

Merriam S. B., & Simpson, E. L. (2000). *A guide to research for educators and trainers of adults* (2ⁿᵈ ed.). Krieger Publishing Company.

Michailidou, A., & Economides, A. (2003). Elearn: Towards a collaborative educational virtual environment. *Journal of Information Technology Education, 2*, 131-152.

Mortenson, S. T. (2002). Sex, communication and cultural values: Individualism-collectivism as a mediator of sex differences in communication in two cultures. *Communication Reports, 15*(1).

Mudur, S. (2001). On the need for cultural representation in interactive systems. In R. Earnshaw, R. Guedj, A. van Dam, & J. Vince (Eds.), *Frontiers of human-centered computing, online communities and virtual environments* (pp. 299-310). Springer.

Muirhead, B. (2000). Enhancing social interaction in computer-mediated distance education. *Educational Technology & Society, 3*(4), 4-11.

Myers, M., & Tan, F. (2002). Beyond models of national culture in information systems research. *Journal of Global Information Management, 10*(1), 24-32.

Nijholt, A. (2005). Human and virtual agents interacting in the virtuality continuum. In *Proceedings of ACTAS II: IX Symposio Internacional de Comunicacion Social, Centro de Linguistica Aplicade, Santiago de Cuba* (pp. 551-558).

Obidah, J. (2000). Mediating boundaries of race, class and professorial authority as a critical multiculturalist. *Teachers College Record, 102,* 1035-1061.

Paulsen, M., & St. John, E. P. (2002). Social class and college costs: Examining between college choice and persistence. *The Journal of Higher Education, 73*(2), 189-236.

Paulus, P. B., Legett, K., Dzindolet, M. T., Coskun, H., & Putman, V. L. (2002). Social and cognitive influences in group brainstorming: Prediction of production gains and losses. In W. Stroebe & M. Hewstone (Eds.), *European review of social psychology* (pp. 299-325). London: Wiley.

Potter, R. E., & Bathazard, P. A. (2002). Understanding human interactions and performance in the virtual team. *Journal of Information Technology Theory and Application (JITTA), 4*(1), 1-23.

Raybourn, E. M. (2001). Designing an emergent culture of negotiation in collaborative virtual communities: The DomeCityMOO simulation. In E. Churchill, D. Snowden, & A. Munro (Eds.), *Collaborative virtual environments* (pp. 247-264). Springer.

Raybourn, E. M., Kings, N. J., & Davies, J. (2003). Adding cultural signposts in adaptive community-based environments [Special issue on intelligent community-based systems]. *Interacting With Computers: The Interdisciplinary Journal of Human-Computer Interaction, 15*(1), 91-107. Elsevier Science Ireland Ltd.

Rich, M. (1997). A learning community on the Internet: An exercise with masters students. In *Proceedings of Americas Conference on Information Systems,* Indianapolis.

Richardson, J. A., & Turner, A. (2000). A large-scale "local" evaluation of students' learning experiences using virtual learning environments. *Educational Technology & Society, 3*(4).

Rovai, A. A. P. (2002). A preliminary look at the structural differences of higher education classroom communities in traditional and ALN courses. *Journal of Asynchronous Learning Networks, 6*(1), 41-56.

Selim, H. M. (2003). An empirical investigation of student acceptance of course Websites. *Computers & Education, 40,* 343-360.

Swigger, K., Alpaslan, F., Brazile, R., & Monticino, M. (2004). Effects of culture on computer-supported international collaborations. *International Journal of Human-Computer Studies, 60,* 365-380.

Turner, Y. (2000). When an unstoppable force meets an immovable object: Chinese students in the UK university system. In *Proceedings of the 5th International Conference on Learning Styles* (pp. 353-384).

Vogel, D. R., Lou, D., van Eekhout, M., van Genuchten, M., Verveen, S., & Adams, T. (2000). Distributed experiential learning: The Hong Kong-Netherlands project. In *Proceedings of the 33rd Annual Hawaii International Conference on System Sciences* (pp. 1-9).

Volet, S. (1999). Learning across cultures: Appropriateness of knowledge transfer. *International Journal of Educational Research, 31,* 625-643.

Walpole, M. (2004). Socioeconomic status and college: How SES affects outcomes. *The Review of Higher Education, 27*(1), 4573.

Watkins, D. A., Adair, J., Akande, A., Cheng, C., Fleming, J., Gerong, A., et al. (1998). Cultural dimensions, gender and the nature of self-concept: A fourteen-country study. *International Journal of Psychology, 33*(1).

Watson, W. E., Kumar, K., & Michaelsen, L. K. (1993). Cultural diversity's impact on interaction process and performance: Comparing homogeneous and diverse task groups. *Academy of Management Journal, 36*(3), 590-602.

Wegerif, R. (1998). The social dimension of asynchronous learning networks. *Journal of Asynchronous Learning Networks, 2*(1), 34-49.

Wenger, E. (1998). *Communities of practice: Learning, meaning, and identity.* Cambridge University Press.

Young, S., Dewstow, R., & McSporran, M. (1999, July). Who wants to learn online? What types of students benefit from the new learning environment? In *Proceedings of the NACCQ.*

Yu, F. (2001). Competition within computer-assisted cooperative learning environments: Cognitive, affective, and social outcomes. *Journal of Educational Computing Research, 24*(2), 99-117.

Chapter XI

Student Motivation in International Collaboration:
To Participate or Not to Participate?

Janice Whatley, University of Salford, UK

Elena Zaitseva, Liverpool John Moores University, UK

Danuta Zakrzewska, Technical University of Lodz, Poland

Abstract

This chapter introduces peer reviewing as a form of collaborative online learning, which can be used in higher education. Peer reviewing encourages students to engage in reflective critical evaluation of each other's work through participation in online discussion with their peers, who may be located anywhere in the world. The advantages of such an activity for students are described, using the experiences from two cases. The chapter highlights the impact that student and tutor motivation has on the successful participation of students in online peer reviewing activities, as well as perceived benefits for students, including acquiring various skills, and development of intercultural awareness. There is a discussion of potential difficulties, such as timing and different expectations, along with challenges for tutors in designing an online peer reviewing activity, culminating in a template that can be used as an aid for tutors to use when planning an online peer reviewing activity.

Introduction

One of the main tasks of the modern education system is to prepare learners for participation in an information society where knowledge is the most critical resource for social and economic development, and where networking for knowledge sharing is an emerging skill. Effective communication skills, an ability to negotiate existing and create new knowledge, to critically evaluate information resources or a product, are among the transferable skills higher education aims to develop in students. Communication technologies based on the Internet give learners the opportunity to "talk" to their peers from different countries, and develop such skills. In this chapter, we investigate the pedagogical benefits afforded by a form of online collaborative learning, called peer reviewing, and we show, from our experience, some of the benefits students in higher education derive from such an activity. We also look at student and tutor motivation, and the challenge posed by overcoming difficulties of involving students in an international collaborative activity.

An important part of learning is reflecting on one's learning of a concept, skill, or a topic, by discussion with one another. Learning together is a model used in higher education to encourage reflection on learning, whether by carrying out joint projects or by helping each other to understand learning material. Stahl (2002) notes that questioning each other, engaging in discussion, and synthesis of findings encourages learners in further questioning, development of hypotheses, and insights into the topic, which results in deeper learning. Dialogue between learners can elicit multiple perspectives and provoke cognitive conflict, encouraging development of critical skills and the ability for professional discussion, objectivity, and discursive reflection (Falchikov, 2001). Collaborative learning is working together in a joint intellectual effort in order to achieve learning outcomes, which may be enhanced when the learning partners bring different perspectives to a problem or topic (Alavi, 1994).

Collaborative activities may include discussing a research paper, joint authoring of a piece of work, practicing communication in a foreign language, giving advice and help, or reviewing products, such as projects or artifacts made by students during their courses. In addition to the subject-related knowledge and skills, through participating in the collaborative activities, students develop a range of generic/transferable skills, such as analytical and team working skills, and communication and organizational skills (Kanuka & Anderson, 1998; Nachmias, Mioduser, Oren, & Ram, 2000). In particular, a learning activity based around reviewing products encourages reflection and criticism, as reviewers need to understand and use the product in order to give meaningful criticism (Gibbs, 2002). A number of different terms exist for collaborative reviewing activities. Peer review and peer evaluation are concerned with giving feedback to the authors to promote deeper learning (e.g., Quinn, 1997). Falchikov (2001) gave the term "peer feedback" to an activity where students engage in reflective criticism of the work or performance of other students, using previously identified criteria, and supply feedback for them. A further term, "peer assessment," is used where reviewing students also give a grade or mark for the products they are reviewing (Ford, 1997). This chapter is concerned with peer review, which may or may not include assessment.

Activities—such as joint authoring of an essay, critiquing of a research document or engaging in discussion of a given topic to group projects—may be regarded as *symmetrical* activities, because both sets of students are working on the same task, and producing the same outputs. Peer reviewing or evaluating is a different type of online collaborative activity, where one set of students present their work for the other set of students to give feedback, using discussion to elaborate and explain any comments made. This type of activity may be regarded as an *asymmetrical* activity, because the two sets of students engage in different types of learning and produce different outputs. Many of these activities may also be performed through online collaboration, supported by tools available on the Internet, such as a discussion forum or chat, which can enable the exchange of ideas, knowledge and experience between students.

The cases presented in this chapter were activities organised within the Collaboration Across Borders (CAB) Project. This was a project funded under the Socrates-Minerva programme to promote European cooperation in the field of open and distance learning, and information and communication technologies in education. The project team was a partnership between higher education institutions from the United Kingdom, Poland, the Netherlands, Spain, and Germany. The goal of the project was to establish a network for online collaboration between staff and students from different countries, with emphasis on critical evaluation and reflection. Students' collaborative activities, mainly comprising peer review activities, were organised on the CAB portal, known as CABWEB (http://www.cabweb.net). These asymmetrical activities involved students in using an online discussion forum to review IT (Information Technology) types of products, such as Web sites, multimedia presentations, or programming projects.

The remainder of the chapter outlines some of the theories underpinning the use of online peer review for learning, followed by a discussion of some of the findings from the activities we organised for peer review of IT products. We suggest that our findings are likely to be applicable to other subject disciplines as well. We also introduce a framework for designing a collaborative peer review activity to help with setting up an international collaboration. These we think are critical for an understanding of the processes involved in changing the teaching and learning culture towards advanced knowledge creation practices through online collaboration.

International Collaborative Activities Based on Peer Review

Peer review or evaluation, as a form of collaboration, is recognised as a very important professional duty of future specialists, and aimed at "…accepting and providing objective, critical, documented review of the work of others" (Kern, 2003). Pedagogic benefits of this form of collaboration include increased student interaction with each other and with the learning materials, providing interesting discussion points and gaining useful information from others. However, Moreira and Da Silva (2003) noted that evaluators and those whose work is evaluated are likely to have different perspectives on the collaborative activity, depending upon their designated task, hence the experiences and benefits each can gain from engaging in the activity may be different.

Evaluation of information systems is an important workplace skill for students studying any subject, either for choosing between different products to select the one that best fits system requirements, or as a part of the development of a product, by giving feedback to improve the design (Bostock, 2002). In the higher education setting, formative feedback can inform the design, or summative feedback may be used to assign a grade or mark to a piece of work or to facilitate a reflection on learning outcomes. Giving feedback to peers as a part of learning may perform either or both of these functions:

- The author receives help to improve the product.
- The evaluators have practice in giving considered and justified feedback, using their own or specified criteria.

Many researchers have talked about the benefits of peer assessment activities, both face-to-face and online (Brown & Dove, 1991; Gatfield, 1999; Purchase, 2000), and peer review and assessment activities have been widely used in teacher education (Sluijsmans, Brand-Gruwel, van Merriënboer, & Bastiaens, 2003). Peer assessment is said to be effective in developing students' critical thinking, communication, and collaborative skills (McLaughlin & Simpson, 2004). Purchase highlighted that such activities can be used to mirror the professional environment in which students will ultimately work, and encourage cooperative, rather than competitive, learning (Purchase, 2000). Pond and Ul-Haq (1997) stated that students who participated in peer assessment activities had increased ownership of the learning process, and they regarded the exercise as effective for learning and group work, and overall considered it to be useful. Brown and Dove (1991) suggest that the main benefits from peer assessment or review are increased student motivation, autonomous learning, and the development of transferable skills.

When peer review is conducted online, using collaboration tools to support the activity, a number of other advantages arise, such as broadening the range of potential evaluators, or exchanging and comparing knowledge, ideas, or experiences with students representing different cultures (Swigger, Brazile, Monticino, & Alpaslan, 2004). Also, in this kind of activity, as well as development of critical reflection skills, students can improve their use of a foreign language.

In addition to benefits for students from the immediate collaborative activity, the diversity of universities' participants across Europe and beyond provides great potential for fruitful collaboration based upon different interests, missions, and strengths. Being involved in a multidimensional dialogue enhances undergraduates' confidence in intercultural communication (Zaitseva, Shaylor,

& Bell, 2004), their ability to work in international distributed (online) teams, and, as a result, competitiveness on the international job market (Silliman, Boukari, & Crane, 2006). From a tutors' perspective, negotiating the curriculum, making academic standards explicit, and reflecting collaboratively on the experiences of students contributes to the internationalisation of higher education. At the same time, adopting the most successful approaches and methods from colleagues abroad, is another important dimension of the internationalisation process (Whatley & Shaylor, 2005).

In Europe, internationalisation is closely linked to the Bologna declaration process, a series of reforms aimed at creating an open European higher education area, by making academic degree standards and quality assurance standards more comparable and compatible throughout Europe. These reforms are also aimed at creating a higher education system that is highly competitive and attractive for European citizens and for citizens and scholars from other continents, while removing the barriers to student mobility (Europeunit, 2006).

Where students meet face-to-face (based on campus), peer review activities are relatively simple to organise, with students sometimes able to bring to the activity complementary knowledge in order to help peers to improve their work. There are drawbacks with face-to-face peer review, because as peers are also friends, they may not apply a critical eye to their review; also, there may not be sufficient breadth of knowledge to review a product from alternative perspectives. Similarly, even well-planned peer assessment activities may fail in the face-to-face situation for such reasons as uneasiness of marking friends' work or through taking unfair advantage through using biased marking. Brown and Knight (1994) distinguished four kinds of biased marking that may be observed during peer assessment:

- **Friendship marking:** Giving an inflated mark to a friends' work.

- **Collusion marking:** All the group members give the same marks, which results in lack of differentiation within groups.

- **Decibel marking:** Students who are popular or have a strong personality dominate groups and get the highest marks.

- **Parasite marking:** Students who fail to contribute benefit from an identical mark being given to the whole group.

To overcome some of the drawbacks of face-to-face peer reviewing and peer assessment, our solution was to recruit peers who are not co-located for the activity, and support the review process with online asynchronous discussion tools. When peers do not know each other, there will be less of a tendency for friendship, collusion, or decibel marking, and peers, who are not friends, are less likely to be embarrassed when giving a critical review of the product. Students from other institutions or other countries are also more likely to have an alternative knowledge base, which can be expressed as a different perspective on the review of the product. The development of the Internet has made the possibility of participating in online review activities with unknown peers from other universities, or even other countries, much easier. Peer review using computer mediated communication (CMC) tools provided on the Internet appears to be easier to access, and possibly more impartial, because in "meeting" online, where peers do not see and do not necessarily know each other, it is easier to be objective than when meeting in a face-to-face situation (Curran, 2002). There are, however, other drawbacks, which might not be present in face-to-face peer reviewing, such as distrust of peers because nonverbal cues are not visible, there is limited opportunity to get to know one's peers, a lack of motivation to participate or the possibility to ignore online messages if the feedback is not what the receiver expects. The necessity to give a grade as part of the peer assessment activity means that students may not concentrate on giving objective feedback for fear of upsetting their peers.

Pedagogical Arrangements for Peer Review Activities

A collaborative peer review activity may or may not be an integral part of the teaching of a subject. It depends upon the planned learning outcomes, the importance of the activity to the teaching of the topic, and the logistics of planning the activity into the teaching schedule. Further, the extent of the students' involvement in the learning process, and their commitment to different aspects of the task, could be different (Ogata & Yano, 1999). We have identified several pedagogical arrangements for online peer review:

- An activity planned well ahead, as an integral part of the learning for a module. For example, one set of students prepare a Web site, a computer program or a report, and the tutor finds another set of students to review these products, and the activity forms a part of the reviewing students' learning as well.

- A planned, but additional activity, not assessed, but providing for extra practice in a subject. For example, students may benefit from practice in a language, so enter into conversation with students from another country, who can talk about any topic related or not to their study.

- Spontaneous activities, not planned into the module, but arising from tutor motivation to provide an online experience for students. For example, we found that some tutors set up an area for discussion on an ad hoc basis, and student groups were enrolled at short notice to give peer review.

- Open activities, initiated by students themselves. For example, we observed students who had enrolled on CABWEB, using it voluntarily to engage in discussion with other students and give feedback.

Any combination of these different arrangements could take place in the framework of a single peer reviewing activity. The first two types of arrange-

Figure 1. Pedagogical framework, showing a common student activity within different organisational contexts (Whatley & Bell, 2003)

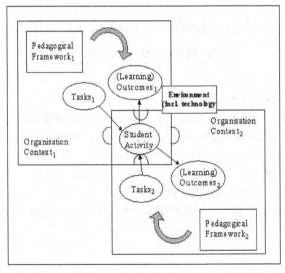

ments, together with students' satisfaction and general learning outcomes. are to be discussed in the following sections.

This diagram (Figure 1) shows that a shared student activity can take place within different organisational contexts, where the pedagogical framework for learning may be different for each of the learning organisations. Amongst a variety of tasks and learning outcomes prescribed for each set of students on their individual modules, a single student activity can be set up to share between the collaborating students, which fits between the organisations, a bit like a piece of a jigsaw puzzle.

Organising Peer Review Activities

For any tutor who would like to include an online collaborative activity, such as peer review, into the course or module activities, the starting point should be that the activity adds some value to the learning on the module. The added value might perhaps be encouraging reflection in a particular aspect of the students' learning (Brockbank & McGill, 1998), or developing skill in evaluation (Bostock, 2002). The content of any taught module will vary between different institutions, according to the stated learning outcomes, and how they build up towards the aims of the programme of study. It is often easier to identify an asymmetric collaborative activity, where the tasks and outcomes may be different for each set of the collaborating students, than to design identical tasks and outcomes for all participants.

Having identified a learning activity that might be enabled by collaborating with other students, the duration and timing for the activity is crucial for its success. Teaching terms and scheduling of modules within them varies between institutions, especially in different countries. It is easier to plan a collaborative activity of short duration to fit into a module, than a collaboration to occupy the whole module. However, there are still problems with ensuring that the activity fits into the whole module, at the most appropriate time to benefit the students.

Programmes of study in different institutions may include similar teaching modules, which would make eminently suitable partnerships, as there would be mutual benefits from the collaborative activity (Whatley & Bell, 2003). In the absence of a similar module, there may be complementary modules of teaching. It may not be necessary for both sets of students to be studying at the same level (i.e., first, second, final year of study, or post-graduate) or studying the same module, as skills gained in one module may be useful for reviewing the work of students studying on a different module at a higher or lower level (Ligorio, Talamo, & Pontecorvo, 2005). However, the background and capabilities of the students must be known and recognised as appropriate for the proposed activity.

The activity may need to be supported by practical or tutorial sessions—for example, giving advice to students on how to critically review a piece of work. It is possible that a session when students are timetabled to use the computer suite is the best time for them to commence the work involved in the collaborative activity. Training or help to get started may also need to be given for using the discussion forum, to the extent of ensuring students have registered to use the discussion tool.

The tutors must agree how long the activity might take, allowing for socialising, time to read essential material, then preparing for the activity and engaging in a discussion. Sometimes one or two weeks may be sufficient, other activities may require four to six weeks, depending upon the complexity and estimated length of time for the discussion to reach conclusions. The arrangement of students participating in the activity can vary from two individuals work-ing together online to any combination of teams working together, and our example cases show two variations in the arrangements.

Tutors need to consider whether the activity is to be assessed in itself, or a product of the activity will be assessed. Our experience suggests that students will only actively participate if they can see an advantage, or are highly mo-tivated. Motivation can take several forms, but nothing motivates more than receiving a grade for an activity. One approach is for the tutor to grade either the actual discussion process, or an output from the peer reviewing process. An alternative is to ask the peer reviewers to provide a graded assessment of the work they are reviewing; the reviewers could also be assessed on the quality of the review they provide for their peers, which might encourage a more considered review (Ko & Rossen, 2001). There could also be models without assessment, in which case a tutor could choose a flexible approach to the learning outcomes—for example, delaying the learning outcomes by running a non-assessed collaboration, and afterwards asking the students to reflect upon their learning. If grading is to form a part of the peer review activity, the main factors that determine the success in achieving the required learning outcomes is how the whole process is set up and managed (Wheater, Langan, & Dunleavy, 2005). In particular, when employing peer assessment, students should not only understand what criteria their peers are assessing, but also the weighting of those criteria, and how the criteria relate to the learning outcomes for the activity (Pond & Ul-Haq, 1997).

As computer mediated communication becomes a recognised means of providing learning experiences, the number of possible ways in which the various tools can be implemented for learning is increasing. Of particular use for online asynchronous learning are discussion forums, which are suitable for peer review learning activities, because asynchronous communication provides time between elements of discourse for students to prepare their postings in a thoughtful way. Managing and moderating a large number of discussions between students can be time consuming for the tutors involved, providing encouraging comments within the discussion, and at the same time ensuring that a minority of participants does not abuse the opportunity. The discussion could be completely unmoderated, and possibly open to abuse, could be moderated by the tutor, who keeps a close eye on the content of messages posted, or moderated by the students themselves, in which case the discussion is kept private from the tutors.

Many online discussion forums are available, both freely and at a price. A discussion forum is also usually provided within the virtual learning environments (VLE) commonly provided by institutions for their students. The downside of the forums provided by the institution is that students not enrolled at the institution cannot usually access the tool. If the collaborative activity is to involve students from other institutions or countries, then a neutral discussion place is needed, which can be accessed by everybody involved in the discussion. Any one of the freely available discussion forums may be suitable, and can be set up by the individual tutors involved. What CABWEB offers is a neutral space already set up for collaborative activities, such as peer review, which speeds up the process of designing the activity.

Intercultural Communication Issues

Information and communication technologies allow students from different countries to take part in distributed collaborative activities. Because the scale of intercultural educational communication is growing rapidly, there is a recognised need to anticipate cultural differences in this type of multicultural learning environment. As Collis suggests, electronic communication across cultures in an educational context could present challenges due to:

- Different recognition of the status of student-student communication compared to instructor-student communication in different cultures.

- The extent of adoption of the social-participative model (learning through communicative interaction with others) in a particular national and institutional culture, and also in a discipline-related context.

- Cultural differences in terms of the network and support infrastructure available to groups of learners and also in the competence and comfort levels they have with using technology.

- Differences in perception of appropriate allocation of responsibilities between students and instructors, in appropriate teaching styles and forms of student behaviour.

- Different responses to the design and layout of the user interface between cultural groups (Collis, 1999).

Chase highlighted that despite the benefits of asynchronous text-based communication technologies, they are lacking the important elements of face-to-face communication, such as a parallel visual channel, context perception, dynamic real-time repair mechanisms, eye contact, gestures information, and, in general, the flexibility we normally expect to obtain or to emerge between conversational partners, especially in intercultural context (Chase, Macfadyen, Reeder, & Roche, 2002). These could contribute to a higher level of anxiety on the part of participants from multicultural teams, as they struggle to interpret a different language, because they are unable to rely on gestures such as nodding approval of correct language usage.

CAB research has demonstrated that a major barrier to communication, as perceived by participants of international collaborative activities, is the requirement for communication to be carried out in a language other than the particpants' mother tongue (Zaitseva et al, 2004). When students are working with peers from a different country, there may not be an obvious common language for communication, in which case a common language will need to be agreed. Sometimes the language may be significant in designing the activity, such as a requirement for students to practice their language skills whilst providing a review for the other students.

Discussion conducted in a second or a foreign language can make peer review more difficult, especially for students with lower levels of language fluency. Native speakers can experience feelings of impatience and frustration when communicating with non-native speakers of a language, whether face-to-face or online (Giles & Robinson, 1990; Wiseman & Koester, 1993; Zaitseva et al, 2004).

There is reported evidence that various factors lead to miscommunication, including culturally contingent differences in conversational style, emotional and appraisal patterns, and use of culture and language specific features for indexing of speaker attitude (Belz, 2003; Chase et al., 2002; Ware, 2005; Zaitseva et al, 2004). Kim and Bonk (2002) discussed differences in social interaction behaviour across cultures, stating that differences in communication styles influenced the students' collaborative behaviour. Some common challenges in intercultural discussion are the same in the traditional face-to-face setting as in a computer-mediated environment. As Spencer-Rodgers and McGovern (2002) stated, intercultural communication barriers arise from group differences in cognition (e.g., fundamental epistemologies, values, norms), effect (e.g., types and levels of emotional expressiveness), and patterns of behaviour (e.g., language, communication styles).

Whilst researchers accept that ethnic, linguistic, communication and other differences are deeply rooted in every educational culture, in order to achieve successful intercultural understanding in an educational context, students must be prepared for this complex learning environment in order to be able to deal with the challenges of language barriers, unfamiliar practices, and cultural variations.

The importance of negotiating different, culturally contingent understanding of the purpose of collaboration was highlighted by Belz and Müller-Hartmann (2003), and Kramsch and Thorne (2002). For example, the following questions from the "multiple cultural model" developed by McLoughlin and Oliver could be a part of collaborative "inquiry" prior to the activity:

- What cognitive and communication styles characterise the target group?
- How does the cultural background of these students influence their use and view of time?
- How do students perceive the role of the teacher in this activity?
- What rewards and forms of feedback will be most motivating for these students? (McLoughlin & Oliver, 1999).

This could be accomplished through a pre-collaboration student socialising discussion and tutors' discussion (it would also help students to master the discussion tool or virtual learning environment if it is new to them). Ware (2005) suggested "… instead of making and acting on assumptions about communication norms, students need to openly discuss their expectations of language use, message length, and response time."

According to Hofstede (1991), cultural dimensions can be used to explain similarities and differences in communication patterns. The set of dimensions is a good background for building a user cultural profile (Wojciechowski & Zakrzewska, 2006). Ware (2005) also advised tutors to involve students in joint analysis of published episodes of successful and unsuccessful intercultural communication before the exchange begins, to open discussions about "missed" communication, and help deflect potential tensions in their own communication.

Online participants of collaboration should be made aware of different language tools (translators, dictionaries, etc.) and allowed more time to process the language in online activities, which may alleviate problems with misunderstandings (Beauvois, 1998; Warschauer, 1996). In planning collaboration, consideration should be given that there might be some participants with a high level of anxiety in their limited language proficiency, and ways to reduce their anxiety level and encourage their participation need to be considered (Kim & Bonk, 2002). For example, in one of the CAB collaborations a special evaluation template was designed for students with limited language skills.

In the preceding sections, we have ascertained the benefits of online peer review as a learning activity, and explained some of the potential difficulties. In the next section, two cases of using a peer review collaborative activity between students from different countries are described, the occurrence of some difficulties is acknowledged, leading to a framework to identify possible problems at the design stage of a collaborative activity.

Examining Cases of Activities

In order to demonstrate how different pedagogic arrangements could influence students' motivation and have an impact on their learning outcomes, we now offer detailed case studies based upon two of our CAB peer reviewing activities. In both activities, students were reviewing their overseas peers' projects, they did not give an assessment of their counterparts' work in the form of a grade, but had a chance to give feedback from their evaluation through their comments and provide advice or give suggestions. Depending on the pedagogical arrangements taking place, tutors gave a grade (or % of a final mark) for the activity, based upon the discussion itself or based upon outcomes of the activity, or it was a non-assessed activity. Although these collaborations were *asymmetrical*, with expected (planned) outcomes for each of the two sets of students being different, it was found that some benefits were common to both sets of students.

Case 1. Salford-Murcia-Lodz Collaboration

The first case study took place between April and May 2004, and was a peer review of prototypes of Web sites for teaching a topic, involving students from three universities: University of Salford (UK), Technical University of Lodz (Poland), and University of Murcia (Spain). Final year UK under-graduate students (studying Information Systems) worked in small groups to develop prototypes of teaching packages for distance learning. The students were able to choose any subject, suitable for adult or children learning and produce a prototype that demonstrated the main ideas of their proposed teaching package. Pedagogically-grounded learning activities, Web design issues, and human computer interaction (HCI) issues were important in producing the prototypes, so reviewers were asked to consider these issues when evaluating the prototypes.

Since the teaching package prototypes were designed for online use, it was felt that reviewers should act as "remote" potential users, and online discussion throughout the process would give the students an experience of working online. Thus, activity for the UK students was planned well in advance and they were relying on their tutor to find a group of online peers to take part in the review process.

The counterpart students who joined the collaboration had particular interests: to see how relevant learning theories are implemented into online packages (educational psychology students from Spain), and to give feedback on aspects of HCI and Web site implementation (computer science students from Poland). Both reviewing groups were also invited to offer advice on design aesthetics, navigation, clarity of the content and usability. Expected benefits for the reviewers were not only an opportunity to apply their own learning to a real world evaluation activity, but also practicing writing and discussion in English language. Both sets of reviewers were working in small groups of two or three students, matching up with the small groups of authoring students to form an arrangement of small groups collaborating with small groups. From an organisational point of view, involvement of the evaluators was rather short notice, so success relied on the enthusiasm of their tutors to encourage their students to participate, foreseeing the possible benefits from the activity.

The prototypes were made available online, and collaboration took place over a period of six weeks on a CAB discussion forum. UK students were assessed by their tutors on a written report on the modifications to their learning packages that they would recommend based on the results of discussion. Students providing the evaluation were not formally assessed in this activity.

Case 2. Lodz-Stuttgart Collaboration

The second case study is based on a collaborative activity that took place in June 2004, between students from Technical University of Lodz (Poland) and Hochschule der Medien, Stuttgart (Germany). As part of their multimedia learning, Polish students working in small groups prepared computer animations (short films on different topics) in 3D Studio Max software.

Reviewers, studying multimedia design, were interested in looking at their peers' projects from the design and HCI perspective, they were asked to work in small groups to provide feedback and initiate discussion to elaborate on any comments and suggestions given. In order to help with the structuring of the feedback, the Polish students were guided towards reviewing the following aspects of their work:

- Design of the multimedia product.
- Meeting the users' needs/quality of information.
- Navigation/presentation.
- Technical problems.

Practicing meaningful discussion in English was an additional learning task for both groups, as English was the second language for both set of students. Because of the large file size of the resulting presentations, 24 projects were recorded on CDs and sent by post to the reviewers in Germany. Although this activity was well planned in advance for both sets of participants, assessment only took place in the Polish case; the tutor gave students who took part in the collaboration additional grades; participation of the German students was not assessed. The activity took place over three weeks in the summer, close to the end of the teaching semester. Since the 3D projects were already completed and had been assessed by a tutor, there was no timing pressure on the Polish students in this activity, and the German students were also relatively free around this time, having completed most of their coursework.

Analysis of Student Motivation and Successes

The two cases described have a lot of similarities, but they have distinct differences in organisation, assessment, language abilities of students, and other aspects having impact on students' satisfaction. At the end of each collaborative activity, participants were asked to complete an online questionnaire to give their feedback. A number of focus groups were also arranged to gain more in depth opinions on peer review activities, and transcripts of some discussion forums were analysed. In this section, we present findings from these cases and other peer review activities under the following headings:

- Overall satisfaction and benefits.
- Organisational issues and timing issues.
- Language difficulties.
- Motivation and students' wish to participate again.

As a result of our research, we have developed a template (Appendix A) to help tutors to design a peer review activity, which guides the user through a series of the issues we have identified as important to consider in the design process.

Overall Satisfaction and Benefits

The level of participants' satisfaction was different in each case (see Tables 1 and 2), but we were able to conclude that the majority of students thought that the peer review activity was useful for them, and they derived some benefit from it, though in different ways. Students valued the critical views of outsiders, and realised that it was an opportunity to make their studies more interesting. As a result, they felt that they had developed a variety of skills, including reflective, analytical skills, communication and language skills, as well as having a chance to improve their subject knowledge. The reviewing students in Case 1 clearly felt that they had benefited from the experience (Figure 2). Only the results from the reviewing institutions are given in Figure 2, because the students from the authoring institution did not complete the online questionnaire. The reviewed students instead participated in a focus group, from which we ascertained that only a quarter of the students thought that the collaborative activity was beneficial to them, a finding that is discussed in the next section.

In contrast, the findings from Case 2 (Figure 3) indicate that both reviewing and reviewed students derived considerable benefit from the activity. Some tutors confirmed this; one of whom, for example, commented:

My observation is that both sides benefited quite a lot from this collaboration...

Students reported that they thought the international activity encouraged a professional attitude, and appreciated the opinions of other students, who may have more experience in a particular area. In many discussion threads, there was a good exchange of ideas, generated from an alternative perspec-

Figure 2. Case 1 (Salford-Murcia-Lodz) Collaboration benefit (reviewing institutions)

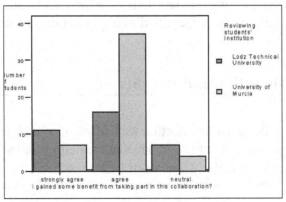

tive, which often prompted action to complete the work. Evaluating other students' work was also perceived as a good exercise in reflection on their own knowledge and experience. For example, over 50% of the Polish students wanted to extend the collaboration into other topics.

Collaboration was regarded as an opportunity to get to know other students from different cultures and different countries. For example, about 90% of the Polish students from the Case 2 activity saw it as valuable to have contact with students from other faculties or from other universities. Their answers suggested that they would prefer to be assessed by higher level colleagues who might be more experienced, or they themselves would prefer to assess younger colleagues. For the majority of students, this is the opportunity to learn about something new, to learn about being objective and about justifying their feedback. One tutor said:

It was a very interesting evaluation. Students were well prepared for their role of reviewing or being reviewed. They established good contacts with students from Germany and wrote not only on the forum but also by the e-mails. Students form both countries exchanged much information not connecting with the projects, they made friends.

Figure 3. Case 2 (Stuttgart-Lodz) Collaboration benefit (reviewing and reviewed institutions)

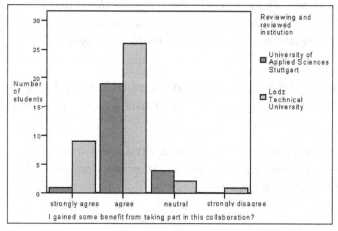

Feedback from both students and tutors on these two activities suggests that an asymmetrical peer review activity can give benefits to both reviewed and reviewing participants.

Organising and Timing Issues

Finding a counterpart set of students (compatible in terms of availability and skills) poses difficulties; tutors meet each other as they network, but even within one country there are limited means of making contact with like-minded tutors. There must be a willingness to help other tutors and their students for this type of activity to be successful.

While no organisational and timing related difficulties were reported in Case 2, the collaboration was more complicated in Case 1, because there were two sets of students carrying out the reviewing, rather than just one, which made the peer review activity more difficult to organise and manage. As described in Case 1, the reviewed students were dependent on the contribution of their reviewers, since they had to complete their final project reports using results from the discussion. The reviewing students did not feel the same pressure and their first postings were perceived by the reviewed students to be rather late and did not contain a level of detail these students anticipated. They had to ask for more clarification, using prompts and guidance:

Could you give us some more detailed feedback about what needs improving. Think about it from the point of view of the user, a purchaser of the system or teacher/tutor using it for learning. Should the website be targeted at a specific age group? What sort of features need adding? Should it be designed for use at school or at home? Please give as many suggestions as you can. The more the better, as long as they're realistic. Regards, Team C.

Later on, the Polish students were able to provide a good level of technical feedback, which in many cases was very useful as an evaluation:

... OK, all of links (besides Storyboard & Prototype) are opening *.doc page, WHY? I don't understand sense of this. Diagram would seen better in Scalable Vector Graphic format (svg)...

...I think that Flash objects are useless in this project, you can use simple java scripts to enlarge those icons on the bottom of the screen.

In addition, since the Salford projects were just prototypes, many authors felt that such levels of detail were not really necessary at this stage, emphasising the importance of considering the students' expectations for the peer review activity.

Due to the limited access of the Spanish students to the computer lab, they were only able to post messages once a week, and this considerably slowed down the interaction between authors and reviewers. This did put the authoring students into a situation where they were unable to use the results of the review in their final reports, or used them in a very limited way. Whilst the majority of the reviewing students enjoyed the experience as reviewers and rated it as beneficial, the reviewed students, who participated in a focus group, admitted that they had a rather stressful experience, which did not contribute to their learning.

Explicit and implicit assumptions about "time" and "punctuality" emerge, and different cultural attitudes towards these become apparent from the ways in which students and their tutors account (or not) for lateness in some of their responses. The short duration of a peer review activity requires the tutors to agree the timing and duration of the activity so that it fits into other teaching and assessment schedules.

Expectations as to the level of detail for feedback and the form it will take should be agreed before the activity, by preparing criteria for evaluation or assessment, and ensuring that the reviewing students know what is expected of them, as well as ensuring the reviewed students know what to expect from their peer reviewers.

Language Difficulties

Both collaborative activities were seen as a good chance for developing language skills for non-native speakers of English and this motivated many students to participate actively. Thus, about 87% percent of the Polish students indicated that this international collaboration was supportive of English language learning. At the same time, partly because of the language barriers, almost 80% of the Polish students said they would prefer to have such an activity in their native language. This is because the language skills of the participants had an impact on the time students needed to prepare their messages before posting, and their understanding of the meaning of messages posted. The reviewed students from Case 1, having this activity incorporated in their module, were expecting in-depth feedback from reviewers, both from the relevance of the pedagogy applied and from a technical or implementation perspective, but reported that the level of language skills of their peers, especially in the case of the Spanish students, was rather low for detailed reviewing. An example of the criticism of their peers' language skills from some native speakers is:

... The foreign students did not possess the language skills required to understand what our development was about.

Another problem that appeared whilst communicating in online international discussions is connected with cultural differences. In planning peer review activities, different communication styles should be taken into account and different patterns of behaviour that are likely to emerge. For example, one survey of Polish students showed that they liked taking part in discussions and forums, but they preferred working individually and regard group work as difficult to perform online.

Students may have problems not only in writing their opinions, but also with understanding their foreign peers' written work. For example, in the survey among Polish students participating in online activities, only 27% of the students had problems with writing in English, but 48% found it difficult to understand their peers from abroad. They suggested that participants of online activities should be made aware of different communication styles across cultures, which could be achieved by placing examples of different communication styles, as part of an online help system, on the Web pages. More than 66% of the students who answered the online survey also used "emoticons" as support for expressing their opinions. As other supportive elements they mentioned pictures, sounds, photos, links, or attachments that may be utilised during online collaboration.

When organizing the collaboration, it would be good to encourage the use of different language tools like dictionaries or translators, which are available online, because more than 74% of the Polish students from both cases used external help for writing and reading messages from their foreign peers. Online language tools were commonly used during both activities (more than 77% used online dictionaries and almost 39% of participants used translators). However, some students still employed conventional resources like printed dictionaries or a friend's help. There follows an example of using language support, from an English-speaking student, who used online translation software to help some Spanish students, who complained about difficulties they experienced with understanding some English terminology:

Hello students of Murcia University,

I am sorry about the complicated language; I hope this has not been too much of a problem. Please let us know if you have any specific comments about the website which might help us for future changes? We have tried to make the website look as professional as possible, please leave any comments. Your English is far better than my Spanish! Traducido usando los pescados de Babel - http://babelfish.altavista.com/babelfish/tr -

Hola estudiantes de la universidad de Murcia,

Estoy apesadumbrado sobre la lengua complicada, yo espero que ŭste no ha sido demasiado de un problema. . ☺ Grazias.

P.S. Apesadumbrado para ninguna errores de la traducciyn, no soy muy bueno con espacol ☺.

The experience of using different languages and recognising different cultural styles was appreciated by both reviewing and reviewed students. Providing access to online translators can make the discussion easier for all parties involved, but students should be made aware of possible differences in expectations of levels of competency in the chosen language for discourse before the collaborative activity starts.

Motivation Issues from Both Cases

Motivation of tutors, and intended learning outcomes in both cases had an impact on students' attitude to the collaborative activity. The level of involvement of tutors in helping, and moderating the discussion can directly affect the level of motivation in the students. We also found that, when the outcome from the activity was assessed, students who took part in the collaboration tended to receive higher grades for the module. We also asked whether the students would be willing to participate in such an activity again in the future. Engagement without assessment was found to affect the students' participation in terms of intensity of postings and their content, but generally these students were able to recognise the potential benefits of such activities, derived many benefits and said that they were inclined to participate again in a similar activity (Figures 4 and 5). On the other hand, we found from the focus groups, that highly motivated students from Case 1, found themselves in a situation where they had to wait for their reviewers to post messages, which were not always complete enough to work from, so their motivation dropped, through frustration, over the period of the activity, and these students were not as keen to participate again in a similar activity.

One interesting finding was that the Polish students wanted to be formally assessed (about 87.5%), rather than being the subjects of informal evaluation in such activities. The idea of assessment is preparation for their future work, where they will have to prepare their projects for different types of users and probably will be assessed by others, or they will have to assess others' projects.

Figure 4. Case 1 (Salford-Murcia-Lodz). Wish to participate in the future (reviewing students)

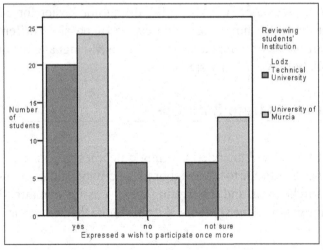

Figure 5. Case 2 (Stuttgart-Lodz). Wish to participate in the future

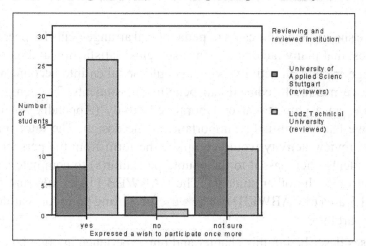

The tutors' involvement during the period of the discussion can vary, from a "hands off" approach, leaving the students to moderate their own discussion if necessary, to an active discussant approach. In Case 1, the tutor of the reviewed students regarded the discussion space as private to the students, and only contributed messages to remind and encourage the students to be active in the discussion. In Case 2, activities took place spontaneously on the discussion forum and by e-mails, without any prompting from either tutor.

Further survey results indicated that this sort of collaborative activity was well suited to IT related work, such as Web pages, programming projects or graphics, but also over half of the students thought that this sort of collaborative activity could be useful in other subjects beyond their immediate curriculum.

The opportunity to learn how to give comments and to justify their opinions was seen as an important preparation for the world of work, giving a sense that assessment does not necessarily mean giving a grade.

Conclusion and Recommendation

We have shown using our cases of pedagogical arrangements for peer review activities, that many factors influence students' satisfaction and motivation to engage in such an activity, which should be taken into account in order to achieve maximum educational benefits for students. The template for designing an asymmetrical collaborative activity (Appendix A) lists the issues we have identified as important for the design. The tutor initiating the peer review activity would complete the form from the perspective of their students, then pass it to the counterpart tutor(s) to complete from the perspective of the other students. The CABWEB Finder's Forum (within the HELP area of CABWEB) can be a useful starting point for searching for counterpart tutors.

The cases described in this chapter and our experience in organizing many online peer review activities, show that achieving success depends on careful design as well as monitoring of all the processes involved in the collaboration. In particular, attention should be paid to the following elements:

- The activity should clearly add some value, like developing skills or encouraging reflection. Students should be aware of the purpose of the peer review activity, and the desired learning outcomes for all participating students, so the mutual benefits of taking part in the activity need to be made known to all the participants. It is preferable to put the focus on reviewing to help, rather than assessing for grades.

- The background and capabilities of the students must be known and recognised, so that there is a reasonable match between the subject matter and the type of evaluation. It is important to know the level of language fluency of the participants in advance, so that, students with limited language proficiency are encouraged and supported by language tools or by other means.

- Cultural differences should be taken into consideration; these may be manifested by differences in communication styles and behaviour. Pre-collaboration or other socialising discussions may help in overcoming difficulties in skill levels and differences in cultural perspectives.

- Attention should be paid to organising the activity, particularly the duration of the activity and timing the discussion so that it fits into the teaching timetable of all the parties involved. Students should be aware of different expectations of other participants, and open discussion between tutors and students may help in adjusting to language use, message length or even expected response times.

- Suitability of the chosen tools for the task cannot be disregarded. It may be useful to support the activity by practical or tutorial sessions in order to familiarise students with the software tool they will be using for the activity. Tutors may be able to customise the interface of the chosen VLE, in accordance with their students' abilities and experience.

Tutors should be prepared that opportunity for personal reflection facilitated by communicating across cultures may or may not have an immediate impact during the actual time of the course (Kramsch, 1993; O'Dowd, 2003). There may also be some potential for arranging peer review activities for the same sets of students in subsequent years, in order to develop skills further.

Benefits of peer review activities include bringing an outside view of the students' work, and an opportunity to practice reviewing skills and language skills. We have also seen learning outcomes, such as communication skills, experience of intercultural understanding, and growing confidence in communication in a foreign or second language. These skills are increasingly important to students in the digital age, in preparation for a future of online working. In our experience, cooperation between institutions, particularly from different countries, offers a means to broaden the teaching and learning experience, for tutors as well as students. Activities we have arranged so far have been mainly in the Information Technology domain, but clearly other disciplines can be successfully integrated into these activities as well, and activities wholly within other disciplines are possible, so although setting up online collaborative activities is time consuming, and at times difficult, it is something well worth pursuing.

Acknowledgment

This work is a result of a project supported by EU Socrates: Minerva funding (Project Number is 110681-CP-1-2003-1-UK-MINERVA-M). We are grateful to the international team of tutors who made these collaborations possible, and the students who took part in the collaborative activities.

References

Alavi, M. (1994). Computer-mediated collaborative learning: An empirical evaluation. *MIS Quarterly, 18*(2), 150-174.

Beauvois, M. H. (1998). Conversations in slow motion: Computer-mediated communication in the foreign language classroom1. *Canadian Modern Language Review, 54,* 2.

Belz, J. (2003). Linguistic perspectives on the development of intercultural competence in telecollaboration. *Language Learning & Technology, 7*(2), 68-117.

Belz, J. A., & Müller-Hartmann, A. (2003). Teachers as intercultural learners: Negotiating German-American telecollaboration along the institutional fault line. *The Modern Language Journal, 87*(1), 71-89.

Bostock, S. (2002). *Keele university innovation project report: Web support for student peer review.* Keele: Keele University.

Brockbank, A., & McGill, I. (1998). *Facilitating reflective learning in higher education.* Buckingham: Open University.

Brown, S., & Knight, P. (1994). Assessing learners in higher education. In J. Stephenson (Ed.), *Teaching and higher education series.* London: Kogan Page.

Brown, S., & Dove, P. (Eds.). (1991). *Self and peer assessment.* Birmingham.

Chase, M., Macfadyen, L., Reeder, K., & Riche, J. (2002, August). Intercultural challenges in networked learning: Hard technologies meet soft skills. *First Monday, 7*(8). Retrieved November 10, 2007, from http://firstmonday.org/issues/issue7_8/chase/index.html

Collis, B. (1999). Designing for differences: Cultural issues in the design of WWW-based course-support sites. *British Journal of Educational Technology, 30*(3).

Curran, K. (2002). An online collaborative environment. *Education and Information Technologies, 7*(1), 41-53.

Europeunit. (2006). Retrieved November 10, 2007, from http://www.europeunit.ac.uk/bologna_process/index.cfm

Falchikov, N. (2001). *Learning together: Peer tutoring in higher education.* London: Routledge Falmer.

Ford, A. (1997). Peer group assessment: Its application to a vocational modular degree course. *Journal of Further and Higher Education, 21*(3).

Gatfield, T. (1999). Examining student satisfaction with group projects and peer assessment. *Assessment & Evaluation in Higher Education, 24*(4), 365-377.

Gibbs, G. (2002). Learning gains in a multi-user discussion system used with social science students: The comentor experience. In R. Hazemi & S. Hailes (Eds.), *The digital university: Building a learning community* (pp. 95-109). London: Springer Verlag.

Giles, H., & Robinson, W. P. (Eds.). (1990). *Handbook of language and social psychology*. New York: John Wiley & Sons.

Hofstede, G. (1991). *Cultures and organisations: Software of the mind.* London: McGraw-Hill.

Kanuka, H., & Anderson, T. (1998). Online social interchange, discord, and knowledge construction. *Canadian Journal of Distance Education, 13*(1), 57-74.

Kern, V. M., Saraiva, L.M., & dos Santos Pacheco, R. (2003). Peer review in education: Promoting collaboration, written expression, critical thinking, and professional responsibility. *Education and Information Technologies, 8*(1), 37-46.

Kim, K. J., & Bonk, C. J. (2002, October). Cross-cultural comparisons of online collaboration. *JCMC, 8*(1).

Ko, S., & Rossen, S. (2001). *Teaching online: A practical guide*. Boston: Houghton Mifflin.

Kramsch, C. (1993). *Context and culture in language teaching*. Oxford: Oxford University Press.

Kramsch, C., & Thorne, S. L. (2002). Foreign language learning as global communicative practice. In D. Block & D. Cameron (Eds.), *Globalization and language teaching* (pp. 83-100).

Ligorio, M. B., Talamo, A., & Pontecorvo, C. (2005). Building intersubjectivity at a distance during the collaborative writing of fairytales. *Computers & Education, 45*, 357-374.

McLoughlin, C., & Oliver, R. (1999). *Instructional design for cultural difference: A case study of the indigenous online learning in a tertiary context.* Paper presented at the ASCILITE99 Conference, Brisbane,

Australia. Retrieved November 10, 2007, from http://www.ascilite.org. au/conferences/brisbane99/papers/mcloughlinoliver.pdf

McLaughlin, P., & Simpson, N. (2004). Peer assessment in first year university: How the students feel. *Studies in Educational Evaluation, 30,* 135-149.

Moreira, D., & Da Silva, E. (2003). A method to increase student interaction using student groups and peer review over the Internet. *Education and Information Technologies, 8,* 47-54.

Nachmias, R., Mioduser, D., Oren, A., & Ram, J. (2000). Web-supported emergent-collaboration. *Journal of Educational Technology & Society in Higher Education Courses, 3*(3), 94-104.

O'Dowd, R. (2003). Understanding the "other side": Intercultural learning in a Spanish-English e-mail exchange. *Language Learning & Technology, 7*(2), 118-144.

Ogata, H., & Yano, Y. (1999). Combining social networks and collaborative learning in distributed organizations. In *Proceedings of the World Conference on Educational Multimedia, Hypermedia and Telecommunications 1999* (pp. 119-125). Chesapeake, VA: AACE.

Pond, K., & Ul-Haq, R. (1997). Learning to assess students using peer review. *Studies in Educational Evaluation, 23,* 331-348.

Purchase, H. C. (2000). Learning about interface design through peer assessment, assessment & evaluation. *Higher Education, 25*(4), 341-352.

Quinn, C. (1997). Engaging learning. *Instructional Technology Forum* [IT-Forum, Paper #18]. Retrieved November 10, 2007, from http://www. listserv.uga.edu/archives/itforum.html

Silliman, S. E., Boukari, M., & Crane, P. (2006, October 28-31). *International student collaboration through projects using common software and field experiences: Foundation to program development.* Paper presented at the 36th ASEE/IEEE Frontiers in Education Conference, San Diego, CA.

Sluijsmans, D. M. A., Brand-Gruwel, S., van Merriënboer, J. J. G., & Bastiaens, T. J. (2003). The training of peer assessment skills in teacher education. *Studies in Educational Evaluation, 29,* 23-42.

Spencer-Rodgers, J., & McGovern, T. (2002). Attitudes toward the culturally different: The role of intercultural communication barriers, affective responses, consensual stereotypes, and perceived threat. *International Journal of Intercultural Relations, 26*(6), 609-631.

Stahl, G. (2002). *Groupware goes to school*. Berlin: Springer.

Swigger, K., Brazile, R., Monticino, M., & Alpaslan, F. (2004). Effects of culture on computer-supported international collaborations. *International Journal of Human-Computer Studies, 60*(3), 365-380.

Ware, P. (2005). "Missed" communication in online communication: Tensions in a German-American telecollaboration. *Language Learning & Technology, 9*(2), 64-89.

Warschauer, M. (1996). Comparing face to face and electronic discussion in the second language classroom. *CALICO Journal, 13*, 7-26.

Wiseman, R. L., & Koester, J. (Eds.). (1993). *Intercultural communication competence*. Newbury Park, CA: Sage Publishing.

Whatley, J., & Bell, F. (2003). Discussion across borders: Benefits for collaborative learning. *Educational Media International, 40*(1-2), 139-152.

Whatley, J., & Shaylor, J. (2005). *CAB: Collaboration across borders: Peer evaluation for collaborative learning*. Paper presented at Informing Science and IT Education, Flagstaff, AZ.

Wheater, C. P., Langan, A. M., & Dunleavy, P. J. (2005). Students assessing students: Case studies on peer assessment. *Planet, 15*, 13-15.

Wojciechowski, A., & Zakrzewska, D. (2006). The influence of cultural preferences on user interface design: Polish case study. In K. Elleithy, T. Sobh, K. Mahmood, M. Iskander, & M. Karim (Eds.), *Advances in computer, information, and systems sciences, and engineering: Proceedings of IETA2005, TeNe2005, EIAE2005* (pp. 465-471). Springer.

Zaitseva, E., Shaylor, J., & Bell, F. (2004). *Peer evaluation in multi-cultural context: Language and culture issues in international collaborative project*. Paper presented at CELDA, Lisbon, Portugal.

Appendix A: Online Peer Review Activity Template

	Student Cohort 1	Student Cohort 2
Institution		
School/Department		
Programme of study		
Module/Course		
Level of study		
Number of students		
Individuals or groups		
Collaborating groups size and number		
Duration		
Dates		
Schedule / timing constraints		
Tutor sessions		
Language of collaborative activity		
Language capabilities		
What each group of students can gain		
What each group of students can offer		
Learning outcomes. At the end of this collaborative activity the students will be able to -		
Description of activity task (some parts may be performed off-line)		
What the collaboration parts will involve		
Moodle Tools	Discussion forum √ Chat WIKI Glossary Other (specify)	
Tools and technical constraints not satisfied within CAB Portal		
Product/ output		
Assessment on module If Yes, details and grading	Process: Yes / No Product: Yes / No	Process: Yes / No Product: Yes / No

Chapter XII

Help Me, Help You:
A Triple Track Approach to Maximizing Collaborative Learning in Complex, Cross-National Virtual Teams

Derrick L. Cogburn, Syracuse University, USA

Nanette S. Levinson, American University, USA

Abstract

Reporting on a nine-year case study of collaborative learning in cross-national and cross-university virtual teams, this chapter calls for what it defines as a triple track approach to the opportunities and challenges of cross-cultural collaborative learning. Such an approach involves the concurrent focus on student, faculty, and administrative roles in developed and developing nations. The authors analyze alternative delivery modes, identify best practices, and highlight critical success factors including trust-building, cross-cultural communication, and collaborative learning champions. Finally, they examine trends such as increasing cross-sector collaboration outside of academe and suggest needed additional research.

Introduction

Some of the most exciting developments in international communication today involve the increasing convergence of lessons learned from the diverse—but related—interdisciplinary fields of computer-supported cooperative work (CSCW), computer-supported collaborative learning (CSCL), and international studies. This convergence is evident in a number of ways, including new studies of how transnational civil society organizations use information and communication technologies to coordinate their geographically distributed participation in global policy processes such as the UN World Summit on the Information Society (Cogburn, 2002; Jordan & Surman, 2005; Klein, 2004; Selian, 2004; Siochrú, 2003), distance-based capacity building for such complex policy areas as Internet Governance (Cogburn & Kurup, 2006; Kleinwächter, 2004), and in the implications of ICT use in cross-cultural distributed environments (Abbott, Austin, Mulkeen, & Metcalf, 2004; Cogburn & Levinson, 2003; Zakaria & Cogburn, 2006). Many of these amazing developments are due to innovative applications of the Internet and the increasing availability of advanced commercial and open source information and communication technologies capable of supporting the synchronous and asynchronous needs of diverse, cross-national collaborative learning teams.

Building on what Hollan and Stornetta (1992) presciently described as the "beyond being there" effect that is possible with the appropriate use of ICT tools to support distributed collaboration, this chapter reports on lessons learned from nine years of offering an advanced cross-national, graduate level interdisciplinary seminar focusing on "Globalization and the Information Society" and facilitated by computer-supported collaborative learning approaches. The *Globalization Seminar* involves graduate students at up to six universities (three in the United States and three in South Africa) who work for a full semester in one of five cross-national, virtual teams called "Global Syndicates." Each "Global Syndicate" represents a different stakeholder group in the "Information Society" and has a mix of students from each of the participating universities and countries.

Reviewing findings from our nine-year study indicates that what we call "triple track learning" is present in these learning environments, and must be considered in any identification of best practices or lessons learned. This "triple track learning" involves a concurrent focus on the perspectives of students, instructors, and administrators as we analyze the opportunities and challenges of collaborative learning in complex, cross-national virtual teams.

We argue that analyses of cross-national collaborative learning experiences that do not include this tripartite focus produce an incomplete picture. Overlooking any one of these three elements of "triple track learning" provides only a partial and misleading representation of what is actually happening and what accounts for successful learning in such complex distributed settings. Thus, this chapter is organized around lessons learned and best practices in the following areas:

- Facilitating effective learning at the *student level,* including an understanding of group process and leadership; gender and diversity; trust-building in virtual learning situations; student satisfaction, socialization, and cross-cultural communication.
- Facilitating effective learning at the *instructor level,* including an understanding of the roles of research and reflection in computer-supported collaborative learning (CSCL) environments.
- Facilitating effective learning at the university *administration level,* including implications for both systems architecture and technology (the appropriate infrastructure for cross-national CSCL) and for key university level administrative support and understanding of the importance and uniqueness of cross-university and cross-national learning environments.

Finally, this chapter highlights the often-overlooked vital interactions and requisite trust-building activities, not just among the student learners in different cultures and teams, but also among the students, professor, and the university administrators involved. It concludes with a look at future trends, options, and opportunities for cross-national CSCL.

Background and Methods

Seminar Structure

From its initiation in the spring of 1999, the Collaboratory on Technology Enhanced Learning Communities (http://cotelco.syr.edu) has organized the

Globalization Seminar, formally billed as "Globalization and the Information Society: Information, Communication and Development," which is taught for thirteen weeks in the spring semester from January–April. Originally, there were two institutions scheduled to participate in the seminar, the University of Michigan: School of Information and the University of the Witwatersrand: Graduate School of Public and Development Management. These two programs were selected primarily on convenience, because the first author and project director had academic appointments at both institutions, and, having lived and worked in South Africa conducting research on globalization and telecommunications policy, was an expert on the country and region. However, the second author, a faculty administrator at the American University School of International Service, learned of the seminar and immediately saw the unique opportunity the seminar presented for students in their international communication and international development programs. So, the first instance of the Globalization Seminar included students from UM, Wits, and AU. Over the years, different configurations of universities have participated, including Howard University, and Syracuse University in the United States, and the University of Pretoria and the University of Fort Hare in South Africa. These different configurations will be described later in this chapter. However, the first three institutions have remained the foundation of the project.

Finally, one additional common element throughout the seminar is that each semester, the students are randomly divided into one of five cross-national virtual teams that we call "Global Syndicates." Each "Global Syndicate" represents a different stakeholder group in the Information Society, namely global and multinational corporations; developed country national governments; developing country national governments; intergovernmental organizations; and nongovernmental organizations/community-based organizations. These Global Syndicates are characterized in our work as highly complex, cross-national virtual teams. For example, these teams include members of different: (1) disciplines, (2) stages in their lives/careers, (3) institutions, (4) levels of technology expertise, (5) levels of technology support, (6) cross multiple time zones, and (7) people from multiple countries, cultures, and languages.

Sociotechnical Infrastructure

The CSCL environment for the seminar is based primarily on models found in the literature on scientific "collaboratories" (Finholt, 2002; Wulf, 1989), as well as the more recent work on "cyberinfrastructure" (Atkins, Droegemeier, Feldman, Garcia-Molina, Klein, Messerschmitt, Messina, Ostriker, & Wright, 2003). We organize the seminar as a "learning" collaboratory, taking a blended approach to designing the infrastructure to support the seminar and our global virtual teams. Again, over the years, the actual hardware and software has changed dramatically, but in general, we make a point to combine advanced, robust, Web-based asynchronous and synchronous communication and collaboration tools. Over the years, our asynchronous infrastructure has included experiments and production use of various open source content management systems (i.e., CourseTools, Sakai, Plone, DotNetNuke) and commercially available learning management systems (i.e., WebCT). For synchronous infrastructure, we have included various presence awareness packages (i.e., MSN Messenger, AOL Instant Messenger, and Skype), and advanced Web conferencing software (i.e., Placeware, Centra, and Elluminate) which help to create a highly-interactive rich media environment of distributed PowerPoint presentations, white boards, application sharing, voice over IP (VOIP), video over IP, polling and decision-making support tools.

In addition to the technology infrastructure, we have paid considerable attention to the social environment. Here, two elements stand out the most, including our drawing from the literature on building trust in virtual teams (Rocco, 1998; Zheng, Veinott, Bos, Olson, & Olson, 2002). Also, in order to minimize the potential for social loafing (Latané, Williams, & Harkins, 1979) in our Global Syndicates, we tried to design the assignments to be as realistic and challenging as possible, and to require the teams to present regularly in order to illuminate the contributions of each team member.

Delivery Models

Over the years, we have experimented with various delivery models for the seminar, including the concomitant instructor roles, and modes of organizing the Global Syndicates. In 1999, we started the seminar using a "circuit-rider" model. In this model, each university would have a designated location—a computer lab in most cases—where the seminar would be held. Each university also has a "site coordinator," which is a staff person assigned to be the primary administrative point of contact for the seminar. In the circuit-rider model, the faculty member moves amongst the various partnering university locations and is physically "present" on one campus, while "virtually" present on the other participating campuses. While this approach has tremendous advantages, allowing the faculty member to spend relatively equal amounts of time physically with each group of students, the costs are generally seen to outweigh the benefits. It is both fiscally and physically costly to move a faculty member around between multiple universities on two continents. However, this foundation allowed us to conceive of and eventually explore alternative delivery models.

We called the second delivery approach we explored the "student socialization" model. Here, the instructor is present at each location only in the "virtual" mode, not meeting physically with any of the students. However, in this model, the students continue to participate in the seminar from a designated computer lab on each campus, taking advantage of the socialization opportunities and assistance from their fellow classmates, even those from different teams. During this phase, we conducted a number of experiments and studies to help us understand the impact of this shift, and the impact of different modes for organizing the Global Syndicates, especially comparing the satisfaction and performance of students working in face-to-face teams with students working only in virtual teams (Cogburn, 2002; Cogburn & Levinson, 2003; Cogburn, Zhang, & Khothule, 2002).

We call the current delivery model the "CyberSeminar." While each university still reserves a computer lab for the delivery of the seminar should any of the students choose to come on campus, this model is the most flexible in terms of physical location; and both the students and the faculty member operate through completely computer-mediated or "virtual" interactions. In other words, neither the faculty member nor the students are required to have any face-to-face contact during the semester. By most accounts, students and the faculty member love this approach because of the tremendous flexibility it offers. When options are presented for students or the instructor to travel to conferences or meetings, no "either/or" decision needs to be made. Both students and the instructor can attend the conference and just plan to log in to the seminar session from wherever they can get an Internet connection (e.g., the hotel room, cyber café, business center). This flexibility has led to some pretty interesting opportunities with the professor being able to attend major international meetings and using the infrastructure to introduce the students to major government, private sector, and civil society players. Administrators, on the other hand, seem to have some difficulty with this model. In some cases, over the last few years of utilizing the Cyberseminar model, administrators in DC or Johannesburg have not "seen" or met with the instructor, sometimes making them question their investment in the seminar.

Data Collection

There are six main sources for the data informing our discussion in this chapter: annual surveys of participants; qualitative, reflective statements compiled by each student; research assistants' observations; computer logs and session recordings; final student performance indicators; and reflective conversations among faculty, administrators and staff support personnel. While one university (Syracuse University) replaced another (University of Michigan) in the course of the six years and several universities joined the Collaboratory (University of Fort Hare in South Africa and Howard University in Washington, DC), the professor (Derrick Cogburn) and two universities (University of the Witwatersrand in South Africa and American University in Washington, DC) have remained constant.

Lessons Learned and Best Practices

Facilitating Effective Teaching and Learning: A Student Focus

During the first three years of the seminar, the technology itself—while straightforward—was, indeed, relatively new. This meant that there was a double impact: students were themselves neither completely familiar with these technologies nor were they as patient with technological glitches or experiments that were bound to occur. Today's students have had more time to acclimate themselves to using technology, both for personal and learning purposes. Thus, they are more comfortable using computers and the Internet for many more aspects of their lives including listening to music and podcasts; communicating through instant messaging using text, voice, and video; purchasing items online; and even tracking breaking news through blogs, RSS feeds and news readers. Many of these technologies were not nearly as widespread in 1999 as they are today (and some barely existed). As a result, the role of the site coordinator, often a research and/ or laboratory assistant physically located at each campus computer site, was vital to the effectiveness of the seminar. These site coordinators not only welcomed students to the lab, fixed technological glitches, and served as key resource persons for the instructor, they also helped to reassure nervous students about the structure of the seminar and to provide a two-way feedback loop on what should be and was going in the lab "classroom."

But the lab classroom truly extended beyond the physical walls of the computer lab. As noted earlier, the professor used the distributed infrastructure to project the students into a wide variety of "real-world" events, from WSIS, to the International Studies Association Annual Meeting in Hawaii, and most recently to the UN Global Alliance on ICT and Development meeting in Silicon Valley. The Global Syndicate teams are critical to these experiences. To create the virtual teams, the professor randomly assigns students on each campus to a Global Syndicate team, making some attempt to control for gender and cross-campus diversity. Learning processes went far beyond the virtual model of an instructor sitting on one side of a wooden log and one student on the other. Yes, there was still the instructor on one side of the "virtual" log, but on the other side was a group/team of individual students distributed across the participating universities and assigned to play a specific team role in the work of the seminar. On-site assistants, working closely with the professor, observed and ensured that the teams were "working."

These early efforts highlight the importance of several critical success factors for students participating in a geographically distributed collaborative learning environment: comfort with using technology and with possible technological glitches (for example, servers going down) and the interest and ability to work in a group (a very different learning skill than that required for one-on-one learning, and one that is amplified in the context of virtual teamwork).

Research on virtual teams, in both academia and the corporate worlds, was very useful in understanding these dynamics (Barrow, 1996; Benbunan-Fich & Hiltz, 1999; Brown & Dobbie, 1999; Guzzo & Dickson, 1996; Ingram & Parker, 2002). Based on both our learning experiences and that of this literature, the instructor soon realized that a vital dimension was needed for successful teamwork: trust. While there is a large literature dealing with the need for trust in a wide range of social relationships from alliance building to social networks (Butler, 1991; Deutsch, 1958; Jones & George, 1998; Holton, 2001; Knoke & Burt, 1983; McAllister, 1995; McKnight & Cummings, 1998; Rocco, 1998), little work focuses on the important connection between trust and effective cross-cultural communication in blended computer-mediated communication environments (Jarvenpaa & Leidner, 1998).

In the first year of teaching the seminar, the instructor observed the importance of a "socialization" period for a cross-national team early on. In many ways, this socialization period is similar to the "getting to know each other" and trust building that occurs in initial meetings in a traditional face-to-face seminar. So, having recognized this importance in the second year of the seminar, we followed Rocco (1998) and instituted a suite of exercises to build trust and to foster effective cross-cultural communication at the very beginning of the course. Without such a foundation early on in the seminar, teams could not "gel" and cross-national communication and learning were hindered. This innovation truly made a difference and provided the skills, respect and motivation to ensure a positive team learning experience for nearly all the students.

Today, the introductory trust-building portion of the course is a taken-for-granted precursor for learning success. It includes a structured period of information sharing and personal disclosure within each team, and within the seminar (including both the students and the professor). Within the teams, there are two early decision-making assignments that are designed to force the Global Syndicates to uncover the diversity of talents, cultures, and perspectives within their teams and to work together to develop a team culture and a specific team charter. These team charters are then presented to the entire seminar.

A final two critical success factors are the realism of the ten tasks required for successful completion of the seminar and the realism of the virtual encounters between professor and student or student teams. This element of assignments and the seminar was developed to reduce the potential phenomenon of "social loafing" (Latané et al., 1979) and to engage students effectively in the work of the seminar. To ensure realism vis-à-vis faculty–student interactions "outside of class," the professor and each site coordinator holds regular virtual office hours, linking to the virtual seminar room at specific, pre-announced and regular times, waiting for any student to enter virtually and chat. Additionally, the professor is available regularly via presence awareness packages such as AOL Instant Messenger, MSN Messenger or Skype, packages with which most of the younger generation are already familiar and already use in their lives outside of any classroom, virtual or not.

Facilitating Effective Teaching and Learning: An Instructor Focus

As noted in the above section, the role of the instructor is quite key in facilitating student learning. Collecting frequent feedback both directly from students and from on-site personnel makes a difference. The burden is greater in situations, such as the current CyberSeminar model, wherein there is no on-site lab presence required (but this is offered as an option) and thus, where there is not always a second source of independent feedback to the instructor. This is why today's seminar design includes numerous opportunities for anonymous feedback on the syllabus and the seminar itself via a discussion thread in the course WebCT site. Initially, students can use this mechanism to provide anonymous feedback on the seminar, but then they may continue to use this mechanism throughout the semester to provide anonymous feedback to the professor at any time. There is also a formal mid-term evaluation of the seminar (including a peer-review mechanism, where the team members anonymously evaluate their own contribution relative to their team members), which is also repeated after the final assignment is submitted.

Additionally, the instructor's research center, Cotelco, tracks emerging trends in collaboratories, CSCW, and CSCL, in order to identify new techniques to support the socio-technical infrastructure of the seminar. Both co-authors are also involved in a number of global information policy processes and are able to bring these experiences into the seminar. In essence, these ongoing research activities help to shape the just-in-time learning environment for curriculum, teaching, planning, and problem solving. The role of research and reflection, especially as it applies to cross-university learning settings and computer-assisted collaborative learning is integral to effective teaching and learning in such settings as the seminar.

Creativity on the part of the instructor is a final success factor for facilitating cross-national team learning. No two teams are exactly alike, no matter what the numerical composition of a team in terms of its participants from different campuses and different countries. Creative interventions and observations can set a team back on track and maximize learning. But, to accomplish this, it is vital to have frequent and just-in-time feedback on seminar learning processes. The instructor can easily glean from the seminar's supporting technology who is, or is not, communicating with whom, how frequently, and to what effect.

Facilitating Effective Learning: University Administrator Level

In ordinary classroom learning situations, university administrators do not often have a direct impact on student learning in any individual faculty member's class. However, university administrators do play an important facilitating role in ensuring cross-national team learning. They do this in the following ways, which are unlike their usual on-campus roles where they intervene only when there is a problem in a classroom, once a class has begun (in these cases, it is only in the most egregious situations where a student will, for example, go to a department chair or dean, to express concern about a course). First, administrators in each participating university have to agree to appoint one faculty member who has a full-time academic appointment in another institution, as a member of the faculty in their own institution. Second, they have to review and accept and assign a course number to the seminar. Each university assigns its own number and related seminar name. Third, they need to review its appropriateness for fulfilling specific degree requirements and delineate the ways in which the seminar contributes to their own curriculum on their own campus. Note that the participating departments are schools of information studies, schools of international studies, and schools of public management, and engineering and computer science, each with their own specific and differing degree requirements. Fourth, they need to provide a physical space, a lab with appropriate technology-related support and often a research or lab assistant, who works together with the instructor as well as counterparts at the other participating universities. These are certainly not ordinary functions on today's campuses wherever they are located in our world.

The key success factor here is the role specific administrators on each campus play as computer and collaborative learning champions on their campus. The above-noted requisite administrative functions do not easily fit existing academic regulations or cultures. Even today, it is unusual to have one faculty member teaching on four or more different campuses, each of which is part of another university, and some of which are public and some private institutions. Such administrators need to have vision and trust; thus, trust also plays a role at the level of instructor and participating university administrators. While there are no exercises similar to those used in trust building for the seminar, there are some factors that do contribute to trust-building at the administrator level. These include the building of a shared vision through the instructor, and the collaboratory's ability to shape an overarching vision that is inclusive of each campus' own distinctive mission and culture. Thus, a key best practice is triple track trust-building; in other words focusing on the interactions among student teams, students and faculty member, and faculty member and administrators. In each case, an understanding of the cultures involved (whether national, ethnic, group, occupational) is important.

Another critical element of administrative success of the seminar has been the choice of technology to support the seminar. Given that the seminar is purposively focused on the active involvement of participants from developing countries, it was important not to select technologies that were only supported by broadband connectivity, or that used overly specialized networks such as Internet2. In contrast, the technologies chosen for the *Globalization Seminar* have focused on being accessible by as little as a 28.8 kbps modem connections and using open source technologies when possible.

The most sophisticated component of the cyberinfrastructure for the seminar is the Webconferencing application, used to create the synchronous (real-time) virtual seminar room. We have had some challenges over the years with this critical component. The Webconferencing application used in the first year (Placeware) did not handle network latencies well and would just drop audio packets when confronted with network congestion. We moved to another application (Centra Symposium), which handled these audio issues much better, and integrated video into our CSCL environment for the first time. However, this application was Windows only, and cross-platform functionality (Windows, Mac, Linux, Solaris) became increasingly important for the professor and the students.

Our Webconferencing infrastructure is now quite stable and robust, with our current virtual seminar room being based on technology licensed from a Canadian company called Elluminate. Elluminate is one of the leading Webconferencing applications and places a high value on accessibility—including cross-platform, low bandwidth accessibility, and high levels of accessibility for people with disabilities (Cogburn & Kurup, 2006).

All of these elements are critical for collaborating in most geographically distributed environments, but are especially critical when working in developing countries. The bandwidth limitations and the so-called "digital divides" in developing countries are well recognized (Heeks & Kenney, 2001; Warschauer, 2002). For example, even at the University of the Witwatersrand, a major English speaking university and our primary partner in South Africa, there are bandwidth limitations. Even though we have a dedicated lab for use by the seminar, the actual bandwidth available to each individual computer sometimes reaches dial-up or less connectivity. At the University of Fort Hare, the initial situation was much, much worse. When we initiated our collaboration with Fort Hare, they had a 64 kbps connection to be shared by the entire university. That connection was subsequently upgraded, but it illustrates some of the bandwidth limitations facing the developing world. So our collaboration tools had to be able to function reasonably well in these environments.

Finally, there is a need, especially at the administrative level, to have champions for the kind of cross-national virtual learning embodied by the seminar. In each university of the collaboratory there has been at least one administrative "champion." As noted earlier, this "champion" plays a particularly important role because CSCL classes that involve multiple universities do not easily fit within existing regulations and practices in most universities today, whether in developing or developed nations.

Future Trends and Research Opportunities

Increasingly there are cross-national inter-organizational collaborations in public, private and not-for-profit sectors. Our students will work in and contribute to these settings. The seminar we describe in this chapter provides students with learning opportunities that closely mirror the settings in which they may some day soon work and matches the requisite skill set for such future settings. Focusing just on the university sector, we believe there will be an increase in future "collaboratories" in a wide variety of fields. In particular, there also will be more multi-disciplinary arrangements, again to match the complex societal and scientific problems we will face.

These two trends alone possess implications, not just for crafting teaching and learning opportunities that make sense, but also for the kinds of concomitant research that need to be rigorously designed and implemented. Examples include quasi-ethnographic studies of learners, instructors, and administrators in cross-national university settings.

Work reviewing various hardware-focused solutions to the digital divide (Heeks & Kenney, 2001; Warschauer, 2002) highlights problems with a unique focus on technology, devoid of an understanding of cultural and social contexts. The work reported here is just a beginning that includes a strong focus on social science research approaches to understand CSCL and its success factors. There is still much to be examined. For example, compared with nearly a decade ago, today's students in some cultural contexts have grown up with their lives saturated with Internet-based technologies and have used computers since early childhood. This appears to lessen the technology-related learning challenges of the seminar and similar learning arrangements.

We need cross-case meta-analyses of learning situations similar to the one discussed in this chapter. While we can consider each semester's offering of the seminar as a self-contained case study and thus have nine cross-case studies for comparison, there is an opportunity to do case studies involving other instructors and subject matter foci, holding cross-national university contexts constant. There also is the opportunity to do longitudinal studies of those who have participated in each seminar offering. What is a student's perspective six years out from the learning experience compared with a student who is, for example, two years out? This, of course recognizes different baselines for each seminar offering.

Finally, there is an important research opportunity to examine student-learning experiences where the seminar is the only, for example, asynchronous learning experience of a student. In other words, all courses but the seminar involve more traditional face-to-face classroom learning on one campus. Will there be a difference in situations where all classes a student experiences involve cross-national virtual teams and a virtual professor, no matter what the subject? Moreover, to what extents do technology-related generational differences influence learning outcomes?

Conclusion

This chapter emphasizes the need for a triple track approach on CSCL, focusing concurrently on student, faculty, and administrative roles in a global perspective. Such an approach ensures that our understanding of student learning goes beyond the focus on traditional classroom or virtual classroom performance measures. It allows for assessing the interaction within teams, across teams, between students and instructor, and between instructor and participating universities' administrative structures. We have emphasized the importance of culture and context, technology and learning, as well as the interactions of our triple track approach.

The case study in all its complexity captures well the broader field of change in higher education worldwide. It is clear that a critical success factor is the presence of change champions on each participating campus. Furthermore, the barriers to change in general in higher education also apply to the change efforts described in the creation and implementation of the CSCL of the seminar. The instructor is the primary disseminator of the innovation. Just as in the diffusion of innovation literature (see, for example, the pioneering research by Everett Rogers, 1962), cultural context plays an important role in determining whether or not the innovation will 'stick' and, indeed, in how it is received and shaped or adapted. As the collaboratory grows, it will be useful to analyze the added cultural contexts and cross-cultural interactions, to see change in higher education at work.

References

Abbott, L., Austin, R., Mulkeen, A., & Metcalfe, N. (2004). The global classroom: Advancing cultural awareness in special schools through collaborative work using ICT. *European Journal of Special Needs Education, 19*(2).

American Council on Education (2000). *Internationalization of U.S. Higher Education, Preliminary Status Report.*

Atkins, D. E., Droegemeier, K. K., Feldman, S. I., Garcia-Molina, H., Klein, M. L., Messerschmitt, D. G., Messina, P., Ostriker, J. P., & Wright, M. H. (2003). *Revolutionizing science and engineering through cyberinfrastructure: Report of the blue-ribbon advisory panel on cyberinfrastructure.* Washington, DC: National Science Foundation.

Barrow, C. (1996). The new economy and restructuring higher education. *The NEA Higher Education Journal.*

Benbunan-Fich, R., & Hiltz, S.R. (1999). Educational applications of CMCS: Solving case studies through asynchronous learning networks. *Journal of Computer Mediated Communication.*

Bos, N., Olson, J.S., Gergle, D., Olson, G.M., and Wright, Z. (2002). Effects of four computer-mediated communications channels on trust development. *Proceedings of CHI'02* Minneapolis, MN: ACM Press, 135-140.

Brown, J., & Dobbie, G. (1999). Supporting and evaluating team dynamics in group projects. *ACM SIGCSE Bulletin, 31*(1), 281-285.

Butler, J. K. (1991). Towards understanding and measuring conditions of trust: Evolution of a condition of trust inventory. *Journal of Management, 17*, 643-663.

Cadiz, J.J., et al. (2000). Distance learning through distributed collaborative video viewing. *Proceedings of CSCW*. Philadelphia: ACM Press, 135-144.

Castells, M (1996). *The Information Age: Economy, Society and Culture, Volume I: The Rise of the Network Society*. Oxford: Blackwell Publishers.

Cogburn, D. L. (2002). Understanding distributed collaborative learning between the United States and South Africa. In *Networked Learning in a Global Environment: Challenges and Solutions for Virtual Education (pp. 144-159)* Berlin: ICSC Academic Press.

Cogburn, D. L., & Levinson, N. (2003). US-Africa virtual collaboration in globalisation studies: Success factors for complex, cross-national learning teams. *International Studies Perspectives, 4,* 34-51.

Cogburn, D. L., Zhang, L., & Khothule, M. (2002). Going global, locally: The socio-technical influences on performance in distributed collaborative learning teams. In *ACM International Conference Proceeding Series, 30* (pp. 52-64). South Africa: South African Institute for Computer Scientists and Information Technologists.

Cogburn, D.L. and D. Kurup (2006). Synchronous collaboration software: A comparative review of webconferencing products that facilitate highly interactive geographically distributed collaborative work. *Network Computing*, 57-63.

Cristian, F. (1996) Synchronous and asynchronous. *Communications of the ACM*, 39(4), 88-97.

Deutsch, M. (1958). Trust and suspicion. *The Journal of Conflict Resolution, 2*(4), 265-279.

Finholt, T.A. (2002). Collaboratories. *Annual Review of Science and Technology, 36*, 73-107.

Govani, T., & Pashley, H. (2005). Student awareness of the privacy implications when using facebook. Unpublished manuscript, found on the Internet on 23 October at: http://scholar.google.com/url?sa=U&q=http://lorrie.cranor.org/courses/fa05/tubzhlp.pdf

Guzzo, R. A., & Dickson, M. W. (1996). Teams in organizations: Recent research on performance and effectiveness. *Annual Review of Psychology, 47*, 307-338.

Hazemi, R., Hailes, S., & Wilbur, S. (Eds.). (1998). *The digital university.* London: Springer.

Heeks, R., & Kenny, C. (2001). *Is the Internet a technology of convergence or divergence?* (Mimeo). Washington, DC: World Bank.

Hiltz, R. (1999) Evaluating the virtual classroom. In L. M. Harasim & M. Turnoff (Eds.), *Online education: Perspectives on a new environment* (pp. 133-183). New York: Praeger.

Hollan, J., & Stornetta, S. (1992). Beyond being there. In *Proceedings of the SIGCHI Conference on Human Factors in Computing Systems* (pp. 119-125).

Holton, J. A. (2001). Building trust and collaboration in a virtual team. *Team Performance Management, 7*(3), 36-47.

House, R. J., Filley, A. C., et al. (1971). Relation of leader consideration and initiating structure to R and D subordinates' satisfaction. *Administrative Science Quarterly, 16*(1), 19-30.

Ingram, S., & Parker, A. (2002). Gender and modes of collaboration in an engineering classroom: A profile of two women on student teams. *Journal of Business and Technical Communication, 16*(1), 33-68.

Jago, A. G. (1982). Leadership: Perspectives in theory and research. *Management Science, 28*(3), 315-336.

Jarvenpaa, S. L., & Leidner, D. E. (1998). Communication and trust in global virtual teams. *Journal of Computer-Mediated Communication, 3*(4).

Johnson, P., Heimann, V., & O'Neill, K. (2001). The "wonderland" of virtual teams. *The Journal of Workplace Learning, 13*(1), 24-30.

Johnson, S. D, Suriya, C., Yoon, S. W., Berrett, J., & La Fleur, J. (2002). Team development and group processes of virtual learning teams. *Computers and Education, 39*(4), 379-393.

Jones, G. R., & George, J. M. (1998). The experience and evolution of trust: Implications for cooperation and teamwork. *The Academy of Management Review, 23*(3), 513-546.

Jordan, K., & Surman, M. (2005, December). *Civil technologies: The values of nonprofit ICT use* (Social Science Research Council Report).

Kiesler, S., et al. (1984). Social psychological aspects of computer-mediated communication. *American Psychologist, 39*, 1123-1134.

Klein, H. (2004). Understanding WSIS: An institutional analysis of the UN World Summit on the information society. *Information Technology and International Development.*

Kleinwächter, W. (2004, February 26-27). *WSIS and internet governance: Towards a multistakeholder approach.* Paper presented at the Workshop at International Telecommunication Union on Internet Governance in Geneva.

Knoke, D., & Burt, R. S. (1983). Prominence. In R. S. Burt & M. J. Miner (Eds.), *Applied network analysis: A methodological introduction* (pp. 195-222). Beverly Hills, CA: Sage.

Latane, B., Williams, K., & Harkins, S. (1979). Many hands make light work: The causes and consequences of social loafing. *Journal of Personality and Social Psychology, 37*, 822-832.

Lewis, J. D., & Weigert, A. (1985). Trust as a social reality. *Social Forces, 63*, 967-985.

Mayer, R. C., Davis, J. H., et al. (1995). An integrative model of organizational trust. *The Academy of Management Review, 20*(3), 709-734.

McAllister, D. J. (1995). Affect- and cognition-based trust as foundations for interpersonal cooperation in organizations. *The Academy of Management Review, 38*(1), 24-59.

McKnight, D. H., & Cummings, L. L. (1998). Initial trust formation in new organizational relationships. *The Academy of Management Review, 23*(3), 473-490.

McLellan, H. (1997). Creating virtual communities via the Web. In B. H. Khan (Ed.), *Web-based instruction: Development, application, and evaluation* (pp. 185-190). Englewood Cliffs, NJ: Educational Technology Publications.

Nass, C., Moon, Y., & Green, N. (1997). Are machines gender neutral? Gender-stereotypic responses to computers with voices. *Journal of Applied Social Psychology, 27*, 864-876.

Norman, K. (1998). Collaborative interactions in support of learning: Models, metaphors and management. In H. Hazemi & Wilbur (Eds.), *The digital university: Reinventing the academy.* London: Springer.

Rocco, E. (1998). Trust breaks down in electronic contexts but can be repaired by some initial face-to-face contact. In *Proceedings of CHI '98* (pp. 496-502). ACM Press.

Reich, R. (1991). *The work of nations: Preparing ourselves for 21st century capitalism*. New York: Vintage Books.

Selian, A. (2004). The World Summit on the information society and civil society participation. *The Information Society, 20*(3).

Siochrú, S. (2003). Global governance of information and communication technologies: Implications for transnational civil society networking (Social Science Research Council Report).

Sproull, L. S., & Kiesler, S. (1991). *Connections: New ways of working in the networked organization*. Cambridge, MA: MIT Press.

Steeples, C., Unsworth, C., Bryson, M., Goodyear, P., Riding, P., Fowell, S., Levy, P., & Duffy, C. (1996). Technological support for teaching and learning: Computer-mediated communications in higher education (CMC in HE). *Computers & Education, 26*(1-3), 71-80.

Stutzman, F. (2005). An evaluation of identity-sharing behavior in social network communities. Unpublished manuscript. Retrieved November 11, 2007, from http://www2.scedu.unibo.it/roversi/FormNet/7420.0.stutzman_pub4.pdf

Tiffin, J., & Rajasingham, L. (1995). *In search of the virtual class: Education in an information society.* London: Routledge.

Tuckman, B. W. (1965). Developmental sequence in small groups. *Psychological Bulletin, 63*(354), 399.

Varghese, N. V. (2004). *Private higher education in Africa.* United Nations Education, Scientific and Cultural Organization.

Veerman, A. L., Andriessen, J. E. B., & Kanselaar, G. (1999, August 24-28). *Computer-mediated discussions through graphically structured interaction.* Paper presented at the 8th European Conference for Research on Learning and Instruction, Göteborg, Sweden.

Warschauer, M. (2002) Reconceptualizing the digital divide. *First Monday, 7*(7). Retrieved November 10, 2007, from http://www.firstmonday.org

Welsch, L. A. (1982). Using electronic mail as a teaching tool. *Communications of the ACM, 25*, 105-108.

Wulf, W. A. (1989, March 17-18). *The national collaboratory: A white paper* (Appendix A in an unpublished report of a National Science Foundation invitational workshop). Rockefeller University, New York.

Yamaguchi, R., Bos, N., & Olson, J. S. (2002). Emergent leadership in small groups using computer-mediated communications. In *Proceedings of CSCL'02* (pp. 138-143). New York: ACM Press.

Zakaria, N., & Cogburn, D. (2006). *Webs of culture: Applying high and low-context theory to understand decision-making behaviors in transnational NGO networks involved in WSIS.* Paper presented at the Annual Conference of the International Communication Association, Dresden, Germany.

Zheng, J., Veinott, E., Bos, N. D., Olson, J. S., & Olson, G. M. (2002). Trust without touch: Jumpstarting long-distance trust with initial social activities. In *Proceedings of CH'02* (pp. 141). ACM Press.

Section V

Looking Forward

Chapter XIII

Developing Shared Mental Models in Computer-Supported Collaborative Learning

Marissa L. Shuffler, University of North Carolina, USA

Gerald F. Goodwin, U.S. Army Research Institute, USA

Abstract

In order to adapt to changing learning environments, instructors must be aware of the challenges that virtuality brings to establishing a shared understanding among online learners. Although developing shared mental models is typically a natural part of learning, it requires significant social and task-related interaction among students, which can be difficult in computer-based environments in which social presence is lacking. This chapter will briefly discuss research related to the development of shared understanding and explore what instructors can do to address challenges and facilitate the development of shared knowledge in computer supported collaborative learning environments.

Introduction

The way we learn has changed immensely over the past several decades. With the advance of technology, the typical face-to-face classroom setting is no longer the only option for learning. Internet and computer technology allows for students to gain knowledge from new sources as well as to work in new forms of interaction, changing the dynamics between instructors and students. Indeed, the proliferation of university and other degree-oriented Internet-based instruction is largely due to the wide-spread use of the Internet and the development of related technology. Instructors in these online learning environments, while still an invaluable knowledge resource, have changed to emphasize more of the facilitation, rather than impartation, of learning. This new role is one that promotes learning not only from the instructor-student relationship, but also through student interactions with one another.

Learning is not simply an instructor to student relay of information. Although classroom instruction has always had the potential for interaction among students as well as between students and instructors, it has also been widely associated—rightly or wrongly—with less learning-enabling forms of instruc-tion (e.g., lectures). Online learning technology does not prevent the use of lecture-style instruction, however it does make more interactive forms of instruction more readily available, and easier to pursue. With the continuous and constant flow of information surrounding us due to changes in technology and communication practices, students now face a world in which learning comes from multiple sources. Today's classroom is often found online or supplemented by online discussions and interactions, where both students and instructors contribute to learning outcomes. However, this is not to say that instructors have become any less necessary; indeed, they remain a vital part of developing and maintaining the flow of knowledge.

In a collaborative environment, it is important that students—as facilitated by the instructor—develop an understanding that encompasses the knowledge being dispersed. In addition to the vast resources available online, the amount of information available in a collaborative environment is bountiful, coming from the experiences and knowledge of students as well as the instructor. During learning, individuals develop and utilize knowledge structures to or-ganize information as it is learned (Anderson, 1983, 1993). These knowledge structures are sometimes referred to as mental models or schemas. When individuals are learning in groups, it can be beneficial for the group to have a common mental representation of the knowledge domain to facilitate sharing of information and discussion. One form of common mental representation is referred to as a shared mental model (Cannon-Bowers, Salas, & Converse, 1993; Klimoski & Mohammed, 1994). There are a variety of cognitive concepts related to the shared mental model concept, which are collectively referred to as forms of shared cognition (Klimoski & Mohammed, 1994; Mohammed & Dumville, 2001; Mohammed, Klimoski, & Rentsch, 2000). These shared cognition concepts include information sharing, transactive memory, shared or team mental models, shared schemas, cognitive consensus, and others (Mohammed, 2001; Mohammed & Dumville, 2001; Mohammed & Ringseis, 2001). Information sharing and transactive memory generally refer to processes in which groups or teams engage, whereas shared mental models, shared schemas, and cognitive consensus generally refer to knowledge content or knowledge structures which are held in common to some extent among group or team members. Although there are important distinctions to be made among these concepts, for the purposes of this discussion, we refer to the collective as shared understanding. Where the distinctions between these constructs are highly relevant to this discussion, the specific shared cognitive construct will be identified.

Although mental model development typically occurs as a natural part of learning, development of "sharedness" typically requires significant social and task-related interaction between group members. As such, their development can be difficult in computer-based environments in which social presence is lacking. This lack of social cues inhibits key aspects of effective learning, such as nonverbal indicators of student confusion and confidence in accuracy of information provided by other students, as will be discussed more extensively later in the chapter. Therefore, it is vitally important that instructors recognize the unique challenges presented to the development of shared understanding in computer supported collaborative learning environments, as they must work hard to overcome these difficulties in order to instill effective patterns of learning within their students.

The purpose of the current chapter is to briefly discuss research related to the development of shared understanding and explore what instructors can do to facilitate this development in collaborative learning environments. We will begin by defining mental models at the individual level, exploring their relevance to learning in general, and examining the different ways that mental models are used to store information. This will be followed by a discussion of the importance of the development of shared understanding, particularly in learning environments. Next, we will present several of the challenges faced in the development of shared understanding in computer supported collaborative learning (CSCL). We will conclude by proposing several ways in which instructors can address these challenges in order to aid in the effective development of shared understanding in virtual learning environments.

What are Mental Models?

The concept of mental models as a key tool in learning and perception is not a new idea. Craik (1943) first proposed the idea that, upon gaining new information, individuals have the tendency to develop a model of reality within their minds that encompasses these new concepts. Mental models allow for individuals to gain a more dynamic understanding of the world through conceptual representations of their surrounding environment (Johnson-Laird, 1983). Holyoak (1984) characterizes a mental model as a "psychological representation of the environment and its expected behavior" (p. 193). This representation incorporates both the specific knowledge content as well as relationships between the concepts being represented (Johnson-Laird, 1983; Rouse, Cannon-Bowers, & Salas, 1992; Rouse & Morris, 1986). For example, when learning about combustion engines in automobiles, a student develops an understanding of the engine components (e.g., pistons, cylinders, drive shaft, carburetor) as well as relationships between the components (e.g., ignition of a fuel-air mixture inside the cylinder moves the piston; pistons turn the drive shaft). Based upon the knowledge the student gains from this mental model development, upon encountering combustion engines in other settings, the student may expect similar components and relationships to be found.

In a broader sense, mental models serve the purpose of allowing individuals to interact with their environment. Cannon-Bowers et al. (1993) characterize mental models as a mechanism used by individuals to "draw inferences and make predictions, to understand phenomena, to decide what actions to take, to control system execution, and to experience events vicariously" (p. 225). Although the original conception of mental models was literally to cognitively represent a physical system (e.g., automobile, computer, airplane), the concept has evolved to address socio-technical systems as well. Thus, mental models can be said to explain both human functioning and human-system interactions (Cannon-Bowers et al., 1993; Johnson-Laird, 1983).

In individual learning, the development of mental models plays a key role in one's ability to compartmentalize, structure, and make sense of the world. By being able structure information, we are able to rapidly recall when needed, as well as add new information to existing mental models. For example, the student referenced above would expect that, based upon the model he has created of combustion engines, he should be able to recognize another combustion engine when he sees one, because while its features may be somewhat different from the one he visited, it still possesses the same general characteristics. Moreover, the student will add to his knowledge of engines as he encounters and links information about other types of engines (e.g., electro-mechanical engines) to the knowledge structure containing information about combustion engines. Based on existing knowledge of combustion engines, the student may be able to predict the functions of some components of a different type of engine as well as have some basis for understanding the relationships between the components of the new engine. Thus by utilizing our mental models, we are able to learn procedures more quickly, retain information more accurately, and work more efficiently (Kieras & Bovair, 1984).

In summary, a mental model provides for the structuring of information in a way that is easily accessed and modified. The development of mental models is necessary to the learning process, as it advances a student's ability to learn and process information. Through the effective use of mental models, students should be more prepared to not only process information, but to make meaningful contributions to the classroom.

How is Cognition Shared?

While students can benefit from having mental representations of information, developing collective forms of understanding information is useful in collective learning environments. Information becomes shared as individuals express their unique experiences and knowledge to the rest of the group. Shared mental models and schemas are a reflection of individual thought, combined and reconstructed so that information is held in common among group members (Klimoski & Mohammed, 1994). Transactive memory, information sharing, and cognitive consensus reflect means of utilizing, storing, and analyzing information as a group or team. All of these concepts reflect aspects of how groups take in, consider, store, and utilize information as a collective. The importance or primacy of these concepts vary depending on the task the group is performing, as well as the extent to which group members have specified roles and are interdependent. Classroom settings are typified by tasks focused on acquisition of knowledge rather than utilization of knowledge to perform another task, although there are certainly exceptions. Virtual classrooms often reflect a greater degree of diversity of individual student backgrounds and background knowledge as well. As such, the concepts of information sharing, cognitive consensus, and shared schema likely play larger roles in terms of better understanding the impact of shared cognition on these settings. However, one form of shared mental model is quite relevant. The "team"-shared mental model reflects a common understanding of the expected and accepted behaviors and dynamics within the team, and is highly relevant to classroom contexts. Additionally, to the extent that class members are expected to regularly contribute information from their own unique backgrounds, some form of "teammate" mental model—reflecting essentially "who" knows "what"—may also be relevant to the development of shared understanding of the group.

Effects of Shared Understanding in Computer-Supported Collaborative Learning

While typically associated with work teams, shared understanding concepts can also be applied to learning environments. As much of the shared cognition literature focuses on team performance and outcomes, our knowledge of shared understanding development specific to the domain of computer supported collaborative learning environments is somewhat limited. However, research in face-to-face collaborative learning environments shows promise for the inclusion of shared cognition as an important facet of both group and individual learning (Jeong & Chi, 2006). We present this information here to illustrate the benefits of effective shared understanding development in CSCL environments, and how this knowledge can be beneficial outside of the classroom as well.

Through the development of shared understanding, collaborative learners are able to gain a greater depth of understanding of the material to be learned. In college populations, shared knowledge resulting from collaborative learning has been directly linked to overall learning outcomes (Jeong & Chi, 1997). Specifically, increases in the level of shared knowledge reflected gains in individual learning, as measured by pre- and post-tests. More recent evidence indicates that convergence of knowledge occurs during collaborative learning and contains information that is over and above what is in the learning material (Jeong & Chi, 2006). Clearly, shared mental models and shared knowledge are important in collaborative learning environments.

The sharing of knowledge is also important in dispersed collaboration, or environments in which individuals are located in different places, often both geographically and temporally (Cramton, 2001). In these types of environments, the ability to gain "mutual knowledge" is vital, as it provides a basis upon which knowledge can grow and expand. If individuals can recognize that they have a certain amount of knowledge that is shared, it provides a starting point for communication, comprehension, and addition of new knowledge. By effectively developing a basis for collaboration, communication lines can be more effectively opened to allow for the flow of new information, as individuals will have an understanding of what their fellow learners do and do not already know. Instructors can take advantage of this understanding of shared knowledge in order to promote interaction among students as well. This leads to another benefit of shared understanding development, in that individual learners are able to gain a deeper knowledge of subject matter based on the unique contributions from group members. This comes both from those who may have greater expertise in the area and those who have unique or different perspectives on the subject matter.

Finally, effective shared understanding development promotes sensemaking skills that can be carried over into a variety of contexts, not just the classroom. By going through the process of developing "sharedness," individuals have a better grasp of the importance and utility of this type of knowledge. Therefore, it is believed that in future situations, they will be more inclined and able to develop sharedness in new group or team contexts. For example, shared understanding plays an important role in face to face work teams, as illustrated through numerous studies of teams and groups in organizations, most of which argue for the benefits of shared mental models and other shared cognition constructs in relation to performance and other outcomes such as team member interaction (e.g., Marks, Mathieu, & Zaccaro, 2001; Mohammed & Dumville, 2001; Orasanu & Salas, 1993). Current research is also beginning to explore the importance of shared cognitive concepts in virtual work environments as well. Shared knowledge is key to overcoming the numerous boundaries of virtual environments, particularly for decision making in distributed teams (Cramton, 2001; Vick, 2003). Clearly, by helping students understand the role of shared knowledge and shared cognition in CSCL environments, instructors will instill them with skills and abilities that will be greatly advantageous in a variety of settings outside of the classroom.

What are the Challenges to Shared Understanding Development in CSCL?

The challenges to shared understanding development in computer-supported collaborative learning environments are really twofold. Not only are the typical challenges to shared understanding development present, but the added component of virtuality creates a new set of challenges that must be overcome in order for learning to occur successfully. In this section, we will explore both sets of challenges, as well as present methods that instructors can utilize to successfully achieve shared knowledge in CSCL environments.

In their exploration of shared mental models, Cannon-Bowers et al. (1993) note several issues which must be considered in mental model development include providing guidance, presenting conceptual models, allowing for practice, addressing individual differences created by prior knowledge, and preventing too much of "a good thing."

Sharedness Challenges

Providing guidance. Simply providing information is not enough for effective knowledge representation development. We are constantly surrounded by enormous amounts of information which must be perceived and processed. Without guidance on which bits are central concepts and critically important and which bits are peripheral, it can be difficult to absorb and interpret all of the necessary information. Rouse and Morris (1986) argue that guidance is key to transferring knowledge into performance. In traditional classrooms, the instructor typically controls the flow of information and is able to provide guidance to students relatively easily. However, providing guidance in an on-line classroom can be quite a challenge. Widely varying backgrounds can make it difficult to provide all students with enough, but not too much, guidance on core lesson information. Because of easy access to the vast amount of information available on the Internet, readily available to online students as they participate in classroom activities, instructors also have lost some of the control they would otherwise possess in being able to structure the flow of information during lessons and class discussions.

Instructors can prepare strategies to cope with these phenomena, particularly if they refocus themselves as facilitator—rather than provider—of learning. One way in which this can be accomplished is to require students to provide information in structured formats so that it can be evaluated effectively. Additionally, as in traditional classrooms, instructors should be prepared to tailor the guidance they provide to individual students to the extent possible. Providing extra guidance to some when necessary, and avoiding over-structuring the learning of others, can assure that individual students continue to contribute to class discussions and remain engaged in the course material.

Presenting conceptual models. It is difficult for an individual to develop a mental model without some type of initial framework. Attention must therefore be paid to the way that information is presented in order for students to develop the most effective means of knowledge organization (Cannon-Bowers et al., 1993). Proper organization of information is key to its usefulness; if information is not stored efficiently and effectively, the resulting mental models will not be valuable as learning tools. These conceptual models can greatly benefit learners when working with very complex information or for those learners who need more guidance in general. However, the development of these conceptual models must be fairly precise, as they do play such an important role in student learning. Instructors must be aware of the impact of these models when designing them, making sure that they accurately represent the information to be presented.

These conceptual models are often viewed as pre-organizers, or advanced organizers (Burke, 1999; Goldsmith & Kraiger, 1997). Advanced organizers are presented early in the learning process in order to provide a basic framework from which students can build. This initial framework can then be expanded as knowledge increases and as other students provide input. Advanced organizers are particularly effective if they contain terms and information that students are already familiar with (Mueller-Hanson, White, Dorsey, & Pulakos, 2005). They are also most beneficial when further instruction closely matches the order presented in the organizer; therefore, instructors should design these in a way that flows in a logical order, and should interject in discussions to relate discussion content back to the organizing framework. These organizers can also be beneficial in redirecting a discussion that has gone astray. Advanced organizers can consist of an outline of the material to be covered, a chart explaining relationships, or an introduction section talking about the organizing framework, among other ideas.

Allowing for practice. Practice is an important aspect of mental model development, but it cannot be the only aspect. While practicing a task can be beneficial, without proper guidance, students will not fully develop their mental models, which can result in inaccurate or incomplete models. Instructors cannot simply assign a collaborative task to students, expecting that the practice alone will produce an effective shared mental model. It must be guided by providing feedback to the individuals, which will promote a richer learning environment. Feedback has been studied for years, as it was one of the first variables found to support learning (Goldstein & Ford, 2002). Feedback has numerous functions, including evaluation of performance and practice, as well as cuing what an individual is doing correctly or incorrectly (Kozlowski, 1998).

Another function of feedback is the type of information provided, typically dichotomized into process or outcome (Goldstein & Ford, 2002). Process feedback provides information about the processes needed to accomplish a task where performed, and provides students with direct information about where changes can be made, building a better collective understanding, and promoting a more successful reception of feedback (Zaccaro, Shuffler, & Hildebrand, in press). Outcome feedback focuses solely on the performance outcomes, typically stating whether or not they were successful. This type of feedback can be less useful as it does not tell students what specific changes need to be made.

Feedback is perhaps the most direct method for instructors to influence members of virtual environments (Tannenbaum, Smith-Jentsch, & Behson, 1998). Both feedback prior to performance and following performance can be beneficial to the development of shared mental models (Burke, 1999; Marks, Zaccaro, & Mathieu, 2000). However, it is important to note that the instructor's role in feedback is not necessarily to always diagnose the reasons for a lack of mastery, but instead, it is the group who must work together to understand how to improve their outcomes (Kozlowski, 1998). An instructor should use process feedback to foster a learning environment that promotes recognition and correction of ineffective behaviors, but still allow room for students to develop their own sensemaking skills.

Prior knowledge. Any time a group of individuals is formed, individual differences and prior knowledge will affect the outcomes. The inclusion of prior knowledge in mental models can be beneficial or detrimental depending on whether or not the information is accurate. If previously developed mental models contain accurate information, students with such models may be greatly beneficial to other learners, as they can provide a conceptual model upon which others can build. However, if the information is incorrect or poorly modeled, this can cause confusion and be particularly challenging, as inaccurate mental models are not easily changed (Rouse & Morris, 1986). Instructors can pay close attention to student contributions in order to determine the accuracy of preformed knowledge, and provide effective feedback that addresses the correctness of the information contributed.

Preventing "too much of a good thing." Much of what we have discussed here focuses on the benefits of sharing knowledge. However, there does appear to be a limit on how much sharedness is appropriate. When there is too much sharedness and agreement among members of any group, little room is left for dissonance and new ideas (Mohammed & Dumville, 2001; Mohammed & Ringseis, 2001). This is similar to Janis's (1972) concept of groupthink, in which groups with high levels of cohesion favor unified decision-making over examining all courses of action. While this is more harmful in decision-making groups, it can also be applied to the learning context. Once sharedness becomes too powerful, students may be unwilling to listen to new ideas or to think for themselves. This can certainly hinder learning, as it leaves no room for growth or change. Successful mental model development will be halted if new information cannot be learned, as the ability to effectively predict from models will be hindered.

In order to prevent or overcome too much sharedness in a CSCL context, instructors can promote the inclusion of new or different ideas in discussions and other learning contexts. One method to do this is to present issues that have numerous solutions or perspectives. Another method could be to have students debate both sides of an issue, introducing them to two sets of relevant—yet different— perspectives (Palloff & Pratt, 2005). By providing opportunities for students to learn new and unique information in a variety of ways, an instructor can decrease the likelihood of groupthink occurring while still promoting a healthy level of sharedness.

Virtual Learning Challenges

By examining the virtual learning and virtual teams literature, we identified several additional and unique challenges that may present themselves in CSCL environments. These include communication issues related to lack of social presence, asynchronous communication, decreased trust, increased conflict, increased availability in information, and issues with communication.

Lack of social presence and communication issues. Much of the current literature on virtual environments focuses on the loss of social presence as measured by decreased verbal, nonverbal, and social cues. As communication media differ, so does the ability of the media to convey social presence, or "degree of salience of the other person in the interaction and the consequent salience of the interpersonal relationships" (Short, Williams, & Christie, 1976, p. 65). Conveying social presence promotes a sense of community and connection among students, allowing for increases in learning outcomes and learning satisfaction (Palloff & Pratt, 2005).

Although social presence is particularly important in CSCL environments, the utilization of technology decreases the ability to convey social presence, easily losing the nuances of communication. This is particularly true for nonverbal aspects of communication, which often convey information about how the accompanying verbal information should be interpreted (e.g., confidence in accuracy or relevance of information). Typically, sharedness develops as a group of individuals interact around a particular task. For example, as points of confusion occur, often due to failure, individuals tend to articulate this confusion via non-verbal cues, such as a shoulder shrug, shaking of the head, or facial expressions. Overall, individuals use a great deal of nonverbal behavior to communicate in everyday situations, such as gestures, intonation, or facial expressions. However, when put into virtual environments, students and instructors are no longer able to communicate these cues, therefore causing ambiguity in the transmission, reception, and interpretation of information.

Another aspect of learning related to a lack of social presence is an understanding or knowledge of the confidence someone can have in the information they are receiving. In normal classrooms, the instructor is usually the one imparting information, and thus the students have reasonably high degree of confidence in the information they are receiving—based on the expected expertise of the instructor. In a virtual learning environment, however, students can just as easily contribute information to the learning environment with fewer indicators of whether or not a learner/student can have confidence in the information they are receiving. This remains a role of the instructor as facilitator, but it is more difficult for information to be filtered after it has already been shared with other students.

In order to overcome issues spawning from a lack of social presence, instructors should take time to convey presence and understand their students. Virtual groups who spend time understanding who the group members are as people, making clear what they expect to gain from group membership, and making known their preferred work styles are typically more successful (Avolio & Kahai, 2003). By providing students with outlets for conveying contextual and social information, such as through ice-breakers or discussion boards for side topics, students will be able to gain a sense of who their fellow learners are. Encouraging students to let one another know that they are confused or do not understand a concept is also important, as this information provides vital cues easily missed by a lack of nonverbal communication. Finally, instructors should set the norms in CSCL in order to establish their social presence. By setting ground rules such as how often students should post online, what to use as supplemental Internet resources, or how to handle conflict, instructors should be able to help maintain an appropriate flow of information that conveys social presence while also overcoming the potential risk of information overload.

Asynchronous communication. As previously discussed, communication in CSCL environments is very different from a regular classroom setting. In a typical face-to-face classroom, students and instructors have synchronous discussions and conversations, allowing for a beginning, middle, and ending point for most learning experiences. For CSCL environments, technology brings a mix of synchronous and asynchronous communication. Asynchronous communication can allow learners to process information more deeply before responses are generated, as students may have days or weeks to formulate responses. However, this type of communication also can stretch discussions beyond the point of coherency. It can be difficult to reestablish the focal point of a discussion after it has been stretched out over days or weeks, particularly if tangents have been introduced.

Instructors should be sensitive to the quality of these discussions, as some may be very productive for establishing collective knowledge. In asynchronous communication, it can be difficult to determine where the cutoff of a discussion should occur, as time is a flexible issue. One way to address this challenge could be to have topic focused discussions (analogous to classroom discussions), and a general discussion board for the class which can absorb additional discussion on a topic when the instructor deems that it has outlived its usefulness in the classroom discussion forum.

Trust. Trust plays a significant role in the sharing of information in virtual environments. If group members fail to share important information, trust can be greatly reduced or diminished (Cramton & Orvis, 2003). However, trust can be very difficult to form in virtual environments (Jarvenpaa & Leidner,

1999). Face-to-face interaction among students promotes the communication of social information more readily than in a virtual environment. This
interaction provides a shared context within which students can begin to build
their relationships. In virtual environments, individuals are more likely to
discuss primarily task-related information and less social information (Jarvenpaa, Knoll, & Leidner, 1998). While sharing personal information aids
in the development of trust and shared context, in virtual environments team
members are less likely to share information about themselves (Zaccaro &
Bader, 2003). This loss of shared context slows the development of trust,
which can in turn increase the likelihood of conflict and decrease opportunities for SMM development (Griffith, Mannix, & Neale, 2003).

In order to overcome the challenges of trust, instructors should be aware of
how trust can effectively develop over time. Zaccaro and Bader (2003) explore
three basic types of trust that exist in virtual environments. *Calculated trust*
emerges first as individuals recognize the potential to gain information from
others in the group for their own personal benefit. It is a time in which students
can learn about how they interact with one another and what resources each
possesses. This is a critical aspect of trust for instructors to identify, as they
can influence future trust development at this point by emphasizing each
individual's contribution to the overall success of the group.

Once students have begun to understand one another, they start to establish
knowledge-based trust, in which they begin to be able to anticipate and predict the actions of their fellow classmates. This is a time in which trust can
easily be derailed, and therefore instructors must pay close attention to the
interactions of the students. Instructors should establish task norms, provide
clear goals and expectations, review student exchanges, and promptly provide
feedback when needed. Encouraging students to share social and personal
information is also key to success, as virtual groups who spend extensive time
discussing topics such as families, interests, or hobbies contain higher levels
of trust than those who do not (Jarvenpaa & Leidner, 1999). By addressing
any potential conflicts in discussions or other interactions, instructors should
aid in the guidance of trust development.

The final aspect of trust development, *identification-based trust*, is perhaps the
most essential in virtual environments. As previously discussed, the sharing of
personal information allow for a deeper development of shared context. This
last stage of identification allows for students to recognize, through sharing
information, that they hold beliefs, values, goals, and intentions in common
with other classmates. This act of identifying with other students promotes

an environment in which students can come to terms with the similarities they hold in common with their classmates, allowing for a shared context to develop. This helps to overcome the dispersed nature of CSCL environments, and allows them to feel comfortable in sharing knowledge or engaging in discussions. In order to facilitate identification based trust, instructors should encourage the sharing of personal and social information, continue to be proactive in monitoring discussions and providing feedback (especially for situations where trust has been broken), and foster a collective identity in the class by emphasizing the common purpose of the group.

Conflict. While numerous factors, including satisfaction, trust, and cohesion, have been linked as problem areas for virtual environments, conflict is perhaps the most recognized of these as being detrimental to both shared knowledge and outcomes (Hinds & Bailey, 2003). Mortensen and Hinds (2001) recognize two types of conflict as emerging in distributed environments. Affective conflict "results from an awareness of interpersonal incompatibilities arising from differences in personality" (p. 213), and is most often associated with detriments in performance. This type of conflict can be extremely harmful to distributed teams, as it prevents teams from performing successfully. On the other hand, task conflict, or conflict which "arises from an awareness of differing opinions and viewpoints about the work being done" (p. 213), has been linked to beneficial effects on performance when occurring in small amounts. This benefit appears to be primarily due to the fact that task conflict promotes the questioning of information and the prevention of a groupthink mentality (Hinds & Bailey, 2003).

Both affective and task conflict play a role in CSCL learning environments, particularly in the establishment of shared understanding. Developing shared understanding cannot be effectively accomplished without some type of conflict arising, yet once it is established, it can aid in faster elimination of conflict, as students should have a better knowledge of one another. Indeed, Hinds and Mortensen (2005) found that as shared processes and shared familiarity emerge over time in distributed teams, the negative effects of conflict can dissipate. When a group can gain a shared understanding of information and cues available in its environment, members should experience less conflict, although some task conflict may still be beneficial.

In order to address issues of conflict, instructors must first be aware of what type of conflict is occurring (Griffith, Mannix, & Neale, 2003). Paying attention to discussion boards, e-mails, and other forms of communication is critical for the prevention of too much conflict. Once the type of conflict has been noted, an instructor must determine how detrimental it is to the overall learning process. If task conflict is occurring, it may actually be beneficial, but it must be carefully monitored so that it does not become affective in nature. As a distributed interface is highly amenable to the types of emotional and personal attacks that are harmful to learning, it is important that instructors create methods to prevent such occurrences. Setting ground rules for respect of opinions, expression of opinions, proper use of language, and other issues will provide clear direction for students that should aid in the prevention of inappropriate conflict.

Increased availability of information. In virtual learning environments, sources of information are richer and more abundant than ever (Berg, 2003). Due to the online nature of CSCL, classes can be more diverse in their knowledge and backgrounds. This can be of great benefit to students, as more heterogeneous groups can provide a greater pool of knowledge upon which shared mental models can be established (Cramton, 2001). However, this increased availability of information is certainly not without its drawbacks. By increasing diversity in groups, the likelihood of task and affective conflict is very high as differences in opinions more easily occur (Hinds & Mortensen, 2005). The information is also more distributed in nature, where some students may have more contextual, task, or social information than others (Cramton & Orvis, 2003). Unfortunately, this distribution can cause information be overlooked or ignored, especially in online environments where an excellent idea or question can get lost in the midst of numerous e-mails or discussion posts.

Overcoming the challenge of increased availability of information is necessary in order to produce richer shared knowledge. As previously discussed, instructors should utilize and enforce ground rules in order to prevent conflict from occurring. Establishing and enforcing policies for the sharing of information can be particularly key, such as through the creation of off-topic areas for continuing side conversations, providing time allotments for how long a discussion can continue, discussing what are appropriate sources for getting information, and providing tips on how to give constructive criticism. Feedback also plays a key role in addressing this issue of information, in that instructors should highlight unique and new contributions from students that are highly relevant, so that it builds the collective knowledge.

Instructor's Role in Developing Shared Understanding in CSCL

As previously discussed, the instructor's role in learning environments is rapidly changing, particularly for computer-supported environments. Much of the current literature on the instructor's role in CSCL environments focuses on the instructor's ability to utilize technology, with little attention paid to the facilitating role these instructors must commonly play (Orvis & Lassiter, 2006). This can certainly be detrimental when it comes to shared understanding development, as the instructor is typically the only person who has contact with all class participants. An instructor's role in developing shared understanding is critical, as their behavior has been found to significantly impact outcomes in shared understanding development (Franz, McCallum, Lewis, Prince, & Salas, 1990). If the instructor does not take the lead in promoting interactions among students, the benefits of sharedness will be inhibited, as they will be slower to develop.

As much of the leadership literature discusses the functional role of leaders, instructors must also serve a similar role. Effective instructors should be able to act as functional leaders, playing a key role in doing "what needs to be done for effective performance" (Hackman & Walton, 1986, p. 77). Further applied to the role of the instructor by Zaccaro and colleagues (in press), instructors should work to the necessary environment for effective learning. For example, this may be fostering a learning climate, acting as a coach or mentor in the learning process, or utilizing resources to increase interaction among students.

Instructors serve as the leaders in such learning environments, as they assist in setting direction and managing the information resources necessary for learning; therefore, they must take action to promote effective learning through shared understanding development. As were the challenges presented previously, the role of instructors in developing shared understanding in CSCL is also twofold. First, instructors must overcome the issues typically associated with working in virtual environments. Secondly, instructors must promote a learning environment that emphasizes collaboration. Instructors having a higher level of behavioral complexity may be more effective performing multiple leadership roles simultaneously (Kayworth & Leidner, 2001). This is particularly important when considering both task consideration and relational skills. It is not simply enough for instructors to design the course; they must be able to handle the interactional processes in such environments

(Orvis & Lassiter, 2006). Overall, instructors must combine their knowledge of the subject to be taught with the ability to interact effectively with their students.

In summary, instructors of computer-supported collaborative learning can facilitate learning through communication and reinforcement of a collective knowledge structure, conceptualized here as shared mental models. While there are challenges that most all instructors will face when working in CSCL environments, there are methods that can be incorporated to overcome them. In order to effectively establish shared understanding in any learning environment, instructors must provide guidance to students through clear, concise formatting of information. These formats should present conceptual models, ideally through advanced organizers which preview what the students will be learning. Providing appropriate time for practice is necessary, but it must be accompanied by effective feedback. While students may have prior experience with a subject, it is the instructor's job to assist in the adequate dissemination of this information to other learners, especially as this information may not always be accurate. Most importantly, instructors must recognize when too much shared understanding is overpowering new and unique contributions and act accordingly by encouraging a constant flow of new ideas into group activities.

Finally, instructors must be aware of the challenges brought about by virtuality. As previously discussed, social presence is a major issue in virtual learning, and instructors must work hard to convey their presence, as well as promote the interaction of students. In order to do so, instructors can facilitate the development and maintenance of a collective knowledge structure through persistence in keeping the level of interaction relatively high among the learners (i.e., not allowing discussions to die out quickly; keeping the learning process active, not allowing the learners to be passive recipients of information only). To maintain trust and prevent negative affective conflict, instructors can highlight contributions and changes to the collective knowledge structure by individual learners (e.g., "Sue brings up a good point that we had not discussed before. If we consider these two concepts from Sue's perspective, we can more easily see how they are related to each other."). They can also encourage the sharing of personal and contextual information so that students gain a sense of the bigger collective in which they are participating. Certainly, interacting in such environments is no easy task for instructors or students, but by establishing a shared understanding, all involved should gain more than just knowledge of the subject at hand.

References

Anderson, J. R. (1983). *The architecture of cognition.* Cambridge, MA: Harvard University Press.

Anderson, J. R. (1993). *Rules of the mind.* Hillsdale, NJ: Erlbaum.

Avolio, B. J., & Kahai, S. (2003). Adding the "E" to e-leadership: How it may impact your leadership. *Organizational Dynamics, 31*(4), 325-338.

Berg, G. A. (2003). *The knowledge medium: Designing effective computer based learning environments.* Hershey, PA: Information Science Publishing.

Burke, C. S. (1999). *Examination of the cognitive mechanisms through which team leaders promote effective team process and adaptive team performance.* Unpublished dissertation, George Mason University.

Cannon-Bowers, J. A., Salas, E., & Converse, S. (1993). Shared mental models in expert team decision making. In N. J. Castellan (Ed.), *Individual and group decision making: Current issues* (pp. 221-246). Hillsdale, NJ: Lawrence Erlbaum Associates.

Craik. (1943). *The nature of explanation.* Cambridge, UK: Macmillian.

Cramton, C. D. (2001). The mutual knowledge problem and its consequences for dispersed collaboration. *Organization Science, 12,* 346-371.

Cramton, C. D., & Orvis, K. L. (2003). Overcoming barriers to information sharing in virtual teams. In C. Gibson & S. Cohen (Eds.), *Virtual teams that work* (pp. 214-229). San Francisco: Jossey-Bass.

Franz, T. M., McCallum, G. A., Lewis, M. D., Prince, C., & Salas, E. (1990). Pilot briefings and aircrew coordination evaluation: Empirical results. In *Proceedings of the 12th Symposium on Psychology in the Department of Defense,* Springfield, VA.

Goldsmith, T., & Kraiger, K. (1997). Structural knowledge assessment and trainingevaluation. In J. Ford, S. Kozlowski, K. Kraiger, E. Salas, & M. Teachout (Eds.), *Improving training effectiveness in work organizations* (pp. 19-46). Lawrence Erlbaum.

Goldstein, I. L., & Ford, J. K. (2002). *Training in organizations: Needs assessment, development, and evaluation* (4th ed.). Belmont, CA: Wadsworth.

Griffith, T. L., Mannix, E. A., & Neale, M. A. (2003). Conflict in virtual teams. In C. Gibson & S. Cohen, (Eds.), *Virtual teams that work* (pp. 335-352). San Francisco: Jossey-Bass.

Hackman, J. R., & Walton, R. E. (1986). Leading groups in organizations. In P. S. Goodman & Associates (Eds.), *Designing effective work groups.* San Francisco: Jossey-Bass.

Hinds, P. J., & Bailey, D. E. (2003). Out of sight, out of sync: Understanding conflict in distributed teams. *Organization Science, 14*, 615-632.

Hinds, P. J., & Mortensen, M. (2005). Understanding conflict in geographically distributed teams: The moderating effects of shared identity, shared context, and spontaneous communication. *Organization Science, 16*, 290-307.

Holyoak, K. (1984). Analogical thinking and human intelligence. In R. J. Sternberg (Ed.), *Advances in the psychology of human intelligence.* Hillsdale, NJ: Erlbaum.

Janis, I. L. (1972). *Victims of groupthink.* Boston: Houghton Mifflin.

Jarvenpaa, S. L., Knoll, K., & Leidner, D. E. (1998). Is anybody out there? Antecedents of trust in global virtual teams. *Journal of Management Information Systems, 14*, 29-64.

Jarvenpaa, S. L., & Leidner, D. E. (1999). Communication and trust in global virtual teams. *Organization Science, 10*, 791-815.

Jeong, H., & Chi, M. T. H. (1997). Construction of shared knowledge during collaborative learning. In R. Hall, N. Miyake, & N. Enyedy (Eds.), *Proceedings of Computer Support for Collaborative Learning* (pp. 124-128). Hillsdale, NJ: Erlbaum.

Jeong, H., & Chi, M. T. H. (2006). Knowledge convergence and collaborative learning. *Instructional Science.* Retrieved November 10, 2007, from http://www.springerlink.com/content/8r3356g682543625/?p=699eb6fe185b4788ba92cd798e42f377&pi=3

Johnson-Laird, P. N. (1983). *Mental models: Towards a cognitive science of language, inference, and consciousness.* Cambridge, MA: Harvard University Press.

Kayworth, T. R., & Leidner, D. E. (2001). Leadership effectiveness in global virtual teams. *Journal of Management Information Systems, 18*(3), 7-40.

Kieras, D. E., & Bovair, S. (1984). The role of a mental model in learning to operate a device. *Cognitive Science: A Multidisciplinary Journal, 8,* 255-273.

Klimoski, R., & Mohammed, S. (1994). Team mental models: Construct or metaphor? *Journal of Management, 20*(2), 403-437.

Kozlowski, S. W. J. (1998). Training and developing adaptive teams: Theory, principles, and research. In J. A. Cannon-Bowers & E. Salas (Eds.), *Making decisions under stress: Implications for individual and team training* (pp. 115-153). Washington, DC: American Psychological Association.

Marks, M. A., Mathieu, J. E., & Zaccaro, S. J. (2001). A temporally based framework and taxonomy of team processes. *Academy of Management Review, 26,* 356-376.

Marks, M., Zaccaro, S. J., & Mathieu, J. E. (2000). Performance implications of leader briefings and team-interaction training for team adaptation to novel environments. *Journal of Applied Psychology, 85,* 971-986.

Mohammed, S. (2001). Toward an understanding of cognitive consensus in a group decision-making context. *Journal of Applied Behavioral Science, 37,* 408-425.

Mohammed, S., & Dumville, B. C. (2001). Team mental models in a team knowledge framework: Expanding theory and measurement across disciplinary boundaries. *Journal of Organizational Behavior, 22,* 89-106.

Mohammed, S., Klimoski, R., & Rentsch, J. R. (2000). The measurement of team mental models: We have no shared schema. *Organizational Research Methods, 3,* 123-165.

Mohammed, S., & Ringseis, E. (2001). Cognitive diversity and consensus in group decision making: The role of inputs, processes, and outcomes. *Organizational Behavior and Human Decision Processes, 85,* 310-335.

Mortensen, M., & Hinds, P. J. (2001). Conflict and shared identity in geographically distributed teams. *International Journal of Conflict Management, 12,* 212-238.

Mueller-Hanson, R. A., White, S. S., Dorsey, D. W., & Pulakos, E. D. (2005). *Training adaptable leaders: Lessons from research and practice* (Research Report 1844). U.S. Army Research Institute for the Behavioral and Social Sciences.

Orasanu, J., & Salas, E. (1993). Team decision making in complex environments. In G. Klein, J. Orasanu, R. Calderwood, & C. E. Zsambok (Eds.), *Decision making in action: Models and methods*. Norwood, NJ: Ablex Publishing.

Orvis, K. L., & Lassiter, A. R. L. (2006). Computer-supported collaborative learning: The role of the instructor. In S. P. Ferris & S. H. Godar (Eds.), *Teaching and learning with virtual teams* (pp. 158-179). Hershey, PA: Idea Group.

Palloff, R. M., & Pratt, K. (2005). *Collaborating online: Learning together in community*. San Francisco: Jossey-Bass.

Rouse, W. B., Cannon-Bowers,J. A., & Salas, E. (1992). The role of mental models in team performance in complex systems. *IEEE Transactions on Systems, Man, and Cybernetics, 22*, 1296-1308.

Rouse, W. B., & Morris, N. M. (1986). On looking into the black box: Prospects and limits in the search for mental models. *Psychological Bulletin, 100*, 349-363.

Short, J., Williams, E., & Christie, B. (1976). *The social psychology of telecommunications*. London: John Wiley & Sons.

Tannenbaum, S. I., Smith-Jentsch, K. A., & Behson, S. J. (1998). Training team leaders to facilitate team learning and performance. In J. A. Cannon-Bowers & E. Salas (Eds.), *Making decisions under stress: Implications for individual and team training* (pp. 247-270). Washington, DC: American Psychological Association.

Vick, R. M. (2003). *Development of shared mental models: Structuring distributed naturalistic decision making in a synchronous computer-mediated work environment*. Unpublished dissertation.

Zaccaro, S. J., & Bader, P. (2003). E-leadership and the challenges of leading e-teams. *Organizational Dynamics, 31*, 377-387.

Zaccaro, S. J., Shuffler, M. L., & Hildebrand, K. (in press). The leader's role in group learning. In V. Sessa & M. London (Eds.), *Group learning*. Mahwah, NJ: Lawrence Erlbaum Associates.

Chapter XIV

Practical Strategies for Assessing the Quality of Collaborative Learner Engagement

John LeBaron, Western Carolina University, USA

Carol Bennett, WRESA Elementary & Middle Grades Curriculum Coordinator, USA

Abstract

Teachers and designers of computer-networked settings increasingly acknowl-edge that active learner engagement poses unique challenges, especially for instructors weaned on traditional site-based teaching, and that such engagement is essential to the progressive construction of learner knowl-edge. "Learner engagement" can mean several things: engagement with material, engagement with instructors, and, perhaps most important, peer engagement. Many teachers of computer-networked courses, who are quite diligent about incorporating activities and procedures to promote human interactivity, are confronted with the challenge of assessing the efficacy of their efforts. How do they discern whether the strategies and tactics woven into their "e-settings" are achieving the desired ends? This chapter outlines issues of self-assessment, including ethical questions. It lays out recommendations for self-assessment in a manner that respects student trust and confidentiality, distinguishing the demands of practical self-assessment from scholarly course research. The institutional pressures from which such assessment emerges are also examined.

Introduction

Computer-supported collaborative learning (CSCL) outlined by Orvis and Lassiter (2006) makes a case for the active engagement of students in their own learning. These authors introduce certain challenges unique to computer-networked vs. face-to-face settings. Their commentary begs the question, "How do we know if our intentions work?" If we are truly committed to active student engagement and peer collaboration, then how do we gauge the achievement of our intentions? Orvis and Lassiter suggest that cognitive growth depends on a successful social construction of knowledge. If this is true, online instructors and designers need to devise techniques to discern the effectiveness of tactics and strategies incorporated into their course settings.

Personal interaction is crucial to the success of all forms of teaching and learning (Laurillard, 2000; Swan, 2002; Vrasidas & McIsaac, 1999). Computer-supported learning allows for many kinds of interactions: one-to-one, one-to-many, or many-to-many. By itself, however, technology does not promote interaction. Technology requires human intervention in design and instruction to assure strong student engagement in networked settings (Harasim, 1993; Harasim, Hiltz, Teles, & Turroff, 1995; Kearsley & Schneiderman, 1999). Roblyer and Wiencke (2003) add that specific, deliberate activities are necessary to promote and support interaction among course participants.

Inquiry into the questions of self-assessment in computer-networked learning environments has progressed little since the day when research concentrated on direct efficacy comparisons between computer-mediated and traditional classroom teaching. As computer-networked education was just emerging,

Verduin and Clark (1991) reviewed 56 studies comparing the academic achievement of students in conventional classrooms to "distance learning" students. While focusing on student performance measured by grades, they found little or no distinction. Continuing this "no significant difference" stream of research, Russell's growing compendium of studies (2001) revealed no significant difference in student performance between learners in conventional classrooms and those enrolled in various types of "distance learning" courses. Based on such "no significant difference" research, findings to date have indicated that distance learning, in a variety of modalities, typically matches or exceeds teaching, at least when effectiveness is gauged by student perceptions or performance measured by, say, their course grades.

These studies, however, provide little insight beyond that indicated by survey results or student transcripts. They fail to reveal much about the qualitative nature of the compared learning environments, and leave unanswered such other questions as: Do different teaching modalities transform traditional instructional media into significantly different learning experiences? What tactics and strategies do particular teaching and learning settings enable to promote the kinds of student growth sought by the course designers and instructors?

Several scholars have decried the persistent failure of scholarly research to analyze academic practice deeply or to improve it (Brown & Johnson-Shull, 2000; Phipps & Merisotis, 1999). Ehrmann (1997) suggests that most research comparing technology-infused with traditional teaching fails to address important substantive questions about distance education. Indeed, comparisons between alternative modes of instruction are meaningless because they typically fail to account for the innumerable and complex variables that distinguish different types of learning environment. As Ramage (2002) points out, the research deficiencies on effective higher education teaching are by no means limited to the analysis of education-at-a-distance. Research on classroom practice is similarly weak.

Comparative "modality research" assumes that technology does little more than assume a simple replication of what is occurring in conventional classrooms. Rather than thinking about technology as the electronic equivalent of the conventional classroom, researchers might instead ask how technology could transform, say, a 100-student introductory physics lecture into a rich multidisciplinary "conversation" that links the humanities and the arts with related concepts in physics where students participate actively and collectively in the distribution of knowledge? In this way, technology becomes *transformative* rather than *adaptive*. Self-assessment attempts, therefore, become multifaceted, formative, and naturalistic as instructors struggle to assess *process*, at least as much as *products* represented in transcripts of student work.

Aside from the common-sense proposition that the quality of teaching and course design is advanced by deliberate attempts to gauge efficacy, the practice of self-assessment is theoretically supported by a more critical application of the rich "reflective practitioner" literature (Bengtsson, 1995, 2003; Schön, 1987a, b). The "reflective practitioner" (RP) concept has informed the education field for several decades. It has its roots in the progressive schooling movement of Europe and America in the 1930s and 1940s, but more recently has been championed by the late Donald Schön. Schön's work is a response to rigidly positivistic accountability pressures so globally prevalent in contemporary educational policy. He urges higher education teaching to focus significantly on "reflective practica," where teacher intuition interplays with "received knowledge" (i.e., formal research) in close coaching environments where the coach assumes more the Socratic role of "critical discussant" than of "knowledge dispenser."

Moving from theory back to common sense for a moment, the argument that thoughtful reflection about one's own practice somehow impedes the objective assessment of efficacy defies logic, so long as such reflection is supported by data and by theory. Rigorous RP is challenging. As Schön has noted, "...The introduction of a reflective practicum ... is an uphill business.... If you think about introducing a reflective practicum into ... education you must work against the view that practice is a second-class activity" (1987a).

A discussion about self-assessment carries implications for evaluative technique, for ethical research behavior, and for the institutional context where the outcomes of these discussions often carry rather high career stakes, especially for instructors. This chapter attempts to advance this discussion and to suggest future directions that it might take. Between them, the authors have been engaged in designing computer-networked learning environments since 1999.

Several online graduate education courses taught between 2003 and 2006 serve as case histories for the ensuing discussion. The first author designed and taught two of these courses through several iterations at two universities. The second author is a former student in two of these courses. She has gone on to design her own online learning projects for the professional development of school teachers. Her particular student perspectives appear in narrative boxes throughout this chapter.

Assessing the Efficacy of Collaborative Learner Engagement

Hill, Han, and Raven (2001) suggest that the use of group work contributes positively to a sense of belonging and connection within Web-based courses. Other pioneers such as Haythornthwaite, Kazmer, and Robins (2000), and Lock (2002) challenge CSCL designers, therefore, to assess the *processes* of interaction and engagement among learners.

Online course instructors and designers need to distinguish between the demands of formative self-assessment and summative public research as they plan to ascertain the effectiveness of the processes they use to promote student collaboration. Self-assessment is formative in nature. Although clear ethical procedures require much care in the collection and analysis of data, the purpose of self-assessment is to determine what works in order to improve future instruction. Research, on the other hand, is by definition a public act, therefore requiring greater rigor and more attention to ethics, not only in reporting results, but also in collecting and analyzing information.

With the growing acceptance in higher education of formal inquiry into teaching, (e.g., the Scholarship of Teaching and Learning (SoTL) as legitimate research for career advancement, online course evaluation might assume that today's private self assessment may become tomorrow's published research (Boyer, 1990; Hutchings, Babb, & Bjork, 2002). We shall return to these issues later, but published research demands more rigorous human subject safety review than does the data collected and analyzed for the private assessment of an individual teacher.

Having said this, important distinctions exist between self-assessment and scholarly research. Research expects to advance disciplinary knowledge in a rigorous manner that observes certain rules of inquiry within a community of critical peers. Self-assessment, on the other hand, is dedicated to the discovery of efficacy and achievement related to more narrowly-conceived instructional purposes. Although such discovery may ultimately become part of a research agenda, observing the relatively harsher rules of research may constrain many useful assessment techniques. For example, self-assessment typically addresses very small subject samples. In most cases, it need not undergo the data coding and analysis required of formal research. There is neither the possibility nor the need to generalize the assessed findings to other settings. The assessor is attempting to find out what is effective in *this course*, with *this population* of students at *this particular time*.

When and where to start? As with most endeavors, knowing how well one does something depends on a clearly-articulated awareness of what was intended in the first place. As banal as this notion may seem, the principle is often overlooked and difficult to sustain. So, if course activities are structured to promote peer collaboration, it makes sense, as Orvis and Lassiter (2006) advise, to embed such activity early in the course and to assess it in several ways as soon after completion of the exercise as possible.

Among the course activities analyzed for this discussion, was an initial "Icebreaker" assignment. Woods and Ebersole (2003) researched the usefulness of personal information-sharing in nonsubstantive discussion boards in an online course. They discovered that the use of autobiographies helped foster positive relationships within the course community for students and instructor alike.

Many learning management platforms (LMS) offer little or no default information to students about their classmates, a glaring deficiency if the instructor means to promote frequent, deep, purposeful dialogue throughout the study period. Therefore, upon enrollment in several of the authors' courses, an early assignment required students to submit more detailed biographical data via a hot-linked browser-based form. Students were asked to list their primary professional and recreational interests and provide more detailed contact information than a simple e-mail address. Most students also capitalized on the option to file-attach a personal photo. This information was then shared on a separate course page, shown in Figure 1.

Based on these online biographies, students were required to undertake a simple "get to know you" assignment, called the "Icebreaker," within the first three weeks of the course. John Cowan, a professor well known for his work on student-centered online learning at the British Open University, has advised that everything an instructor truly values should be assessed as part of the overall calculation of student performance (personal communication, June 10, 2001). Therefore, 10% of the course grade was attributed to the completion of this assignment, even though it was not directly associated with the course content. It should be noted here that this aspect of the grade depended only on assignment completion; in no way was the content of the

Figure 1. The instructor provides an online form through which students submit contact information and biographical data. Additionally, they send photos of themselves as e-mail attachments. From these submissions, the instructor created a "student mini-biography" Web page to post as a course resource for several collaborative group assignments.

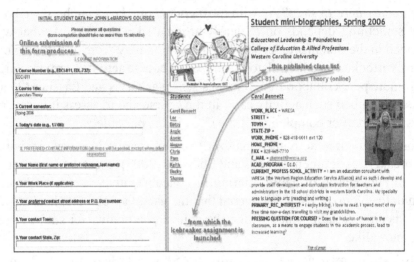

student contributions judged—it was only reported. Students were asked to review the online student biographies and begin a dialogue within private small teams created by the instructor within the asynchronous discussion boards of the LMS.

Former student perspective on the course Icebreaker assignment

The Icebreaker activity was a comfortable way to quickly get involved in the course. Right from the start students had an assignment deadline; but one with which we could almost certainly be successful. It was an authentic way to get us actively engaged from the get-go. An additional benefit was that I found I learned more about my classmates than I had in other classes where we met face-to-face on a weekly basis. As our coursework projects progressed throughout the semester, I frequently referred back to the student biographies to get a clearer understanding of my classmates' perspectives.

The major purpose of this activity was to build an immediate sense of community within the course as a foundation for subsequent, substantive knowledge construction. To ascertain whether this purpose was met, the instructor surveyed the students anonymously through an online form that asked on a four-point Likert scale, among other questions about this exercise, if the activity promoted the intended sense of community. The scaled questions were supplemented by an open-ended textbox question requesting additional comments about the Icebreaker.

Over several course iterations, on the scaled questions, 96% of respondents answered affirmatively that, yes, the assignment promoted a sense of community. Zero percent responded negatively, and 4% selected "N/A" for reasons that are not clear. Prominently mentioned comments offered in response to the open-ended textbox question were, "The icebreaker was a good way to launch the course"; "The Icebreaker offered a good method to meet classmates"; "The Icebreaker encouraged longer-term dialogue among students"; and "The expanded student list, with photos, was useful."

A helpful way to obtain information on student perceptions about various aspects of teaching and design is through the use of online forms that ask questions keyed explicitly to instructional purpose. In this case, students were asked directly if the intent of the exercise was achieved. Such forms need not be long. They may be used repeatedly for the instructor to build knowledge about the relative success of their intentions formatively and incrementally. Provided that the forms are neither onerous nor excessively time-consuming, students appreciate being asked about their perceptions, especially if they see mid-course instructor corrections made in response to them.

Former student perspective on multiple polling about student perception

As a student, I especially appreciated the fact that the instructor cared enough to elicit student feedback during the course, rather than waiting until the end, when any changes would have little effect on current students. It was a highly effective strategy for initiating student-teacher trust.

Online forms allow for a wide variety of question types to be asked of students in a single sitting, from scaled ratings to open-ended textbox narratives. By encouraging students to comment in their own words in addition to rating preformatted statements about course design and teaching, instructors can obtain a relatively deep, personalized sense of their student's authentic feelings about their experiences. The usefulness of different kinds of information-gathering in online course evaluation is stressed by a host of researchers, including Hammond and Winiyapinit (2005), Hara, Bonk, and Angeli (2000), and Naidu and Järvelä (2005). Our assessment of the Icebreaker, however, could have employed even more robust data sources than it did. For example, transcripts of the students' conversations in this activity could have been qualitatively analyzed according to objectives established in advance for the exercise by the instructor or the course designer.

Like, we were saying; yes, really saying... Student learning is enhanced when diverse media of expression are made available in online course settings. As a result of infusing media streaming into her undergraduate biology courses, Michelich (2002) reports anecdotally on improved student class participation and performance on assignments and exams. Literally giving an audible "voice" to students provides a naturalistic environment for discussion and collaboration. By themselves, most learning management systems fail to offer students such "voice," but after-market conferencing tools such as Centra™ or Elluminate™ may be power-linked to most learning management systems to provide diverse channels of dialogue in a variety of media.

In this case, the instructor established team and whole class dialogues in the conventional text-based asynchronous discussion boards in a manner that challenged students to respond not only to the weekly questions posed by the instructor but also to one another in progressive threads. There is nothing unusual about this kind of activity, but through an asynchronous voice tool, powered by Horizon/Wimba™, students were led directly from the text discussion to a threaded voice environment where students were encouraged to talk directly together in their real voices.

Because this voice communication capacity is not seamlessly integrated with other LMS communications tools, navigation between the text and the voice utilities is awkward, requiring students to back out of one communication protocol and redirect their steps into a different one. The challenge for instructors, therefore, is to make this cumbersome procedure more seamless so that students would actually use it and benefit from doing so. With the help of University technical staff, an HTML script was created that could be inserted into any text discussion message with the result that a simple click would instantly open a new Wimba window side-by-side with the original text message. Students then had the choice of pursuing the conversation by voice or in text, with no prejudice attached to their choice. Figure 2, below, shows the screen appearance of this procedure.

Former student perspective on linking text discussions to voice threads

This was an effective strategy to encourage student engagement and collaborative peer interactions. The asynchronous discussion boards facilitated our getting to know one another at an even deeper level and made our discussions much richer. Additionally, the daily postings encouraged our frequent participation, partly through curiosity about what our peers were saying and additionally, from our innate desire to excel in the class.

Two assessment techniques were used to assess whether this technique met its major purpose: one formative and one summative. Shortly after Wimba was launched for the purpose outlined above (midway through the course), a threaded discussion group was established for anonymous postings. The instructor asked students to respond anonymously to the following question: "I am using voice messaging ... for my responses to your discussion postings.... I'd like to know how it's working for you. I have added two discussion

Figure 2. The instructor indicates in the standard text discussion board (lower left corner of the figure) that he has responded by voice. On opening his message to this effect, the student opens a message containing a hot-link taking her or him directly to the voice board where the message resides.

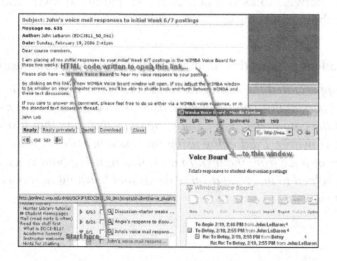

topics explicitly requesting your feedback. These topics enable anonymous postings. I will not know the originator of any message unless you choose to sign your posting.... Please use your own words to respond."

Former student perspective on the use of voice messaging

I enjoyed the voice messages because it felt like personal feedback from the instructor. Often in face-to-face classes, there is little time to speak to the instructor one-on-one. The voice messages felt more like I was getting individual attention. When students started adding their voice messages, it added another dimension to the dialogue and strengthened the lines of cooperative communication. If another classmate left a voice message for me, I felt compelled to answer in a more effectual manner than I did with just the text messages.

Supplementing this request for anonymous student narratives were one open-ended and two scaled questions about the use of Wimba during the course. Thus, three data sources were employed for this one procedure that the instructor had used for the first time. The results reflected the "rookie" status of this undertaking. In their scaled end-of-course evaluative responses, six students agreed that this use of Wimba "helped create a personal dimension in [their] dialogue with the instructor"; five disagreed. Five agreed that Wimba "was a useful medium for [them] to make good use of instructor feedback"; an equal number disagreed. Two representative comments in the open-ended summative student evaluation were, "Make Wimba required for discussions and chats (otherwise folks will default to the traditional text)" and "Either use Wimba throughout course or not at all."

Former student perspective on mandated use of voice communication

I actually appreciated the choice the instructor provided for us to use text or Wimba. I personally would not have liked Wimba to have been mandated throughout the course because I enjoy the reflective time that text messaging allows. However, I did enjoy using the voice boards occasionally as a nice change of pace from the text. In my opinion, using both voice and text messaging helped to meet the diverse needs and learning accommodations of different students.

Narrative student responses in the midterm anonymous discussion board comments reinforced the judgments conveyed in the final online student evaluation. Excerpts from several randomly selected comments appear below:

- "I appreciate the fact that you are extremely active in the course.... The only thing I find a little frustrating is that there are so many places [within the course setting] to look."
- "I like receiving voice messages. However, I am a visual learner so when I ask specific questions, I like to have an answer written out for me that I can print and place in my notebook for this class."
- "I do like the Wimba option. However, I must agree with some of the other responses that with email, and several discussion boards going at one time that I often get overwhelmed with all the things going on in this class."
- "[Text] discussion threads and e-mail are currently better for me."

One student chose to identify herself in her response. She wrote, in part, "I am getting used to the Wimba chat feedback, although I am much more familiar with the text chat. I like the fact that I can print, review and keep the text responses. I also feel more comfortable responding to a text chat."

The salient points here are not so much what the students indicated as how the instructor interprets the information and what he does with it. Assessing instructional efficacy can seem harsh when the instructors fail to remove their egos from the information conveyed. In this case, the message seemed clear. Although students appeared to appreciate the effort put into this innovation, it was not promoting student satisfaction or the peer dialogue intended. The varied data sources pointed to the highly plausible interpretation of a collective student perception, namely a lukewarm endorsement. As a result, the exercise either had to be improved or abandoned.

Not yet convinced that abandonment was indicated, for his next online course, the instructor decided to follow one specific direction suggested in the end-of-course student evaluations, and to reject another. He enabled the Wimba asynchronous tool immediately as the course was launched, and maintained its use throughout the semester. However, because a major purpose of using it was to give students communicative choices according to preference and style, he did not require it.

Thus, the revised Wimba discussion seemed more confident and less tentative. Students accepted it from the outset, and their end-of-course evaluations reflected substantially higher levels of satisfaction. From a total of 11, nine students agreed that the use of Wimba "helped created a personal dimension in [their] dialogue with the instructor" (four strongly); two disagreed (none strongly). Eight agreed that Wimba "was a useful medium for [them] to make good use of instructor feedback" (three strongly); three disagreed (none strongly). In this way, an end-of-course evaluative summation became formative for improving the next course iteration. Assessment results of these and other strategies embedded in the authors' courses are found in several other publications (LeBaron & Miller, 2004; LeBaron & Miller, 2005; LeBaron, Pulkkinen, & Scollin, 2000; LeBaron and Santos, 2005).

Broader Discussion of CSCL Efficacy

The examples provided above prompt a more general dialogue about quality assessment of instructional strategies to promote student collaboration. In the foregoing discussion, we have touched upon issues of purpose, ethics, and the use of multiple data sources and application of assessment results. The importance of keeping keenly mindful of the process intentions was stressed, so that queries about efficacy could be keyed specifically to these intentions. Put another way, if one wishes to know what students think about something; find different, safe ways to *ask them about that particular thing* (Henri, 1991).

Transcript analysis. To deepen the authenticity of the assessments described above, more can be done. For example, assessment of the Icebreaker and the asynchronous Wimba discussions depended largely on various expressions of student perception gleaned through ratings and comments submitted via Web-based interactive forms provided by the instructor either at a mid-point or at the end of a course. Assessment depth, however, would be enhanced by a focused analysis of the transcripted conversations actually undertaken during the Icebreaker. Such transcripts might be supported by performance rubrics describing various levels of depth, responsiveness and relevance embedded in the student postings. Rubrics need not be used for grading student performance (although they may be). In this scenario, they would be used to assess how well the instructor has designed an exercise to achieve the goals originally established for it.

In depth, qualitative transcript analysis has been promoted for instructional self-assessment by much commentary in the field (Gerbic & Stacey, 2005; Mason, 1991; Naidu & Järvelä, 2006). Successful transcript analysis depends on knowing what information is desired. For example, is the assessor seeking evidence of the collective construction of knowledge, evidence of critical thinking, social engagement, depth of dialogue, substantive analysis of course content, or some combination of the above? For the purpose of this discussion, the choice does not matter much. What matters is that assessors know exactly what they're looking for so that they might develop a coding system that accurately produces the answers geared to informational categories determined in advance.

Third-party interviews. Although transcript analysis offers a potentially rich leg on the triangulation tripod, an equally valuable strategy is the third-party interview. Such interviews are conducted under the overall guidance of the instructor or course designer seeking to secure "richer, thicker" insights into student perceptions about particular instructional purposes. Such interviews are best conducted within the month after a course has ended. Conducting them in-progress can seem threatening to students, no matter how convincing the assurances of confidentiality and anonymity.

The third party may be an unbiased faculty colleague, a teaching assistant, or a peer student—someone who understands the course and its intentions but has no vested interest in the responses or the identity of those making them. Interviews may be conducted in-person, by telephone or through e-mail. Typically, such follow-up is undertaken only with a relatively small sample of a whole course enrollment. A randomly-selected "A list" of subjects is identified, with "B list" substitutes if students initially selected are unable or unwilling to participate. This assisting assessor reveals only the raw aggregated results of the interview. It is then up to the instructor to code and interpret the results according as rigorously as deemed necessary for the assessment purpose.

LMS "log counts." Campos (2004) and Mason (1991) have pointed out that simple "log counts" of discussions provided by most LMS tracking tools are of limited value because they indicate nothing about the content, relevance, scholarship, or responsiveness to instructional purpose of the student postings. This is not to say that logs should not be used, just that if they are used, it should be understood that they offer little more than unqualified counts. They may, however, serve to reinforce other, richer sources of information.

As Garrison, Anderson, and Archer (2001) suggest, any single data source is by definition unacceptably limiting for deep understanding.

Outside the formal assessment box. There are many ways outside a formal program of assessment for online course designer-instructors to gain information about the degree to which their intentions are being achieved. Here, the assessor must be particularly attentive to ethical issues. For example, private e-mail provides a very rich vein of information; because it is private, however, it is not the business of public research; indeed, it may concern private assessment in only a limited way. E-mail among students should not even be viewed by the instructor, and a message directed to the instructor in a moment of frustration is best forgotten as a deep indicator of anything beyond the momentary frustration. The same principle applies to student chatter in private chat rooms, or "virtual cafés" established explicitly for their socialization, but visible to the instructor.

More appropriate, though more challenging, are longitudinal assessment techniques, undertaken, again through third-party interview or anonymous survey, a significant period of time after a course has ended. In some of the applied sciences, for example, many graduate course syllabi contain certain goals of workplace application (Boyer, 1990). A curriculum course typically proposes that the theoretical scholarship tackled in class will be applied in subsequent professional curriculum work. One or more years after the course, it is useful to return to the course syllabus, to extract the goals of scholarly application, and to ask the former enrollees incisive questions about their particular applications to practice.

Ethics. How can assessors assess, and how should they not? Is what they *can* do, what they *ought to* do? Clearly, the success of any online instructional assessment, especially when it comes to CSCL, depends on faculty-student trust. Deep trust emerges from course to course over time. It is difficult to build, but it can be lost in a split second. Trust is related to a respect for regulation and policy, but it is much more than that. As discussed above, rules of human subjects' research apply in greater measure to evaluations destined for broad publication, than for the private application to course improvement. If research is intended, or even remotely anticipated, Institutional Review Board (IRB) human subjects' rules should be observed. Even here, however, the rules are less important than trust, laboriously earned and scrupulously maintained.

Elements of trust include confidentiality, anonymity, and intellectual honesty in interpreting the information gleaned. As a rule of thumb, all evaluative data should be aggregated for any public discourse about the efficacy of course activity. There should be no possibility, directly or by implication, of connecting any individual student to any particular sentiment. This is especially true when student scholarly performance is being used to assess the quality of course activity. To greater or lesser degrees, the same may be said of student content analysis and postings in open or closed discussion forums.

The literature on computer-networked assessment ethics is quite rich. Browne (2003), King (1996), and Anderson and Kanuka (2003) suggest the student permission is *sine qua non* for any published research related to course activity. If such permission is withheld for any reason, the transcripts of those students must be excluded from analysis whether or not it compromises the substantive integrity of the conversational thread. The problem here, of course, is that the ethical "bathwater" might jettison the informational "baby" (Rourke, Anderson, Garrison, & Archer, 2001). A more flexible approach may be taken toward unpublished private self-assessment, but assessors must protect themselves by anticipating the possibility of future research. As King points out, all self-assessment using the content of student work as a measure must be accompanied by informed consent, outlining the assurances of anonymity and confidentiality, the potential harm that the students might endure, even in the remotest circumstances, and procedures for the student to opt out.

In order for assessed student information to carry legitimacy, it should not, in most cases, be traced to individual students. Lack of confidence in anonymity may corrupt the integrity of any student's comment, even after a course terminates because the same student may be enrolled in a future course, or the course of a friendly colleague. As Anderson and Kanuka (2003) affirm, the debate on ethics in assessing course attributes based on student work is still emerging. Human subjects' research guidelines offer some guidance in this respect. It may be best to assure safety of students and assessors by erring on the side of caution.

Closing the conversational circle. The foregoing discussion presents a workload potential capable of filling an instructor's entire professional time card. As Hara, Bonk, and Angeli (2000) suggest, in-depth online instructional assessment can be so exceedingly time-consuming that it fails to get done. Fortunately, strategies exist for managing time without unduly compromising assessment results. For example, "mountain" of data can be reduced to more manageable "hills" through various sampling techniques. Transcripts may be selected from representative segments of a course, for example, every third week of a fifteen-week course (Pena-Shaff & Nicholls, 2004; Santos & LeBaron, 2006). Interviews may be conducted with a random sample of enrolled students. Qualitative information may be coded for efficient analysis. The question of personal ego was raised earlier, with the suggestion to strip it away from the analysis of assessed student perceptions. This is not entirely true, however. Professional educators must trust their own deep intuitive sense about the meaning of the information they collect. For example, Virginia Michelich's sense (2002) about the efficacy of streamed media in her undergraduate biology course is based largely on evidence she calls anecdotal. By "anecdotal," she means her experienced, expert, professional analysis of student work quality. For the purposes of formative self-assessment, such conduct is perfectly acceptable. Michelich appears confident enough to know (and report publicly) what works well in her courses when she sees it.

The Institutional Stakes

The practical implications of the foregoing discussion occur in the real world of higher education policy. The usefulness of assessing CSCL or even attempting to integrate it into learning environments in the first place, depends on the prevailing scholarly values of its sponsoring institutions. Typically, but not always, these institutions are colleges or universities. Universities pose special challenges. Alex Wright (2005) recently penned a discussion about online learning's metamorphosis from a speculative entrepreneurial bubble in the 1990s into mainstream higher education practice today.

Parts of Wright's article, "From Ivory Tower to Academic Sweatshop," are troubling to faculty who are passionate about teaching quality. Reporting on one particular university's business model for online learning, Wright declared that this institution "has built its business through economics of scale, developing a course once and then replicating it, so that many teachers can administer the course to the school's 200,000-plus student body." Such an approach to online education has been described as a "package and deliver" approach where course components are bundled into deliverable products requiring only token human facilitation to service student access and keep instruction moving within defined timeframes.

Recognizing the threat of commercial competition from nontraditional newcomers to higher education, institutions developing computer networked learning programs need to engage in deep developmental thinking, guided by their educational missions, to compete effectively with the lower-cost "package and deliver" strategies of learning distribution so common in certain marketplace sectors (Pulkkinen, 2005). For institutions committed to personalized teaching excellence, viable markets will continue to exist for high-quality post-secondary teaching (Twigg, 1998). Designers and instructors in such institutions require support for assessing the collaborative processes they build into their courses.

Universities following the lure of scholarly commoditization embrace a model reminiscent of that voiced by Arizona State University's Steve Salik who opined to Wright (2005), "Our professors are content experts. *That's all they are*" (emphasis ours). Such a sentiment can come only from someone who knows exponentially less about teaching and learning than about marketing. While universities can ill-afford to ignore market conditions, doing so at the expense of their core educational missions embodied in highly skilled teaching faculty members harms students and demeans the scholarly integrity of educational institutions. In such a setting, the professor is divorced, among other things, from the pedagogical creation of processes to promote learner collaboration. Such a setting renders discussion about collaborative learning, and the assessment of it, entirely moot in a world that may indeed be new but not particularly brave.

Conclusion and Future Trends

While we do not deny the value of rigorous research in the process of efficacy evaluation in online teaching and course design, we point out that useful self-assessment procedures are available which may not meet the most rigorous standards of scientific research. Nonetheless, these may give online instructors valuable information about how they are doing with their efforts to promote computer-supported learner engagement. We encourage teachers and designers judiciously to undertake such measures, because if we hold all self-assessment to the strictest rigors of pure research, then we may end up with very little of it, much to the detriment of teaching quality.

This chapter has advocated the use of multiple data sources collected over time, formatively and summatively. We have particularly urged the use of various data-gathering techniques to assess the efficacy of designs to promote learner engagement. We have focused on student perception polling. As a sole data source, the value of student perception may be limited. Actual student performance must also be taken into consideration. In doing so, however, assessors and designers need to think about what they mean by "performance," distinguishing in their own minds the relative virtues of process vs. product outcomes. In some courses, process is very important. Indeed some courses are primarily *about* process.

Strategies for the effective assessment of learner engagement apply to all instructional formats, whether computer-enabled or not. Fortunately for conscientious online teachers and developers, networked computing not only provides ever-richer potential for promoting learner engagement, it also offers more robust tools for assessing the efficacy of such engagement. Synchronous and asynchronous discussion and conferencing tools enable powerfully-mediated channels for communication during any course, at its termination, and retrospectively after the ostensible benefits of study have "sunken in." Qualitative software support for the analysis of discussion transcripts, interviews, and open-ended narratives encourages increasingly sophisticated synthesis of assessment results (di Gregorio, 2000). In short, the future for the enrichment of online learner engagement and for the assessment of it appears bright indeed.

References

Anderson, T., & Kanuka, H. (2003). *E-research: Methods, strategies and issues*. London: Allyn and Bacon.

Bengtsson, J. (1995). What is reflection: On reflection in the teaching profession and teacher education. *Teachers and Teaching, 1*(1), 23-32.

Bengtsson, J. (2003). Possibilities and limits of self-reflection in the teaching profession. *Studies in Philosophy and Education, 22*(3/4), 295-316.

Boyer, E. (1990). *Scholarship reconsidered: Priorities of the professoriate*. Princeton, NJ: The Carnegie Foundation for the Advancement of Teaching.

Brown, G., & Johnson-Shull, L. (2000, May/June). Teaching online: Now we're talking. *The Technology Source*. Retrieved November 10, 2007, from http://technologysource.org/article/teaching_online/

Browne, E. (2003). Conversation in cyberspace: A study of online learning. *Open Learning, 18*(3), 245-259.

Campos, M. (2004). A constructivist method for the analysis of networked cognitive communication and the assessment of collaborative learning and knowledge building. *JALN, 8*(2). Retrieved November 10, 2007, from http://www.sloan-c.org/publications/jaln/v8n2/index.asp

di Gregario, S. (2000). *Using NVivo for your literature review*. Paper presented at the Strategies in Qualitative Research: Issues and Results from Analysis Using QSR NVivo and NUD*IST Conference, London. Retrieved November 10, 2007, from http://www.sdgassociates.com/downloads/literature_review.pdf

Ehrmann, S. (1997). Asking the right questions: What does research tell us about technology and higher learning? In *Engines of inquiry: A practical guide for using technology to teach American culture*. Retrieved November 10, 2007, from http://www.georgetown.edu/crossroads/guide/ehrmann.html

Garrison, R., Anderson, T., & Archer, W. (2001). Critical thinking, cognitive presence and computer conference in distance education. *The American Journal of Distance Education, 15*(1), 7-23.

Gerbic, P., & Stacey, E. (2005). A purposive approach to content analysis: Designing analytical frameworks. *The Internet and Higher Education, 8*(1), 45-59.

Hammond, M., & Wiriyapinit, M. (2005). Learning through online discussion: A case of triangulation in research. *Australasian Journal of Educational Technology, 21*(3), 283-302.

Hara, N., Bonk, C. J., & Angeli, C. (2000). Content analysis of online discussion in an applied educational psychology course. *Instructional Science, 28*(2), 115-152.

Harasim, L. (1993). Networlds: Networks as social space. In L. Harasim (Ed.), *Global networks: Computers and international communication* (pp. 15-34). MIT Press: Cambridge, MA.

Harasim, L., Hiltz, S. R., Teles, L., & Turroff, M. (1995). *Learning networks: A field guide to teaching and learning online*. Cambridge, MA: MIT Press.

Haythornthwaite, C., Kazmer, M., & Robins, J. (2000). Community development among distance learners: Temporal and technological dimensions. *Journal of Computer Mediated Communication, 6*(1). Retrieved November 10, 2007, from http://www.ascusc.org/jcmc/vol6/issue1/haythornthwaite.html

Henri, F. (1991). Computer conferencing and content analysis. In A. R. Kaye (Ed.), *Collaborative learning through computer conferencing*. The Najaden papers (pp. 117-136). New York: Springer-Verlag.

Hill, J. R., Han, S., & Raven, A. (2001, November). Build it and they will stay: A research based model for creating community in Web based learning environments. In *Proceedings of the National Convention of the Association for Educational Communication and Technology*, Atlanta, Georgia (pp. 192-199).

Hutchings, P., Babb, M., & Bjork, C. (2002). The scholarship of teaching and learning in higher education: An annotated bibliography. *The Carnegie for the Advancement of Teaching*. Retrieved November 10, 2007, from http://www.carnegiefoundation.org/dynamic/downloads/file_1_196.pdf

Kearsley, G., & Schneiderman, B. (1999). *Engagement theory: A framework for technology-based teaching and learning*. Retrieved November 10, 2007, from http://home.sprynet.com/~gkearsley/engage.htm

King, S. A. (1996). Researching internet communities: Proposed ethical guidelines for the reporting of results. *The Information Society, 12*(2), 119-127.

Laurillard, D. (2000). New technologies, students and the curriculum: The impact of communication and information technology on higher education. In P. Scott (Ed.), *Higher education re-formed* (pp. 133-153). London: Falmer Press.

LeBaron, J., & Miller, D. (2004). The teacher as "agent provocateur": Strategies to promote community in online course settings. In T. Latomaa, J. Pohjonen, J. Pulkkinen, & M. Ruotsalainen (Eds.), *eReflections: Ten years of educational technology studies at the University of Oulu* (pp. 109-125). Oulu, Finland: Oulun yliopiston kasvatustieteiden tiedekunnan. Retrieved November 10, 2007, from http://gse.uml.edu/lebaron/Oulu-TAPfinal_030922.pdf

LeBaron, J., & Miller, D. (2005). The potential of jigsaw role-playing to promote the social construction of knowledge in an online graduate education course. *Teachers College Record, 107*(8), 1652-1674.

LeBaron, J., Pulkkinen, J., & Scollin, P. (2000). Promoting cross-border communication in an international Web-based graduate course. *Interactive Electronic Multimedia Journal of Computer-Enhanced Learning*,

2(2). Retrieved November 10, 2007, from http://imej.wfu.edu/articles/2000/2/01/index.asp

LeBaron, J., & Santos, I. (2005). Authentic engagement of adult learners in online settings. *MountainRise, 2*(1). Retrieved November 10, 2007, from http://facctr.wcu.edu/mountainrise/archive/vol2no1/html/authentic_engagement.html

Lock, J. V. (2002). Laying the groundwork for the development of learning communities within online courses. *Quarterly Review of Distance Education, 3*(4), 395-408.

Mason, R. (1991). Evaluation methodologies for computer conferencing applications. In A. R. Kaye (Ed.), *Collaborative learning through computer conferencing: The Najaden papers* (pp. 105-116). New York: Springer-Verlag.

Michelich, V. (2002, January/February). Streaming media to enhance teaching and improve learning. *The Technology Source.* Retrieved November 10, 2007, from http://technologysource.org/article/streaming_media_to_enhance_teaching_and_improve_learning/

Naidu, S., & Järvelä, S. (2006). Analyzing CMC content for what? *Computers & Education, 46*(1), 96-103.

Orvis, K. L., & Lassiter, A. R. L. (2005). Computer-supported collaborative learning: The role of the instructor. In S. P. Ferris & S. H. Godar (Eds.), *Teaching and learning with virtual teams* (pp. 158-179). Hershey, PA: Information Science Publishing.

Pena-Shaff, J. B., & Nicholls, N. (2004). Analyzing student interactions and meaning construction in computer bulletin board discussions. *Computers & Education, 42*(3), 243-265.

Phipps, R., & Merisotis, J. (1999). *What's the difference? A review of contemporary research on the effectiveness of distance learning in higher education.* Institute for Higher Education Policy for the National Education Association and the American Federation of Teachers. Retrieved November 10, 2007, from http://www2.nea.org/he/abouthe/diseddif.pdf

Pulkkinen, J. (2005, March 14). *Online learning: Enablers and barriers for educational technology.* Paper presented as visiting scholar at Western Carolina University, Cullowhee, NC.

Ramage, T. R. (2002). *The "no significant difference" phenomenon: A literature review.* Retrieved November 10, 2007, from http://www.usq.edu.au/electpub/e-jist/docs/html2002/ramage.html

Roblyer, M. D., & Wiencke, W. R. (2003). Design and use of a rubric to assess and encourage interactive qualities in distance courses. *The American Journal of Distance Education, 17*(2), 77-98.

Rourke, L., Anderson, T., Garrison, D. R., & Archer, W. (2001). Methodological issues in the content analysis of computer conference transcripts. *International Journal of Artificial Intelligence in Education, 12*, 8-22.

Russell, T. L. (2001). *The no significant difference phenomenon: A comparative research annotated bibliography on technology for distance education* (5th ed.). Montgomery, AL: The International Distance Education Certification Center (IDECC).

Santos, I., & LeBaron, J. (2006). Ethical constraints in the valid interpretation of transcribed communication in online study. *The Internet and Higher Education, 9*, 191-199.

Schön, D. (1987). *Educating the reflective practitioner: Toward a new design for teaching and learning in the professions.* San Francisco: Jossey-Bass.

Schön, D. (1987a). *Educating the reflective practitioner.* Paper presented to the American Educational Research Association, Washington, DC. Retrieved November 10, 2007, from http://edu.queensu.ca/~russellt/howteach/schon87.htm

Schön, D. (1987b). *Educating the reflective practitioner.* Paper presented at the American Educational Research Association annual conference, Washington, DC. Retrieved November 10, 2007, from http://edu.queensu.ca/~russellt/howteach/schon87.htm

Swan, K. (2002). Building learning communities in online courses: The importance of interaction. *Education, Communication and Information, 2*(1), 23-49.

Twigg, C. (1998, May 2). A regulated monopoly enterprise gives way to competition. *AAHE Bulletin.* Retrieved November 12, 2007, from http://www.aahe.org/bulletin/bull_2may98.htm#Twigg

Verduin, J. R., & Clark, T. (1991). *Distance education: The foundations of effective practice.* San Francisco: Jossey-Bass.

Vrasidas, C., & McIsaac, M. S. (1999). Factors influencing interaction in an online course. *The American Journal of Distance Education, 13*(3), 22-35.

Woods, R., & Ebersole, S. (2003). Using non-subject matter specific discussion boards to build connectedness in online learning. *The American Journal of Distance Education, 17*(2), 99-118.

Wright, A. (2005, January 26). From ivory tower to academic sweatshop. *Salon.com.* Retrieved Novembet 10, 2007, from http://www.salon.com/tech/feature/2005/01/26/distance_learning/print.html

About the Contributors

Donna Ashcraft earned her PhD in Social and Personality Psychology from The State University of New York at Albany and is currently a Full Professor of Psychology at Clarion University of Pennsylvania. She, and her co-author Thomas Treadwell, developed CORAL: Collaborative Online Research and Learning, a teaching method that integrates two course topics through assignments teams of students at two universities must complete together by utilizing video conferencing and other online tools. (For more information on CORAL, see http://coral.wcupa.edu.) She is the author of *Personality Theories Workbook*, a number of articles on CORAL and collaborative learning, and has presented dozens of papers, posters, and workshops on these topics.

Carol Bennett is a doctoral student at Western Carolina University. She works as Elementary and Middle School Curriculum Coordinator at the Western Region Education Service Alliance (WRESA) in Asheville, North Carolina, where she provides professional development for K-8 educators. Her specialty areas are language arts with emphasis in integrating the content areas with reading and writing. Carol has worked in public education for 20 years. She was as an elementary teacher and Teacher of the Year in Asheville City Schools prior to becoming an education consultant. She is the author of several (currently unpublished) children's picture books.

Stephanie L. Brooke, PhD, NCC, teaches sociology and psychology online at Western International University, Excelsior College, University of Maryland, and Capella University. She also has written books on art therapy and edits books on the use of the creative therapies. In October 2006, she was the chief consultant for the first Creative Art Therapy Conference in Tokyo, Japan. Dr. Brooke continues to write and publish in her field. Further, Dr. Brooke serves on the editorial boards of PSYCCritiques and the *International Journal of Teaching and Learning in Higher Education*. She is Vice Chairperson for ARIA (Awareness of Rape and Incest through Art).

Kursat Cagiltay is Associate Professor of Computer Education and Instructional Technology at the Middle East Technical University, Ankara, Turkey. His research focuses on human computer interaction, serious computer games, distance education and sociocultural aspects of technology. He can be contacted by e-mail at kursat@metu.edu.tr or via post at Department of Computer Education and Instructional Technology, Faculty of Education, Middle East Technical University, 06531, Ankara, Turkey

Stephanie Cawthon is a Faculty Member in the School of Psychology at Walden University. Dr. Cawthon earned her master's degree in psychology from Stanford University and her doctorate in educational psychology from the University of Wisconsin-Madison. She has worked as an online instructor and mentor for graduate students for over three years. Dr. Cawthon seeks to provide students with the opportunity to participate in rigorous research projects as part of their online higher education experience. She is grateful to all of the support provided by Walden University to the ongoing success of the Online Research Lab.

Derrick L. Cogburn is Assistant Professor in the School of Information Studies at Syracuse University. He is also Director of the Center for Research on Collaboratories and Technology Enhanced Learning Communities (http://cotelco.syr.edu) and is Senior Research Associate at the Moynihan Institute of Global Affairs at the Maxwell School of Citizenship and Public Affairs. His current research and teaching agenda explores transnational social networks and global governance, as well as geographically distributed collaboration and learning by designing and evaluating accessible cyberinfrastructure and collaboratories. He holds a bachelor's degree from the University of Oklahoma and master's and doctoral degrees from Howard University.

Anastasios Economides received a degree in Electrical Engineering from Aristotle University of Thessaloniki in 1984. Holding a Fulbright and a Greek State Fellowship, he received a MSc and a PhD in Computer Engineering from the University of Southern California, Los Angeles, in 1987 and 1990, respectively. He is currently an Assistant Professor and Vice-Chairman in the Information Systems Postgraduate Program at the University of Macedonia, Thessaloniki, Greece. His research interests are in adaptive, mobile, and collaborative learning. He has published more than 70 papers.

Katherine Ely is a doctoral student in Industrial and Organizational Psychology at George Mason University, where she earned her master's degree in 2006. She also works as a Research Fellow at the Advanced Distributed Learning Co-Laboratory, consulting with Department of Defense organizations on evaluating Web-based training. Her research interests include training and development, specifically the use of technology to enhance training effectiveness, the role of self-regulation in improving learning outcomes, and understanding the meaning of training evaluation data. She is a member of the Society for Industrial and Organizational Psychology and the Academy of Management.

Eileen B. Entin is a Senior Research Psychologist at Aptima. She has experience in the development of quantitative, informative performance measures for assessing cognitively-based performance in individuals and teams, in the development simulation-based training programs, and in the design, conduct, and analysis of information processing and decision making experiments. Dr. Entin received her PhD in psychology from Ohio University and her MA and BA from the University of Michigan.

Gerald Goodwin is a Senior Research Psychologist at the U.S. Army Research Institute for Behavioral and Social Sciences. He received his MS and PhD in Industrial/Organizational Psychology from Pennsylvania State University.

Dr. Goodwin's current research focus is on leader and team effectiveness issues in joint, interagency, and multinational teams context. Previous work included test development, employment litigation support with an emphasis on statistical analysis, training evaluation, and performance modeling. He currently serves as an ad hoc reviewer for the *Journal of Applied Psychology, Military Psychology* and *Human Performance*, and is a member of the editorial board for *Human Factors*.

Alycia Harris is enrolled in the PhD General Psychology program, specializing in research and evaluation, at Walden University and an employee of the ITT Corporation. Her research interests include adult learning, workplace learning, technology supported learning, online education, and community of practice.

Evelyn S. Johnson, EdD, is an Assistant Professor of Special Education at Boise State University and part-time faculty for Walden University. She began working as an online instructor in 1999, has developed online courses for Laureate Education, Inc., and served as a consultant for state and national organizations seeking to expand online education.

John LeBaron is the Jay M. Robinson Distinguished Professor of Educational Technologies at Western Carolina University. He has held two Fulbright awards in Finland, and served as the Gulbenkian Visiting Professor in higher education studies in Portugal. Author of several books and articles on educational technology, John has served as Executive Director of Massachusetts Educational Television and Education Faculty Chair at the University of Massachusetts Lowell. Four decades ago, he traveled solo via rail from Hong Kong to Helsinki through China, Mongolia, and the former USSR. He looks forward, at last, to documentation of this travel from disorganized shoeboxes of photographs and notes about lands now changed beyond recognition.

Nanette S. Levinson is Associate Professor and former Senior Associate Dean, School of International Service, American University. Currently Chair of the International Studies Association's International Communication Section, her research and teaching focuses on communication and development, knowledge transfer and innovation in cross-national alliances, and internet governance issues. She received her bachelor's, master's, and doctoral degrees from Harvard University.

Anna Michailidou holds a MSc in Information Systems from the University of Macedonia, Greece. She is a teacher of computer science in secondary education. Her M.Sc. thesis was about virtual educational environments that support collaboration. She has also participated as a research scientist in a project funded by the Greek Ministry of Education concerning the usage of new technologies in secondary education. In particular, the theme of her work was educational software for teaching computer science. Her research interests are the use of information and communication technologies in education and especially the use of collaborative virtual learning environments. She has published six papers, in four of which she was the leading author. She has also contributed to the publishing of a book in the Greek Open University by submitting a chapter concerning the "Evaluation of Collaborative Virtual Environments."

Lisa Neal is an Adjunct Assistant Clinical Professor of Public Health and Family Medicine at Tufts University School of Medicine, where she teaches a course on Online Health Communities. She is Editor-in-Chief of *eLearn Magazine*, published by ACM, and a consultant who designs and evaluates online communities and online courses for a variety of clients including Michael J Fox Foundation, Charles River Analytics, and Aptima. Lisa holds a PhD in Computer Science from Harvard University. Her Web site is at http://www.lisaneal.com.

Ellen L. Nuffer, EdD, is a Professor of Education at Keene State College, Keene NH. She practiced as a school psychologist before coming to higher education and currently specializes in issues of faculty development, pedagogy, and learning theory. She is interested in applications of technology to enhance both teaching and learning.

Orlando J. Olivares is Professor of Psychology at Bridgewater State College, Bridgewater, Massachusetts and a consultant to Aptima, Inc., Woburn, Massachusetts. His areas of interest are performance assessment, motivation, organizational culture, and leadership. He has published a number of peer-reviewed articles in areas such as leadership, personality, and student and teacher performance.

Jane Pitcock is a doctoral student in Educational Technology at Walden University and a counselor and instructor for Umpqua Community College in Oregon. She began her career in education in 1973 as a teacher and has worked in various capacities, including counselor, assistant principal, and dean of students.

Marissa Shuffler is a doctoral student in Organizational Science at the University of North Carolina at Charlotte, and received her MA in Industrial/ Organizational Psychology from George Mason University. As the TIAA-CREF Doctoral Fellow in Organizational Science, her research primarily examines leadership and communication issues in geographically distributed contexts, particularly as these issues affect work teams. Other current areas of research include shared mental model development and sensemaking in high reliability teams and organizations, as well as exploring the effects of international work assignments on leader performance.

Jason Sidman leads the Instructional Technology and Design Team at Aptima. He has experience in the development of cognitive skills training systems, including conducting knowledge elicitation sessions with subject matter experts, developing scenario-based multimedia training content, and developing performance measures for assessing cognitively-based performance in individuals and teams. Dr. Sidman received his PhD and M.S. in psychology from Tufts University and his B.A. from the University of Massachusetts.

Traci Sitzmann is a Research Scientist at the Advanced Distributed Learning Co-Laboratory. She provides consulting services to the Department of Defense for evaluating their training and improving the quality of their Web-based training courses. Traci's research focuses on understanding self-regulatory processes, developing interventions for increasing motivation and learning in Web-based training, and assessing the relationship between training evaluation criteria. Her research has been published in *Personnel Psychology*, *Journal of Occupational Health Psychology,* and *American Society of Training and Development T + D* magazine. She completed her PhD in Industrial and Organizational Psychology at the University of Tulsa in 2005.

Thomas Treadwell earned his EdD from Temple University in Health Behavior and Group Psychology. He is a Full Professor of Psychology at West Chester University in West Chester, Pennsylvania. and Clinical Associate in Psychiatry at the Center for Cognitive Therapy, Department of Psychiatry, University of Pennsylvania School of Medicine, in Philadelphia. He enjoys his work as a facilitator of groups or teams in the collaborative action-oriented environment of CORAL (Collaborative Online Research and Learning). The CORAL pedagogy fosters the development of skills in using computer and video-technology as tools to enhance effective collaboration in college courses. The mutual atmosphere gives individuals the opportunity to share familiar experiences with fellow human beings in a cohesive educational community.

Janice Whatley has lectured in computing and information systems for over eight years, using various forms of computer-mediated communication to support learners. At present, she is a lecturer at the University of Salford, UK, where her current research interests include studies into tools which may be used to support collaboration in online learning and peer review, and innovative uses of multimedia in learning. She is also interested in developing transferable skills in students, in particular the design of software systems to support skill acquisition through student team working.

Robert Wisher is Director of the Advanced Distributed Learning Initiative in the U.S. Department of Defense. He previously was a Senior Research Psychologist at the U.S. Army Research Institute and a Scientific Officer at the Office of Naval Research. Dr. Wisher's research interests are in the areas of instructional technology, training effectiveness, and skill retention. He received a BS in Mathematics from Purdue University and a PhD in Cognitive Psychology from the University of California, San Diego.

Erman Yukselturk is working as a Research Assistant at the Internet Based Education Project (http://idea.metu.edu.tr) of Middle East Technical University. His main areas of interest are distance education, designing online learning environments, online collaboration, and instructional technology. He can be contacted by e-mail at ermany@metu.edu.tr or via post at Department of Computer Engineering, Middle East Technical University, 06531, Ankara, Turkey.

Elena Zaitseva is an Educational Researcher with more than 15 years experience of online teaching and learning in Russia and Japan. Her research interests include collaborative and peer learning, and intercultural aspects of computer-mediated communication. She was previously a researcher for the Collaboration Across Borders Project, and is now a research officer at the Liverpool John Moores University's Centre for Excellence in Teaching and Learning.

Danuta Zakrzewska is Assistant Professor at the Institute of Computer Science, Technical University of Lodz. She received her PhD in Mathematics in 1987. Her current research interests focus on information management in organizations, as well as intelligent methods that may improve it, including techniques such as data warehousing and data mining. She has been also involved in organizing international students' collaborative activities, with emphasis on peer review. She has published more than 30 articles in conferences, journals, and books.

Index